THE
QUEST HUMAN FOR GOD

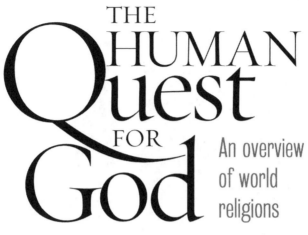

An overview
of world
religions

JOSEPH STOUTZENBERGER

TWENTY
THIRD 23rd
PUBLICATIONS

Quotes from the Koran are from Ahmed Ali, *Al-Quran: A Contemporary Translation* (Princeton, NJ: Princeton University Press, 1988).

The Scripture passages contained herein are from the *New Revised Standard Version of the Bible*, Catholic edition ©1989, by the Division of Christian Education of the National Council of Churches of Christ in the U.S.A. Used by permission. All rights reserved.

Twenty-Third Publications
A Division of Bayard
One Montauk Avenue, Suite 200
New London, CT 06320
(860) 437-3012 or (800) 321-0411
www.23rdpublications.com

ISBN-10: 1-58595-566-3
ISBN 978-1-58595-566-4
Library of Congress Catalog Card Number: 2005935877
Printed in the U.S.A.

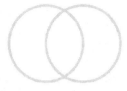

Contents

CHAPTER 1

OUR QUEST FOR GOD
Religion and Religions

Mostly we live day to day, keeping to our routine, not thinking too much about "the big picture." We find fleeting pleasure in our families, our work, our games, our favorite TV shows, and our time with friends. But perhaps one starry night we gaze at the heavens and marvel at the grandeur and expanse of the universe. Perhaps the birth of a child or the death of a loved one causes us to pause and wonder. Perhaps a news report of suffering in the world, if we let it touch us, leads us to ask larger questions. Perhaps a religious ceremony or holy day, a particularly meaningful movie, or song lyrics hint that there is a loving presence in life and the message seeps into our consciousness.

During these times, moments hidden behind our everyday reality, we enter into the realm of religion. The religions of the world represent a record of what human beings in different places and at different times have said about these deeper experiences such as we have when we feel more alive, more attentive, and more in touch with a reality that we may seldom even know exists. A study of the world's religions takes us on a journey both around the world and into the depths of human consciousness. Spiritual guides await us. Through such a study we learn about others; but also, since we share a common spirit with all of humanity, we will learn about ourselves as well.

Overview

- Religion begins with our experience of ultimate mystery.

- In the Catholic perspective, every valid religion offers a ray of truth, found in its fullness in Jesus Christ.

- Different religions emerged in different parts of the world.

- Learning about other religions can help us know ourselves and our world more deeply.

- How to use this book.

Throughout this book, you will be invited to write your thoughts and reactions, to discuss ideas, perhaps even to draw pictures. These exercises are your chance to respond to the various concepts related to some aspect of a religion or a particular religious tradition. By doing a number of them you will in a sense engage the various religions in conversation, hearing from them and offering your own perspective on topics.

ACTIVITY

Before we begin...
1. First, write down three scientific questions.
2. Then, write down three religious questions.
3. Describe how the two sets of questions are different.
4. Based on the differences, compose a definition of religion.

I. Religion
Our Response to Ultimate Mystery

A cursory glance at ancient history shows clearly how in different parts of the world, with their different cultures, there arise at the same time the fundamental questions which pervade human life: Who am I? Where have I come from and where am I going? Why is there evil? What is there after this life? These are the questions which we find in the sacred writings of Israel, as also in the Veda and the Avesta; we find them in the writings of Confucius and Lao-Tze, and in the preaching of Tirthankara and Buddha; they appear in the poetry of Homer and in the tragedies of Euripides and Sophocles, as they do in the philosophical writings of Plato and Aristotle. They are questions which have their common source in the quest for meaning which has always compelled the human heart. (Pope John Paul II, Fides et ratio *[on the relationship between faith and reason], number 1)*

Religion versus Science

We human beings are creatures who wonder. Indeed, a case could be made that, when our capacity to wonder is diminished, so too is our humanity. Wondering serves no apparent practical purpose. Unlike scientific knowledge, which provides answers, wonder leads us into the realm of mystery. From the beginning of the human enterprise we have been on a quest for meaning in the face of the great mystery that envelops us. Modern science has not quenched our thirsting after meaning and purpose. Our science helps us grasp and make sense of the finite. The search for meaning knocks at the door to the infinite. Science can solve the problem of how to build a nuclear bomb. We need to rely on more than science to determine whether or not to use one. Science can detail every stage in our physical development, and yet we still wonder: Why are we here? Were we made under the gaze of a loving creator or merely by chance? Has creation been a blessing or a curse? Science provides us with partial truths, and yet we long for ultimate truth.

Life is a mystery to be lived, not a problem to be solved. This saying has become a cliché. Nonetheless, living the statement is still terrifying. Can we trust that, ultimately, we are not alone in the universe and that our brief lifetime has meaning? Do the actions we take actually make a difference? Is there anything that sustains us, gives us hope, clears up the muddied glass through which we can look into the depths of things?

Religions address these overwhelming questions. The world's religions are a composite of the insights into ultimate mystery that people who struggled with these lofty questions have gained. Each religion proposes its own basis for fundamental trust, a belief that life has meaning. Religion, then, is our response to ultimate mystery. Put another way, religion is ultimate mystery's breaking through into human consciousness. Religious giants have come before us. We are not alone in our own search for meaning and hope.

> *Each of the great religious traditions affirms that as well as the social and natural world of our ordinary human experience there is a limitless greater and higher Reality beyond or within us, in relation to which or to whom is our highest good.* (John Hick, The World's Religious Traditions, *edited by Frank Whaling [New York: Crossroad, 1986], pages 158-59)*

ACTIVITY

A. Think about a time when you experienced wonder.

If you have never experienced wonder, what do you think might bring about such a response from you?

B. Explain the difference between "problems" and "mystery."

Give examples of each.

C. Do you agree or disagree with the following statements?

1. I can't imagine making it through life without religion.

2. I look to my religion to help me make sense out of life.

3. Religion is more for older people than for young people.

4. Because of scientific advances, religion is now outmoded.

5. Science asks more important questions than religion does.

Catholicism and the Religious Quest

But I through the greatness of your love
have access to your house.
I bow down before your holy temple,
filled with awe. (Psalm 5:8, Grail translation.)

In the Hebrew Bible's Book of Exodus, Moses notices a burning bush. Thinking that God may be present in the bush, Moses immediately takes off his shoes as a sign of reverence. In our journey into the mystery of life, we need to cultivate a spirit of reverence. In studying the world's religions, we are stepping onto holy ground. We will be discovering where and how people encounter the sacred according to their particular tradition. Therefore,

Moses before the burning bush

we need to "take off our shoes" in reverence and awe as we study the beliefs and practices of each religion. Such an attitude does not mean that there aren't flaws and shortcomings in the religions we will study. One set of beliefs is not as good as any other. In recent years, popes and other Catholic leaders have warned against relativism ("No absolute truth exists; it's all a matter of perspective.") and religious indifferentism ("Religion isn't important and, besides, one religion is as good as any other.").

During the Second Vatican Council (1962-1965) the world's Catholic bishops laid out a balanced approach toward other religions when they examined the Church and its place in the modern world. The council produced its "Declaration on the Relation of the Church to Non-Christian Religions." In it the bishops point out that, "Humanity forms but one community" and that today "people are drawing more closely together" (no. 1). Therefore, "We cannot truly pray to God the Father of all if we treat any people as other than sisters and brothers, for all are created in God's image" (no. 5). The bishops propose that:

> *The Catholic Church rejects nothing of what is true and holy in*
> *these religions. It has a high regard for the manner of life and con-*

duct, the precepts and doctrines which, although differing in many ways from its own teaching, nevertheless often reflect a ray of that truth which enlightens all men and women. (no. 2)

The council also "proclaims and is in duty bound to proclaim without fail, Christ who is the way, the truth and the life (John 1:6). In him, in whom God reconciled all things to himself (see 2 Corinthians 5:18–19), people find the fullness of their religious life" (no. 2). In other words, we encounter the fullness of the ultimate mystery that all human beings seek in the person of Jesus Christ. In fact, Christ is at work in the world wherever people honestly seek meaning and truth. The bishops call upon Catholics to "acknowledge, preserve and encourage the spiritual and moral truths found among non-Christians" even while "witnessing to their own faith and way of life" (no. 2).

One author describes the Catholic perspective on the centrality of Christ for Catholics and non-Catholics alike in these words:

Does the Catholic Church teach that God wishes the salvation of all? Yes. Does the Catholic Church teach that salvation was made possible for the world through the cross of Jesus Christ? Yes. Does the Catholic Church believe that there is salvation for those who do not know Christ? Yes. Does the Catholic Church believe that the salvation of those who do not know Christ is somehow made possible by Christ, whether or not those saved have ever heard of him? Yes. Does the Catholic Church believe that this puts all those saved in some relationship to the Catholic Church? Yes. (George Weigel, The Truth of Catholicism [New York: HarperCollins, 2001], pages 144-45)

ACTIVITY

A. Describe in your own words the perspective on other religions currently advocated by the leaders of your religion.

B. How do you view other religions?

C. What are relativism and indifferentism in regard to religion? How common are these positions in the world today? Do these positions help or hinder an appreciation for the world's religions?

Vatican Council II had much to say about the relationship between Catholicism and other religions. You might look at the following passages to gain a sense of the spirit of dialogue and respect for others advocated by the Council.

• The Dogmatic Constitution on the Church, paragraphs 8 and 15–16
• The Dogmatic Constitution on Divine Revelation, paragraph 3
• The Constitution on the Sacred Liturgy, paragraph 1
• The Dogmatic Constitution on the Church in the Modern World, paragraphs 1–3, 11, 23–24, 28–29, 40, and 59
• The Decree on Ecumenism, paragraphs 3, 4, 11–12, and 14
• The Declaration on the Relationship of the Church to Non-Christian Religions, paragraphs 1–2 and 4–5
• The Decree on the Church's Missionary Activity, paragraphs 1–12

ACTIVITY

Elements of Religions

In many ways, throughout history down to the present day, men have given expression to their quest for God in their religious beliefs and behavior: in their prayers, sacrifices, rituals, meditations, and so forth. These forms of religious expression, despite the ambiguities they often bring with them, are so universal that one may well call man a religious being:

From one ancestor [God] made all nations to inhabit the whole earth, and he allotted the times of their existence and the boundaries of the places where they would live, so that they would search for God and perhaps grope for him and find him—though indeed he is not far from each one of us. For "in him we live and move and have our being" (Acts 17:26–28). (Catechism of the Catholic Church, #28)

There does appear to be among human beings a universal religious quest—a "groping for God," in the words of the Acts of the Apostles. However, we need to be cautious about fitting religions into a set pattern. For instance, not all religions place a high value on scriptures. Not all religions believe in a god. Some religions emphasize spoken prayers more than rituals acted out, while others emphasize quiet meditation. Nonetheless, to varying degrees religions tend to share certain elements in common. Identifying these common elements can help us better under-

Myth—A Word with Many Meanings

"Myth" plays an important role in all religions. However, in popular usage it has a variety of meanings. Three common uses of the term are the following:

- a popularly accepted falsehood ("It's a myth that the moon is made of green cheese.")

- a collective name for a variety of stories that have a longstanding tradition in a particular culture ("Legends, fairy tales, and parables are all examples of myth.")

- stories of profound religious significance for a religion or culture—the way the term is defined in this book. ("The Exodus story is the central myth describing the Jewish understanding of God, liberation, and the relationship between God and the Jewish people.")

stand the religions we will read about in this book, even when a particular religion doesn't clearly exhibit one or another characteristic.

Religious Experience. People are religious insofar as they are open to the possibility that there is more to life than what is observable by the senses. Religions begin with some kind of breakthrough, an awareness of a spiritual reality that can be overlooked while we go about our daily business. Religious experience is an encounter, a relationship rather than a strictly intellectual pursuit. Religion entails saying "yes" to something (or someone) greater than our minds can normally comprehend. In contrast to the Hollywood version of what such an experience is usually like, read 1 Kings 19:11–12 in the Bible. In this brief but telling scene, the prophet Elijah searches in vain for God in a hurricane, an earthquake, and fire. Instead he meets God in "a sound of sheer silence" or as sometimes translated, "a still, small voice." Every religion would agree: the world of the spirit is always there, whispering in our ear, if we would listen.

Sacred Stories. Among certain Native American groups, some dreams are not just private affairs but contain a message for the entire tribe. Similarly, in every religious tradition some stories are so revealing of a community's place in the universe that they are considered sacred. Sacred stories symbolically portray people's origins and destinies, their values and duties, as well as their relationship to what they consider to be the ultimate, all-encompassing reality. A term for stories that describe the fundamental beliefs and worldview of a particular religion or culture is **myth**.

"Myth" plays an important role in all religions. However, in popular usage it has a variety of meanings. Three common uses of the term are:

- a popularly accepted falsehood ("It's a myth that the moon is made of green cheese.")
- a collective name for a variety of stories that have a long-standing tradition in a particular culture ("Legends, fairy tales, and parables are all examples of myth.")
- stories of profound religious significance for a religion or culture: the way the term is defined in this book. ("The Exodus story is the central myth describing the Jewish understanding of God, liberation, and the relationship between God and the Jewish people.")

This painting of the Holy Grail, by Dante Rossetti, depicts a popular Christian myth

Creed. Especially for Judaism, Christianity, and Islam, formulating a statement of exact beliefs became an important dimension of their religious tradition. You may be surprised to discover that clarifying and listing a set of beliefs are not considered essential to many religions. However, all religions do possess basic beliefs and teachings that we can examine.

Rituals and Symbols. People tend to act out their beliefs symbolically rather than express their beliefs verbally. Ceremonies and celebrations help people enter into the shared experience of their religion. Religious rituals, such as a Jewish Sabbath meal or Muslim daily prayer, create sacred time and space, a way of being in the world that is out of the ordinary. As the *Catechism of the Catholic Church* points out, religious rituals are so important in every culture and in every historical era that we can say that human beings are religious by nature.

Ethical Behavior. Religions do have an impact on how people live their lives. Religious beliefs provide direction about how to treat others and about what behaviors are valued or shunned. When Moses and the Israelites encountered God in the desert they received a set of commandments spelling out attitudes and values that were consistent with belief in their God. People's religion is too important to be tucked away and brought out only on special occasions. Rather, a religion provides the guiding principles for how to live life.

Community. You have probably either said or heard the following comment sometime in your life: "I'm spiritual but not religious." The statement contrasts spirituality with organized, structured religion. A religious person goes to a mosque, temple, or church; a spiritual person strolls alone along the beach or communes with nature during walks in the woods. "Religion" sounds confining; "spirituality" sounds freeing. In fact, religious experience begs to be shared. People who have profound religious insights want to share them with family, friends, and anyone else they meet. It's hard to hold onto spirituality. Trying to go it alone is particularly difficult and can even be problematic in many ways. There's a great difference, for instance, in praying "My Father" rather than "Our Father." Religious communities can be very messy, but they also sustain and support their members. Being part of a religion connects people to a larger group—past, present, and future.

ACTIVITY

A. Look up the word "myth" in a dictionary. Describe the various meanings it has. Explain the role myths play in religion.

B. Give examples of the six elements of religion. Are some elements more or less emphasized in your own religious tradition?

C. Would you question or eliminate any of these characteristics of religion or add other ones?

D. Do you believe that human beings are "religious by nature"?

Vocabulary

myths: Stories that describe the fundamental beliefs and worldview of a particular religion or culture.

II. The Geography of the World's Religions

You may have heard the terms "Western culture" and "Eastern culture." East refers to the continent of Asia; West designates Europe and parts of the world where European culture dominates, such as North America. Traditionally, many scholars of reli-

gion also divided the world's religions into those of the East and those of the West. Actually, *all of the world's major religions began in Asia.* Therefore, another way to group religions is to talk about the "three rivers" of religious traditions.

One river runs through the great sub-continent of Asia known as India. India gave birth to Hinduism and Buddhism. (In a sense, Hinduism is the parent religion; Buddhism is its child.) Thus these two religions share much in common. For the most part, Buddhism in India came to be submerged into Hinduism, but it spread throughout the Far East. Buddhism has touched all countries of Southeast Asia. We will look at Hinduism and Buddhism in chapters 5 and 6.

Another river is that which runs through China. Taoism and Confucianism are the traditional religions of China, balancing each other for most of Chinese history. These two religions also influenced neighboring areas, such as Korea and Japan. For centuries, Buddhism lived side by side with Confucianism and Taoism in China. We will examine these two religions in chapter 7.

The third river is that of Southwest Asia or the Middle East where Judaism, Christianity, and Islam first began. Although Judaism was actually a minor religion in the area for many centuries, nonetheless it has continued to be a strong presence in the world today and also directly influenced Christianity and Islam. As we will see, these three religions share many beliefs in common and even lay claim to a common history. Judaism, Christianity, and Islam are the subjects of chapters 2, 3, and 4.

What About the Rest of the World?

Identifying the place of origin of these great religions does not give us a complete picture of the geography of the world's religions. For one thing, Christianity began at a time when European (Western) cultures reigned over the Middle East. Politically, the Roman Empire ruled the lands where Jesus and his first followers walked. However, Greek was the dominant language and culture of the time. Christianity soon moved beyond its Jewish, Middle Eastern roots and blended into Greek and Roman cultures. (The gospels were first written in Greek. Even today, the Catholic Church is divided into dioceses—a term derived from Roman Emperor Diocletian.) So successful was Christianity in the West that it became its dominant religion; Christianity and Western culture have been intertwined ever since. However, early forms of Christianity also remained strong in the Middle East and in parts of Northern Africa. In fact, evidence suggests that first-century Christian missionaries even made their way into India! Thus, Christianity is bigger and broader than that which is associated with the West.

Islam also moved beyond its Middle Eastern origins. Today, only a minority of Muslims are from Arabia, the area of the Middle East where the religion began. Indonesia has the largest Muslim population. There are Muslims of practically every race and on every continent.

What about Africa, Australia, and the Americas? Traditionally, religious expression on these continents was tribal. That is, each group had its separate and unique beliefs and practices. (We will identify common features of tribal religions in chapter 8.) Christianity came to dominate the South Pacific, Australia, and the Americas along with European colonization of these areas. The vast majority of people in North Africa are Muslim. In sub-Saharan Africa, Christianity and Islam have made great inroads into what had been tribal cultures. Tribal religions do continue to exist in Africa and among the indigenous people of the far north, the Americas, and the South Pacific. At times, elements of tribal religion have blended with either Christianity or Islam, creating unique expressions of each.

Finally, new religions have emerged over the past two centuries that have made a significant impact on the world's religious geography. We will look at a number of these in chapter 8.

ACTIVITY

Look at a map of the world and identify the dominant religion or religions in each section.

How Many People Belong to Each Religion?

Counting how many people belong to the various religions is a dangerous game. Invariably, one group will feel short-changed. Few religions are as structured as Catholicism, so getting exact numbers is difficult. Even determining how many people in the world are Catholic is subject to dispute. (Is anyone who has ever been baptized a Catholic? Are only people officially registered in a parish Catholic?) Nonetheless, we can make some generalizations about how large the various religions are.

For one thing, Christianity is the world's largest religion. Around thirty percent of the world's population is Christian. Within Christianity itself, Catholicism is by far the single largest group. Over seventeen percent of the world calls itself Catholic. Islam is home to nearly twenty percent of the world's population. Islam has also seen rapid growth in recent decades, and a number of Muslim scholars argue that their religion has more members than most surveys indicate.

India and China are two countries with a large and growing population. India is predominantly Hindu, making up over thirteen percent of the world's population. The religious picture in China is more difficult to describe. For one thing, most people in China traditionally practiced Confucianism, Taoism, and Buddhism all at the same time. For another thing, China has been under Communist rule for over half a century. Communism is stridently anti-religion. However, for over a decade now the Chinese government has allowed much religious freedom, and a variety of expressions of religion—old and new—can now be found there.

Of the religions that we will study in depth, Judaism is by far the smallest. One hundred years ago, there were around 12 million Jews. Tragically, six million Jews were murdered under

ACTIVITY

Look at recent statistics on membership in the various world religions today. What is most surprising to you about these statistics?

the Nazi reign of terror during the 1930s and 40s. Today there are fourteen million Jews worldwide, making them less than one-fourth of one percent (approximately .22%) of the world's population. By contrast, there are twice as many Sikhs as Jews in the world. (We will touch on Sikhism briefly in the chapter on Hinduism.)

One question related to religion and population figures is the number of people who are either atheists or non-religious. The number of atheists in the world shot up when Communism ruled Eastern Europe, Russia, and China. Today, atheists and non-religious together make up the third largest "religion" category after Christianity and Islam.

III. Why Study the World's Religions?

We must become familiar with the outlook of the separated churches and communities. Study is absolutely required for this, and it should be pursued in fidelity to the truth and with a spirit of good will. (Vatican Council II, "Decree on Ecumenism," no. 9)

Expanding Our View of the World. In the 1950s an author titled a book on religion in America, *Protestant, Catholic, Jew.* Today a book on American religions would have to take into account that some former Protestant churches are now Vietnamese Buddhist temples, some doctors at our hospitals are Pakistani Muslims or Indian Hindus, and Jehovah's Witnesses occasionally show up at our door wanting to talk about the end of the world. Members of the world's many religions are now our neighbors. Also, thanks to increased communications, we are much closer to our neighbors throughout the globe. If we want to live thoughtfully and compassionately in our global village, we would certainly benefit from learning the beliefs of the various groups of people with whom we live, work, and share resources.

Deepening Our Self-Understanding. If we wanted to find out more about what it means to be an American, one good way would be to travel to other countries. We would discover differences that reveal much about our own culture. For instance, in some places people rest for a few hours in the middle of the day. Elsewhere, the practice of supplying free shopping bags when people purchase groceries is considered wasteful. Many homes throughout the world feature a religious shrine situated in a prominent position. While learning these things tells us about other cultures, it also points out what Americans tend to value and believe. We might overlook characteristics about ourselves or simply take them as natural unless we encounter differences in other cultures.

Similarly, the study of world religions helps us understand ourselves better. For instance, Catholics can better appreciate the uniqueness of the Mass when they learn about what most Protestant Sunday services are like. Christians can understand Jesus better when they compare and contrast him with Muhammad, Gautama the Buddha, or the Hindu notion of God. Christians can also come to a greater realization of the roots of their religion by studying Judaism. In other words, by stepping outside of our religious world, entering into another's, and then returning to our own, we grow in awareness and understanding of our own faith and beliefs.

> You know well that dialogue does not ignore real differences, but neither does it deny our common state as pilgrims bound for a new heaven and a new earth. Dialogue is also an invitation to strengthen that friendship which neither separates not confuses….With [God's] help, may the men and women of every people on the earth continue with renewed determination on the path of peace and mutual understanding! (Pope John Paul II, "Message to Cardinal Cassidy: Interreligious Dialogue" Origins 30 [October 19, 2000]: 298-99)

Encountering the Wisdom of the Ages. A popular character from the *Star Wars* movies is Yoda. He is made out to be the embodiment of ancient wisdom. Such figures are appealing since they give us a sense that in the end all is right with the world. By studying the world's religions, we will indeed encounter ancient wisdom. Into the modern era the words of the Hebrew prophets have inspired more than just Jews. Both Gandhi and Martin Luther King, Jr., are among the many who have found inspiration in the Christian Beatitudes. Confucius and Lao Tzu introduce us to traditional Chinese thought. Although more complex and challenging than the words of Yoda, the world's religions are a true wellspring of wisdom.

Establishing Partners for Justice and Peace. More than ever, ours is an interdependent world. Either all of us learn to get along together, or else we chance destroying ourselves. Unfortunately, religions have at times been causes of conflict rather than partners for peace. The solution is not to do away with religions. Instead, we need to appeal to and build upon those elements present in every religion that foster justice and peace. The study of the world's religions assumes that by learning about other religions, we will discover potential friends and allies rather than enemies.

List goals that you would like to achieve by studying the world's religions.

How to Use This Book

This book is designed to be interactive. By reading the book you will find out some basic information *about* the world's religions. However, it is also designed to help you learn *from* them as well. Truth-seeking through a study of the world's religions is not meant to reduce all religions to a nebulous lowest common denominator, as if they're all essentially the same or one is as good as another. However, it does reflect the belief that we can grow in our faith and in our understanding of our faith. The man who became Pope Benedict XVI had a lifelong passion for seeking religious truth. In a book on world religions he posed the following question:

> *Can or must a man simply make the best of the religion that happens to fall to his share, in the form in which it is actually practiced around him? Or must he not, whatever happens, be one who seeks, who strives to purify his conscience and, thus, move toward—at the very least—the purer forms of his own religion?* (Joseph Cardinal Ratzinger, Truth and Tolerance [San Francisco, CA: Ignatius Press, 2004], 54)

Stepping into the realm of the world's religions leads to questioning. It also fosters clarification, purification, and development. To assist you in deepening your understanding of other religions as well as your own faith, after major sections of each chapter there are a set of questions labeled "For Review." These questions refer directly back to the information presented in that section to help you identify key ideas addressed there. Also, interspersed throughout the text are suggestions for reflection, discussion, and further study. These questions and exercises are there for you. Choose the ones that most appeal to you. If nothing else, simply reading them can help you in your own exploration into the ideas presented in the text.

The search for truth is a lifelong journey. Looking into the world's religions is not a detour but a valuable pathway along that journey. A treasury of wisdom awaits the thoughtful traveler.

For Review

1. After reading this chapter, how would you define religion?

2. What attitude toward other religions was proposed by the bishops of Vatican Council II? How do they view the relationship between Jesus Christ and the various religions of the world?

3. Define relativism and indifferentism applied to religion.

4. What are five elements typically found in religions?

5. What continent was the birthplace for all of the world's major, universal religions?

6. What are the "three rivers" of Asian religious traditions?

7. What religion became dominant in Western culture?

8. What are the world's two largest religions?

9. How large a percentage of the Muslim population is Arab?

10. What two factors make it difficult to describe the religious makeup of China?

11. What ideology helped the spread of atheism during the twentieth century?

12. What reasons does the chapter give for studying about the world's religions?

Prayer

Let us pray...

Oh God, we are one with you. You have made us one with you. You have taught us that if we are open to one another, you dwell in us. Help us to preserve this openness and to fight for it with all our hearts. Help us to realize that there can be no understanding where there is mutual rejection. Oh God, in accepting one another wholeheartedly, fully, completely, we accept you, and we thank you, and we adore you, and we love you with our whole being, because our being is in your being, our spirit is rooted in your spirit. Fill us then with love, and let us be bound together with love as we go our diverse ways, united in this one spirit which makes you present in the world, and which makes you witness to the ultimate reality that is love. Love has overcome. Love is victorious. Amen.

(Thomas Merton, The Asian Journal of Thomas Merton [New York: New Directions, 1975], 318-19)

CHAPTER 2

JUDAISM
A People Struggles
with Their God

Nearly two thousand years ago a man gathered together all the members of his household and set off for a distant land. Of itself his decision doesn't sound particularly earth shattering. However, because of the inspiration behind the move his family's journey would transform history ever after. The man in question we know as Abraham. He left his homeland because his God told him to do so. Unlike the many gods whom his neighbors worshipped, this God exhorted Abraham to be faithful to him alone. In turn this God promised to be faithful to Abraham and to his descendants, who would grow to become a great nation. The saga of the Jewish people, descendants of Abraham of old, has definitely not been the story of a straight march from wandering clan to powerful and populous nation. God's singling them out to be God's chosen people has more often brought struggle than comfort to members of the religion. Nonetheless, Jews insist that their story is a constant, albeit perplexing and at times desperate, encounter with the one, true God of the universe. Despite some differences in interpretation, Christians and Muslims agree that to know their story, the story of the Jewish people, is to know the very workings of God.

Overview

- Throughout history Jewish beliefs and practices take shape in the encounters of the Jewish people with their God.

- After the first century, Judaism emphasizes scripture, the leadership of rabbis, and Jewish communities spread throughout the world.

- Jews celebrate God's presence through the weekly Sabbath and annual holy days.

- Ceremonies mark the holiness of significant events in the life cycle of Jews.

Before we begin...

As we will see, a core teaching of Judaism is that God made an agreement with the Jewish people. God promises to remain faithful to this agreement forever. The task of being Jewish, then, is to work at remaining faithful to the agreement during shifting historical circumstances. As the Jewish religion clearly states, believing in God implies that God has something to say to people—even to people today.

Start with the premise that there is God and then answer the following questions.

A. What do you think are the terms of God's agreement with the people of our time? That is:

  1. What does God promise us?

  2. What does God expect of us?

  3. What is the relationship, if any, between the promises and the consequences?

B. What would you say are God's promises and expectations as the Jewish Bible presents them? Based on your knowledge of the Bible, are the terms of the agreement stated there still in force today? Explain.

I. The People, Their History, and the Covenant
Key Themes of Judaism

I will place my dwelling in your midst, and I shall not abhor you. And I will walk among you, and will be your God, and you shall be my people. (Leviticus 26:11–12)

The Religion of a People

According to the traditional law code of Judaism, to be Jewish means either: (a) to be born of a Jewish mother, or (b) to convert to Judaism. Although modern Jews interpret the law differently, this designation of membership sets Judaism apart from all other religions. For instance, while we might say that someone is born a Christian or a Muslim, in fact something must happen in order for someone to become a member of either of these religions. Essentially, a person must make a statement of faith before he or she becomes Christian or Muslim. (Some Christian groups do permit infants to become official members through an initiation rite known as baptism. In this case others—parents or godparents—make their affirmation of faith for them. Even in the case of infant baptism, however, one is not born Christian but becomes Christian.) What exactly does this traditional designation about who is Jewish imply?

Above all it means that *Judaism is the religion of a people*—specifically the Jewish people. A person is Jewish by birth. It is also possible to become Jewish. Conversion to Judaism does not simply mean accepting a set of beliefs but also means identifying with the Jewish people past and present. Islam sees itself as a universal community; it is a religion meant for everybody. This is also the case with Christianity. Judaism, on the other hand, is a religion strictly for Jews. While Islam and Christianity are **proselytizing** religions, Judaism typically is not. This doesn't mean that Jews perceive their religion as the only true religion. Rather, it means that Judaism is the religion for Jews while other religions are for other people. In fact, it is difficult to separate Judaism the religion from other aspects of Jewish life. On the one hand, "Jewish" is not a racial or ethnic category. There are Jews of African, Asian, and European descent. On the other hand, "Jewish" is also not easily confined to being a religious category either. Attempts have been made to distinguish the religion from other ways of identifying what it means to be Jewish. For instance, some Jewish leaders suggest referring to the religion as "Judaism" and social and cultural aspects of the Jewish people as "Jewishness." However, since the religion—Judaism—is the religion of the Jewish people, exact distinctions fail.

ACTIVITY

A. If you are a member of a religion, make two lists.
In one list name aspects of the religion that you would consider strictly religious. In the other list name social and cultural aspects of the religion. Then circle items on your lists that do not fit neatly into one category or the other. Explain why. (For instance, in which list would you place "Christmas shopping" and "Easter bunny"? Why?)

B. Write a paper on the following questions:
1. Do you believe that people should actively seek converts to their own religion? Why or why not?

2. What kinds of programs and activities would you recommend to members of religions who seek converts?

3. If you are a member of a religion, have you ever tried to convert others to your religion? If not, would you ever try to do so? Why or why not?

4. Do members of a religion with which you are familiar actively seek converts? What are some of the approaches that these people use to encourage conversion to their religion?

C. Are the religions with which you are familiar more communal or individualistic in emphasis? Explain.

Judaism Finds God in History

History plays a minor role in the religions of the Far East. In a sense, for Hinduism and Buddhism history belongs to the realm of illusion and appearances. True reality lies beneath the constant fluctuations of historical circumstance. The enlightened one concentrates on the unchanging essense, not its surface manifestation in history. This is not the case for Judaism. From a Jewish perspective *history itself is sacred*; in the tragedies and triumphs of the human story we meet God. Jews view themselves as God's chosen people, called forth from the nations to play an important role in history. As the chosen people, Jews have been given the task of serving as constant reminders of God's concern for all creation and of how human beings, and in particular themselves, should respond to God. God's selection of the Jewish people for this role appears at first to be a highly unlikely choice—the ancestors of the Jews were a tribe without a homeland who for centuries were slaves in Egypt! However, their lowly origins seem to be an important ingredient in the message God wants to convey—God's special care is for everyone, especially for those who can otherwise be overlooked.

Sophronius, Patriarch of Jerusalem

Another important insight into history that shapes Judaism is that *history is dynamic*. In other words, from the Jewish perspective the past is not dead and disconnected from the present. Past, present, and future are intricately interconnected. For instance, Jews do not say, "Our ancestors were slaves and set free." Instead they say, "We were slaves and set free." Since history has not always been kind to Jews, this belief in God's presence in their midst presents a great challenge to Jewish faith. Since the Jewish religion is so closely bound (a) to the story of the Jewish people, and (b) to God's presence in that story, we can situate major beliefs of the religion in the historical context in which they emerged.

A. **A key theme in Judaism is that history is sacred.** That is, the hand of God lies behind the workings of history, even if we can't comprehend it. Imagine your own life's story as "sacred history." Draw a line across the top of a sheet of paper. On the left end of the line write your birth date. On the right end write today's date. Then mark off specific events or time periods that might be considered sacred. (These do not need to be religious in a narrow sense of the word. For instance, moving to a new neighborhood or changing schools could be viewed as the hand of God at work, enabling you to meet new friends.)

B. **Choose one of these events or time periods and illustrate the sacredness of it in a drawing, song, poem, or story.**

ACTIVITY

Covenant: "I Am Your God; You Are My People"

> *Moses came and told the people all the words of the Lord and all the ordinances, and all the people answered with one voice, and said, "All the words that the Lord has spoken, we will do." And Moses wrote down all the words of the Lord. He rose early in the morning, and built an altar at the foot of the mountain, and set up twelve pillars, corresponding to the twelve tribes of Israel. He sent young men of the people of Israel, who offered burnt offerings and sacrificed oxen as offerings of well-being to the Lord. Moses took half of the blood and put it in basins, and half of the blood he dashed against the altar. Then he took the book of the covenant, and read it in the hearing of the people; and they said, "All that the Lord has spoken we will do, and we will be obedient." Moses took the blood and dashed it on the people, and said, "See the blood of the covenant that the Lord has made with you in accordance with all these words." (Exodus 24:3–8)*

Covenant is a key term for understanding Judaism. You might find the word defined as "contract," but more recently scholars suggest that in the Jewish religion covenant has a less legalistic and more relational meaning— an agreement between two parties. Judaism has its roots in the nomadic culture of the ancient Middle East. Nomads are people without a specific homeland. They wander from place to place, travelling through territory claimed by other groups of people. If a tribe of nomads stops at an oasis and drinks from a well placed there by another tribe, then it had better have an agreement with them to do so. Contracts, or covenants, played an important function in the interaction among Middle Eastern peoples where necessary resources were scarce. Covenants also laid out the terms of agreement between a ruler and subjects within a nation. **Judaism as we know it began with the application of this ancient practice of making covenants to the relationship between God and a particular people.**

In the Hebrew Bible, clearly God is the one who initiates the covenant. In fact, most references to the covenant indicate that God promises to remain faithful to it even though the Jewish people are frequently portrayed as not keeping up their end of the bargain. The Hebrew Bible is essentially the story of how the people suffer or prosper in relation to their keeping the covenant. Meanwhile God remains faithful and loving, becoming manifest especially when the Jewish people face particularly dark times.

Israel is a people like no other, for it is the only one in the world which, from its earliest beginnings, has been both a nation and a religious community. In the historical hour in which its tribes grew together to form a people, it became the carrier of a revelation. The covenant which the tribes made with one another and through which they became "Israel" takes the form of a common covenant with the God of Israel. (Martin Buber, The Way of Response *[New York: Schocken Books, 1966], 189)*

Vocabulary

covenant: An agreement between two parties. In Judaism, the agreement that God made with the Jewish people.

proselytizing: Actively seeking converts to a religion.

The Church Speaks

When she delves into her own mystery, the Church, the People of God in the New Covenant, discovers her link with the Jewish People, "the first to hear the Word of God." The Jewish faith, unlike other non-Christian religions, is already a response to God's revelation in the Old Covenant. To the Jews "belong the sonship, the glory, the covenants, the giving of the law, the worship, and the promises; to them belong the patriarchs, and of their race, according to the flesh, is the Christ (Rom 9:4–5), for the gifts and the call of God are irrevocable." (Catechism of the Catholic Church, #839.)

For Review

1. According to traditional Jewish law, what identifies someone as a Jew? How is this designation of membership in the religion different from that of Islam and Christianity?

2. What does it mean to say that Judaism is typically not a proselytizing religion?

3. What confusion does distinguishing between Judaism and Jewishness attempt to address?

4. Name the two perspectives that Judaism has toward history. How is the perspective on history different from the perspective held by Hinduism and Buddhism?

5. Why does the word "agreement" rather than "contract" better define covenant as Jews understand the concept?

6. What is the origin of the concept covenant?

7. According to the Bible, who initiates the covenant between God and the Jewish people?

II. The History of Judaism
The Biblical Era

The God of the Jews is not the God of philosophers and scientists. That is, God did not create the world and then step back and no longer take an active part in its course. (During the early modern period when science was coming to the forefront, some thinkers spoke of God as initially creating the universe and then no longer taking an active part in it. This perspective on God is known as **deism**.) In contrast to a deistic God, the Jewish God continually intervenes in human history. Ultimately God will also judge history. Christians and Muslims inherit this view of a God actively present in world affairs. The Jewish Bible catalogs the most significant events in the history of the Jewish people, always from the angle that it is God who oversees and judges them. In that sense the Bible combines myth (stories with deep meaning for a people) with history (stories based on fact). It's not always easy to distinguish between myth and history in the Bible, and the biblical authors themselves aren't interested in such distinctions. As we will see in the story of the Exodus, the Bible presents actual historical events as mythic tales. The stories found at the very beginning of the Bible—about Adam and Eve, Cain and Abel, Noah and the great flood—are not based on identifiable historical events. Instead they address in more symbolic fashion grand mythic themes such as creation, alienation, and human wickedness. In this way they set the stage for the biblical stories that do refer to historical events, beginning with Abraham.

Look over the great mythic stories in Genesis, the first book of the Hebrew Bible. Choose one of these stories and make a videotape presentation of a modern adaptation of the story's theme.

Abraham and the Patriarchs

Now the Lord said to Abram, "Go from your country and your kindred and your father's house to the land that I will show you. I will make of you a great nation, and I will bless you, and make your name great, so that you will be a blessing." (Genesis 12:1–2)

By saying yes to God's command, Abram—whose name changes to Abraham to signify the complete change that he undergoes—does become a great blessing. Modern-day Judaism, Christianity, and Islam are all Abraham's children. The concept of monotheism evolves largely from Abrahamic roots. The Ten Commandments and a strong sense of morality and justice in dealing with people also come from this tradition. According to the biblical text, Abraham is seventy-five years old when he begins this journey! He and members of his household are known as **Hebrews**, a word simply meaning "strangers," thus identifying them as a people without a homeland. (Egyptians were from Egypt. Babylonians were from Babylon. Hebrews were from nowhere in particular; they were always aliens in other people's territory.)

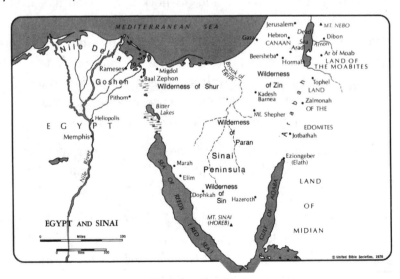

Map of ancient Sinai

When Abraham arrives in the vicinity of what today is Israel he asks God to give him a sign that God's promises will come true. He decides to "cut a covenant." At the time agreements were not sealed by signatures and witnesses. Instead animals were sliced in half and both parties to the agreement walked between the bloody carcasses to affirm their commitment to the agreement. Once Abraham cuts the animals and the stage is set for making a covenant, nothing happens at first. Abraham spends the day fighting off vultures. Then at night Abraham envisions a flaming torch and a smoking fire pot pass through the cut animals: God seals the covenant! Abraham himself does not walk through, as would be customary in a covenant between two parties. This covenant is entirely God's doing. God will remain faithful to it no matter how unfaithful Abraham's descendants are. Later, when Abraham is ninety-nine, God again spells out the terms of the covenant for Abraham and requires that henceforth all male children at the age of eight days should undergo **circumcision** as a sign of the covenant. That day Abraham and all male members of his household are circumcised. Ritual circumcision continues to serve as an initiation rite for male Jews, identifying them as members of the Jewish people.

Later leaders of Abraham's household, known as **patriarchs**, both prosper and struggle as they attempt to keep alive the covenant and find hope in God's promises. One story involving Abraham's grandson is particularly revealing about what it means to be a member of the Jewish religion. Through cunning and wise practices, Jacob does indeed prosper. While returning with his family and his flock to the land that God had promised to Abraham, he comes across a stranger. Since a stranger might be a messenger from God, Jacob asks for his blessing. The stranger refuses, but Jacob remains adamant. Sending his entourage ahead of him, Jacob struggles all night long with the stranger, refusing to let him go until he receives his blessing. The fight is so intense that Jacob's hip is knocked out of joint. In the end the stranger relents and says:

> *"What is your name?" And he said, "Jacob." Then the man said, "You shall no longer be called Jacob, but Israel, for you have striven with God and with humans, and have prevailed." (Genesis 32:27–28)*

Here we have the origin of the name by which Abraham's descendants would be known—**Israelites**, or the children of Israel. It also identifies how they view themselves. The people of Israel are literally those who struggle with God and with humans, seeking God's blessing.

Israel has twelve sons who father the "twelve tribes of Israel." One of his sons is Judah from whom Judaism gets its name. The son written about most, however, is Joseph. You may be familiar with stories about him—his coat of many colors, his being sold into slavery only to become chief advisor to the pharaoh himself, his forgiving the brothers who plotted his death. Joseph plays an important role in determining the fate of the people of Israel. Following him, the Israelites make their way to Egypt where they reside for four hundred years—most of those years as slaves.

A. **The Bible typically transforms historical events into myths, presenting them as saying something about God, about the human condition, and about the people of Israel. For each of the following incidents, describe possible deeper meanings that the story might possess:**

1. Abraham leaves his homeland.

2. To seal an agreement, people walk through animals cut in half.

3. Abraham spends a day fighting off vultures who want to eat the animals he has readied for God's covenant with him.

4. A smoking pot and a flaming torch pass through the covenant animals.

5. God seals the covenant but Abraham doesn't.

6. Jacob fights a stranger throughout the night.

7. The people of Israel are those who struggle with God.

8. Left for dead, Joseph rises to the top of Egyptian society.

B. **Name either a personal, national, or international event of some significance that has happened recently.** How might you present it in order to underscore the deeper meaning of the event?

C. **Have you ever found yourself trying to make a bargain with God?** If so, why did you? What characteristics does a God who can be bargained with possess?

ACTIVITY

Exodus, Liberation, and Nation Building

The Exodus is such a well-known story that it hardly requires retelling here. It is truly one of the world's great stories. It is also the pivotal story of the Jewish religion. During the course of about fifty years a group of slaves, many of them descendants of the Israelites, are liberated from slavery, undergo an arduous desert journey, and arrive in a beautiful and bountiful land as a united people. Here are thematic highlights of that story.

Liberation. Left alone, people are enslaved; thanks to God's intervention, people are set free. Jews celebrate this important theme on a daily, weekly, and annual basis. The Exodus story is *their* story. For Jews, liberation from bondage didn't happen only once three thousand years ago. Even though life's journey today is difficult, God provides guidance and will in the end bring people home. Christianity adopted this theme, sometimes calling it **redemption.** (According to the original meaning of the word, being "redeemed" means to be set free from slavery. Someone who pays to free a slave is a "redeemer.") Islam also contrasts the dire conditions resulting from humanity's rejection of God with the freedom that comes from being true to God.

Yahweh. The greatest figure in Jewish history, Moses is told God's name when God speaks to him from a burning bush. In the Hebrew Bible, God's name is written YHWH. (The Hebrew language does not write out vowels.) During public reading of the scriptures, Jews do not say this word; it is much too sacred. Instead they say *Adonai*, which means "Lord." When the Bible was first being translated into English, YHWH was written as "Jehovah." An early English translation of the Bible known as the King James Version uses Jehovah for YHWH. Scholars today believe that **Yahweh** is a more likely pronunciation, but essentially it is a word that cannot be pronounced. Since it means something like "I am who am," this name for God maintains the dual nature of the Jewish understanding of God. On the one hand, God is unfathomable mystery. On the other hand, God exists and is an active presence in the world. The Exodus story makes clear that God's presence is a caring, liberating presence who battles the forces of injustice and fiercely intervenes on behalf of the downtrodden.

Ethical Monotheism. The freed slaves don't automatically enter the Promised Land. They spend forty years in the desert. As you can imagine would happen from such an experience, during that time they come together as a people with a shared identity. A major event in the fashioning of their identity is God's giving them the Ten Commandments. The Ten Commandments clarify what it means to believe in the one true God. The story contrasts a god named **Baal** with Yahweh. Baal, often represented as a golden bull, demands ritual sacrifices. By contrast, Yahweh proclaims that worshipping the true God means treating people in just and moral ways. In other words, belief in God cannot be separated from morality: honor your parents, do not steal or murder, do not commit perjury or adultery. Therefore, Judaism is not simply monotheism, belief in one God. More importantly it is **ethical monotheism**, recognition that believing in God has ethical implications. Following in the Jewish tradition, both Christianity and Islam believe in ethical monotheism.

The Promised Land. Many of us today have come to think of the Promised Land as the state of bliss that awaits us upon death, at least if we have lived a good life. For the Israelites the Promised Land was an actual place, the land of their ancestors, a place where they could work the land for themselves and not for slave owners. It is easy to see, however, how the image of the Promised Land would grow beyond meaning a mere stretch of earth. As we will see, the concept continues to hold much meaning for Jews of today. It has also inspired many people who suffer under oppression and dream of a better life, such as slaves in the American South two hundred years ago and, in more recent times, civil rights leaders such as Martin Luther King, Jr.

A. **Read through the book of Exodus, at least the first twenty chapters.** Given the fact that this story is the foundational story of Judaism, what would you say the religion stands for? Refer to the Exodus account to explain and illustrate your answer.

B. **Have you ever shared a "desert experience" with a group of people?** That is, have you ever spent time away from home and experienced a challenge or hardship with others? What was the experience like? How did it affect your relationship with these people?

C. **Judaism is not just monotheism but "ethical monotheism."** Explain the difference. Is it possible to have belief in God that does not have ethical implications? Explain.

D. **Read through a speech or sermon given by Martin Luther King, Jr.** Identify any references that he made to the Exodus theme.

ACTIVITY

Kings and Prophets

The Israelites do not simply walk into the Promised Land and claim it for their own without confrontations with local people. For years the Israelites battled other groups to gain control of the land. Leaders emerged, men and women known as **judges**, who temporarily led the fight. Eventually "Israel" referred both to the people and to an identifiable nation. Once that happened the people wanted what other nations had—a king. However, didn't they already have a king, namely Yahweh? This dilemma represents a conflict that Judaism, as well as other religions, continues to struggle with: does our exercise of power contradict God's almighty power? Does a human ruler detract from God's rule? Should a holy nation have no king but God? Samuel, a holy man of the time, reluctantly anoints one of the Israelite military leaders as king. Now Israel can take its place within the community of nations.

The first king of the nation, Saul, does not fare very well. The second king, however, is someone special. David is young, creative, and dynamic. He is a charismatic leader in a way that Saul is not. Under David, Israel does become a great nation, even with a stately capital city—Jerusalem. David's son, Solomon, proves to be a wise and successful ruler as well. He builds a great temple in Jerusalem that deserves to be considered one of the wonders of the ancient world. However, after Solomon the nation splits in two—Israel in the north and Judah in the south. Even despite this division the Jewish nation would probably not have been a match for the powers who in succession conquered the Middle East: Assyria, Babylonia, Persia, Greece, and then Rome. During this period the Jewish people always lived under the domination, or the threat of domination, by other nations. Nonetheless, it still proved to be a very fruitful time in the development of Judaism. Four facets of the Jewish religion emerged during this time period: temple worship followed by the emergence of synagogues, the longing for a messiah, the great outburst of prophetic preaching, and the Bible's becoming the central focus of the Jewish religion.

ACTIVITY

Look at three recent political speeches. Do the politicians involved appeal to God or religion in any way? If so, how? Do you believe that politicians in the United States should refrain from making references to God or religion? Why or why not?

Temple Worship. King Solomon built Jerusalem's great temple. It was a place where Jews worshipped God by offering animal sacrifices at the hands of their priests. The temple became the focal point of the religion, at least the official expression of it. Jews everywhere longed to make their way to the temple, purchase a young sheep or a few doves from the sellers outside its walls, and bring them to the priests for sacrifice. When Babylonians destroyed the original temple and carried off the Jewish leaders into slavery, the religion was changed forever. By the time a second temple was built, another phenomenon had emerged to kindle the Jewish religious spirit—the **synagogue.**

While there was only one temple, there were many synagogues. While the temple required priests and animal sacrifices, synagogues centered around the scriptures and teachers of scripture who came to be known as the rabbis. The temple was in Jerusalem alone; synagogues were meeting places found wherever at least ten men (a **minyan**) would gather to read and pray the scriptures. After Romans destroyed the temple for good in the year 70 CE, the rabbis, the synagogues, and most importantly the scriptures held the Jewish people together.

Messiah. As the people of Israel suffer the hardships and indignities of being a conquered people they begin to long for someone who will restore peace and prosperity to the nation. They long for a new righteous ruler, a new King David. This longing materializes into the concept **messiah.** Messiah means "anointed one," since a person becomes king through an anointing with oil. Messiah in Greek is **christ** from the Greek word for oil, chrism. While the idea of a messiah is not as central to the Jewish religion as the concept covenant and other beliefs, nonetheless it has played an important role in Jewish history ever since this time. In the first century of the Common Era one messianic movement resulted in many Jews attempting an armed revolt against the Romans. The failure of this revolt greatly transformed Judaism, as we will see. Another person considered by some to be the messiah became the focus of a religious movement that split from Judaism and became a great religion in its own right—Christianity.

Prophets. Another important concept that came out of this period is that of prophecy. We will encounter this term again in our study of Islam. A prophet is one who speaks for God. However, in nations of the ancient Middle East official "prophets" were court-appointed and served as advisors to rulers. During the period when the Jewish nation was divided in two and struggling to exist, a different kind of prophet emerged. These prophets spoke in no official capacity. Kings and wealthy members of soci-

The Words of the Prophets—
Do They Continue to Speak to Us?

Read over the following passages from the great Hebrew prophets. For each one, write a brief statement about how it might be applied today. Then choose one statement and illustrate it with a drawing or a poem.

If you remove the yoke
from among you,
the pointing of the finger,
the speaking of evil,
if you offer your food to the hungry
and satisfy the needs
of the afflicted,
then your light shall rise
in the darkness
and your gloom be like
the noonday.
(Isaiah 58:9–10)

With what shall I come before the Lord,
and bow myself before God on high?
Shall I come before him
with burnt offerings,
with calves a year old?
Will the Lord be pleased with
thousands of rams,
with ten thousands of rivers of oil?
Shall I give my firstborn for my
transgression,
the fruit of my body for the
sin of my soul?
He has told you, O mortal,
what is good;
and what does the Lord
require of you
but to do justice, and to love kindness,
and to walk humbly with your God?
(Micah 6:6–8)

To whom shall I speak and give warning,
that they may hear?
See, their ears are closed,
they cannot listen.
For from the least to the greatest of them,
everyone is greedy for unjust gain;
and from prophet to priest,
everyone deals falsely…
yet they were not ashamed,
they did not know how to blush.
(Jeremiah 6:10, 13, 15)

The wolf shall live with the lamb,
the leopard shall lie down
with the kid,
the calf and the lion and the fatling
together,
and a little child shall lead them.
The cow and the bear shall graze,
their young shall lie down together;
and the lion shall eat straw
like the ox.
The nursing child shall play over
the hole of the asp,
and the weaned child shall put
its hand on the adder's den.
They will not hurt or destroy
on all my holy mountain;
for the earth will be full of the
knowledge of the Lord
as the waters cover the sea.
(Isaiah 11:6–9)

ety tried to silence them or to do away with them. These unofficial prophets challenged the king and the people to keep the covenant. They condemned putting trust in weapons and in ritual sacrifices. They pointed out that God requires special treatment for orphans, widows, strangers, and others who aren't making out so well. Read through the books of the prophets in the Jewish Bible and you will find eloquent pleas for justice by some of history's greatest preachers. You will also find, in the end, not a message of despair but one of hope.

Scriptures. One event that occurred at the end of this period that caused a re-thinking about how to practice Judaism was the Babylonian Captivity. For fifty years, 587-536 BCE, most of the leading citizens of the Jewish nation were forced to live in captivity in Babylon. As you can imagine, living away from their homeland was both a hardship and a challenge. During their captivity these Jews came up with ways to hold onto their culture and their beliefs so that they would not be absorbed into the culture in which they were living. They gathered together to tell the stories of their homeland, to pray together to their God, and to reaffirm the rules of conduct that had sustained them for so long. Since they could not rely on worship at the temple to serve as the center of their religion, they emphasized more and more their sacred writings. During this time much of the Hebrew Bible took the shape we find it in today. Writings that had been around for centuries were edited, added to, and placed in a more formal arrangement. From the time of the Babylonian Captivity on, many of the Jewish people revered the Bible as the focal point of their encounter with God. After the first century CE, it became the focal point for all religious Jews.

The Meaning of "Torah"

The word "Torah" is sometimes translated as "the Law," and that translation is certainly not incorrect; on the other hand, it only begins to tell the story. The word "teaching" probably captures the richness of association that the concept "Torah" brings with it. Torah has both a narrow and a broad sense. In its narrow sense, it is the Pentateuch—the Five Books of Moses—the first five books of the Bible. In the broader sense, Torah encompasses everything that flows from the Pentateuch, from the other books of the Bible, to the words of the ancient rabbinic sages, and to the writings of inspired teachers. In other words, Torah really means Judaism. Thus, Torah is central to Jewish life—as an object, as our history and folklore, as our law, as a statement of our ethical values, as a symbol of our relationship to God. (Stephen J. Einstein and Lydia Kukoff, Every Person's Guide to Judaism [New York: UAHC Press, 1989], 41)

The Hebrew Bible: God's Word in Three Parts

The centerpiece in every synagogue is a cabinet that houses a set of scrolls read during public worship. The scrolls are handwritten on sheepskin carefully sewn together. They are also covered with fine cloth and topped with a crown—adorned as a Jewish priest of old would be. Today, priests are not the intermediaries between God and the people; rather, the scriptures are.

The Hebrew Bible, or Jewish Scriptures, consists of three sets of writings. By far, the first five books of the Bible are the central writings of these scriptures. In Greek they are known as the Pentateuch, meaning five books. Jews refer to them as the Torah, meaning law or teachings. They are also known as the five books of Moses, since they are associated with the greatest Hebrew prophet and the one who received "the law" from God on Mount Sinai.

The second set of books found in the Jewish Scriptures describes the actions and the inspiring words of the prophets. These writings tell about those figures who spoke God's word during the rise and fall of the nations of Israel and Judah. We discover through them that God kept a concerned watch over all of the historical events taking place at the time. For Jews the messages of the prophets have become timeless, and portions of these books are read along with the Torah at each Sabbath service.

The third set of writings is a more diverse collection that includes songs, proverbs and wise sayings, and inspiring tales. Together they are called simply the writings. Jews associate the one hundred and fifty songs, or psalms, with David, the servant boy who became king but sang and danced before the Ark of the Covenant nonetheless. The wisdom literature, such as the book of Proverbs, is associated with David's son King Solomon, himself known for his wisdom.

In Hebrew the words for Torah, prophets, and writings begin with T-N-K, respectively. Thus the Hebrew Bible collectively is called TANAKH.

One frequently asked question is...

- Is the Hebrew Bible the same as that which Christians call the Old Testament?

Generally, yes, although books are ordered slightly differently. The official Catholic Bible—because it follows a different early Jewish source—includes a few writings not included in either the Protestant Old Testament or the Hebrew Bible.

Vocabulary

Baal: A popular god, imaged as a golden calf, worshipped by many of the people inhabiting the Palestine region conquered by the Israelites.

Christ: Greek term for messiah. After the time of Jesus, came to be applied exclusively to Jesus Christ and no longer used by Jews.

circumcision: Designated by God to be the sign of the covenant for male Jews.

deism: Belief that God creates the universe but then never again takes an active part in it.

ethical monotheism: The recognition that belief in one God has ethical implications.

Hebrew: "Stranger" or "foreigner." A term for nomadic tribes of the ancient Middle East, one of which became the Jewish people.

Israel: Means "one who fights with God." The name given to the patriarch Jacob after he wrestles with a stranger.

Israelites: The descendants of Israel who become slaves in Egypt and whom God fashions into a people following their liberation from slavery.

judges: Charismatic leaders of the Israelites who led them in their conquest of Palestine.

messiah: Anointed one—a king; a charismatic ruler who will restore peace and prosperity to Israel, as King David had done. Jews today speak more of a "messianic age" than of a particular person.

Vocabulary (continued)

minyan: Originally ten men who could form a synagogue or who needed to be present to hold a public synagogue service. Most communities no longer require only men or hold fast to the ten-person requirement to begin synagogue service.

patriarch: Head of a Hebrew tribe. The Bible names Abraham, Isaac, Jacob, and Joseph as patriarchs.

redemption: Literally "to buy back," applied originally to paying to free someone from slavery. For Judaism, God's intervention to free the Israelites from slavery.

synagogue: A place of worship centered on the reading and study of scripture begun during the Babylonian captivity when exiled Jews could not worship at the temple. Synagogue also refers to those who belong to a synagogue's community.

Yahweh: The name for God given to Moses, means "I am who I am" or "I will be who I will be." This name is held sacred and is not spoken by pious Jews.

For Review

8. How is Judaism different from deism?
9. What does the term "Hebrew" say about the ancestors of the Jewish people?
10. What does God ask of Abraham as a "sign of the covenant"?
11. What is the origin and meaning of the word "Israel"?
12. What is the pivotal story of the Jewish religion?
13. How do Jews today view the Exodus experience of liberation?
14. What is the meaning of the name "Yahweh"?
15. What does it mean to say that Judaism believes in ethical monotheism?
16. What role did the people known as judges play in the formation of Israel?
17. Who were the three kings during the period of a united Israel?

18. What is the difference between the temple and synagogues?

19. What does "messiah" literally mean? What is the Greek translation of the word?

20. How were the prophets extolled in scripture different from official prophets?

21. Name the three parts of the Hebrew Bible.

III. The History of Judaism
The Rabbis, the Diaspora, and the Modern Era

A major event took place in the first century of the Common Era that transformed Judaism ever after. That event was not the life and death of Jesus, himself a pious Jew whose followers came to accept him as messiah and Son of God. The impact that Christianity would have on Judaism would come a few centuries later. In the year 66 CE a band of Jewish warriors decided that the time had come to try to drive the Romans from the Promised Land and to reclaim Israel as independent of the Roman Empire. A war between these poorly equipped Jewish forces and the mighty Roman army waged until 70 CE. The Roman army crushed this rebellion and in the process leveled much of Jerusalem, including the temple—center of Jewish worship. Only the **Western Wall** of the temple remained standing after Rome was through with it.

The destruction of Jerusalem's temple symbolizes a shift from Judaism of old to the Judaism that continued through the Middle Ages and into the modern era. Ever since the Babylonian Captivity, Jews lived not only in their homeland but also throughout what became the Roman Empire. This dispersion of Jews throughout the world is known as the **Diaspora**. Beginning around the same time, synagogues took on greater and greater importance in the religious life of Jews. Jews of the Diaspora could not always make the journey to Jerusalem to offer sacrifice at the temple; they could, however, attend the services held at their local synagogue. Synagogues centered around study of the Torah. Scholars and teachers of Torah, who came to be known as rabbis, grew in ever increasing importance in the Jewish community—rivaling the priests of the temple in their authority. Once the temple was destroyed, the rabbis were able to keep Judaism alive and thriving by interpreting Torah laws for changing times.

ACTIVITY

Prepare a class presentation on synagogues and synagogue services either by visiting one, by interviewing a Jewish person who attends synagogue services, or by reading about what synagogues typically contain.

Talmud: The Oral Law Is Written Down

Jews looked to the Torah as their guidepost for living. Scholars identified 613 laws, or **mitzvah**, in the Torah. However, as with all law, people needed help in interpreting and applying these laws to particular situations. For instance, the Torah prohibits work on the Sabbath. But what exactly is work? Is cooking allowed? Can a priest perform sacrifice on the Sabbath? Can a doctor tend to the sick? (If you are familiar with the Christian Scriptures, you will recall that Jesus was criticized by some of his fellow Jews for healing on the Sabbath.) Great rabbis set down rules for carrying out the rituals called for in the Torah and interpreted the meaning of laws so that the Jewish people could remain faithful even as their circumstances changed.

At first the teachings of the rabbis were not written down. The Torah alone was the *written law*. The teachings of the rabbis were *oral law*. The early rabbis wanted to keep the distinction clear. However, even though rabbinic teachings continued to be referred to as the "oral law," early in the Common Era they were written down. The vast collection of legal pronouncements made by the most highly regarded early rabbis is known as the **Talmud**. (The first complete edition of the Talmud appeared in 425 CE.) Although every Jew would accept the Talmud as secondary to the Torah, nonetheless Jewish scholars came to view the Talmud as the most important doorway through which to enter the holy Torah. A delightful aspect of the Talmud is that it contains fables and witticisms about daily life; it is filled with "lore" more than law. In the spirit of its living tradition, later rabbis would continue to shed new light on the law, building onto the understanding of how it is to be applied to the practical business of life.

In a sense, then, Jewish law is something like the Constitution of the United States. The Constitution is the basis for all American law. However, judicial rulings from the time of its adoption until the present help Americans understand and apply the Constitution. In similar fashion, Jews have an entire tradition of interpretive pronouncements to help them understand and apply Torah law. For over two thousand years rabbis have debated and discussed fine points of the law to help Jews live lives faithful to their original covenant.

The Torah, the sacred teachings of Judaism

> *The Talmud is primarily concerned with law, because the Jews looked upon the legislation in the Bible as its most important element. But the Talmud is also rich in many copious discussions in the field of religion, ethics, social institutions, history, folk-lore and science. Thus we define the Talmud as an encyclopedia of Jewish culture; in form, a supplement to the Bible, and in its contents, a summation of a thousand years of intellectual, religious and social achievement of the Jewish people.* (Rabbi Ben Zion Bokser, The Wisdom of the Talmud [New York: Citadel Press, 1951], 5)

The Talmud helps Jews interpret the meaning of their scriptures. Is anything available in your religion that helps you understand and apply its scriptures? If so, how is this function met?

ACTIVITY

Judaism in Lands Governed by Christians and Muslims

Without a homeland to call their own, Jews developed centers of Jewish life in other parts of the Middle East, northern Africa, and particularly Europe that became more important. By the eighth century, Jews resided in lands controlled either by Muslims or Christians. Jews living in Muslim-controlled lands, especially in southern Spain, belonged to what is known as the Sephardic tradition, **Sephardim**. Those who lived in Christian-controlled lands, especially in Germany and Eastern Europe, belonged to what is known as the Ashkenazic tradition, the **Ashkenazim**. The language and to a lesser extent the practices of the two groups differ somewhat.

Branches of Judaism

Orthodox	Conservative	Reform	Reconstructionist
Follow traditional Jewish practices most closely	Hold onto traditional Jewish practices but are open to change, such as acceptance of women rabbis, men and women sitting together in synagogue, and some use of vernacular languages during worship services	Seek to hold onto the essence of Judaism while accepting change in non-essentials	Identify Judaism as a developing culture

In general, Jews fared better under Muslim rule. In fact, in Muslim-controlled Spain Jews thrived to such a degree that this period is often called a "golden age" of Judaism. The great Jewish philosopher Maimonides wrote *Guide for the Perplexed*, one of the great works of medieval philosophy, to explain how Judaism makes sense in terms of pure reason. He originally wrote the work in Arabic. This golden age ended in 1492 when Christians gained control of Spain. The Christian rulers, Queen Isabella and King Ferdinand, called for the conversion or expulsion of non-Christians. Either alternative, staying or leaving, brought hardship to Spanish Jews. Few countries welcomed Jews. Even Jews who converted to Christianity were subject to the **Spanish Inquisition**, trials set up to punish anyone suspected of undermining or rejecting the Christian faith.

Ashkenazic Jews experienced a much more precarious existence in Christian-dominated Europe. Evidence exists that in many communities during the early Middle Ages Jews and Christians lived together peacefully. However, the position put forth by the influential Christian writer Saint Augustine of Hippo (fourth century) suggests why Jews could never feel fully secure living in a Christian world. Augustine proposed that Jews should be allowed to exist in the Christian world to serve as a living reminder of Christianity's roots, but that Jews should always be second-class citizens to serve as a reminder that Christianity has superceded Judaism. When European Christians underwent a series of crusades to drive Muslims out of the Holy Land beginning in 1095, Jews—who lived closer to home and who were easier targets—were frequently attacked as well. In short, into the modern era Jews experienced periods of toleration with restriction, with intermittent periods of active persecution.

Modern Judaism

European Jews faced a crisis during the time of the French Revolution. In 1791 France granted emancipation to Jews. Jews could now live outside of their restricted area. They no longer were required to wear distinctive clothing, as was the law in many places. They could claim citizenship in the country where they were living. Many Jews welcomed their emancipation and began experimenting with ways to be French or German citizens while maintaining their Jewish identity as well. Some Jews built places of worship that they called temples, even though traditionally there was only one possible temple—the one that lay in ruins in Jerusalem. Mimicking their Christian neighbors, some Jews introduced organ music and communal singing into their temple services and conducted those services in French or German rather than in Hebrew. Some even held their services on Sundays rather than on Saturday, the Sabbath!

The movement to adapt Judaism to the modern world was known as the Reform movement, or **Reform** Judaism. Other Jews cautioned that making changes and blending in with their non-Jewish neighbors could eradicate their identity as Jews. Weren't Jews chosen by God, set apart to be a light to the nations? Jews who proposed staying as close as possible to traditional ways in dress, lifestyle, and worship were **Orthodox** Jews. Later in the nineteenth century some members of the Reform movement felt that the

The Church Speaks

This century has witnessed an unspeakable tragedy which can never be forgotten: the attempt by the Nazi regime to exterminate the Jewish people, with the consequent killing of millions of Jews. Women and men, old and young, children and infants, for the sole reason of their Jewish origin, were persecuted and deported. Some were killed immediately, while others were degraded, ill-treated, tortured and utterly robbed of their human dignity, and then murdered. Very few of those who entered the camps survived, and those who did remained scarred for life. This was the Shoah. It is a major fact of the history of this century, a fact which still concerns us today…

In addressing this reflection to our brothers and sisters of the Catholic Church throughout the world, we ask all Christians to join us in meditating on the catastrophe which befell the Jewish people, and on the moral imperative to ensure that never again will selfishness and hatred grow to the point of sowing such suffering and death.
(Commission for Religious Relations with the Jews, *We Remember: A Reflection on the Shoah*)

movement had gone too far. They wanted to conserve more of their Jewishness. They came to be known as **Conservative** Jews. Even later, in the twentieth century, Rabbi Mordecai Kaplan began the **Reconstructionist** movement. He proposed that, "The past has a vote, not a veto." Reconstructionist Jews see Judaism as constantly evolving throughout history. They wish to create a religious civilization by building on the past while also being open to contemporary developments within the Jewish community and the world.

Zionism and Shoah: Two Events That Shaped Contemporary Judaism

For nearly two thousand years Jews had no homeland to call their own. At different times during that period some Jewish leaders called for the reestablishment of a nation where the ancient kingdom of Israel had stood. This dream became an active movement in the late nineteenth century under Theodor Herzl. He called the movement **Zionism.** Some European Jews made their way to Palestine. One Jewish couple called for the exclusive use of Hebrew in Jewish schooling and started speaking only Hebrew in their family so that the ancient language would not die out.

One of the great tragedies of human history catapulted the Zionist call for a nation of Israel into the world's consciousness. During Nazi rule of Germany, six million Jews were killed—over a third of the Jewish population of the world at that time. Nazi leaders, trying to figure out what to do with the Jews of Europe, decided upon what they termed a "final solution"—systematic murder of all Jews. In addition to the six million Jews murdered in their attempt at genocide, Nazis killed approximately five million other innocent people—Gypsies, Poles, Slavs, homosexuals, Jehovah's Witnesses, the handicapped, and others. Together, these mass murders have come to be known as the Holocaust. Jews refer to the murder of their people in the Holocaust as the **Shoah.**

In 1948 the modern state of Israel came into existence on the site of Israel of old. Through this new nation, Jews now had a voice in the world's political arena. Interestingly, not all Jews welcomed formation of the state of Israel. Some felt that Judaism was meant to be a spiritual presence in the world, not a material, political one. Jews worldwide support the nation in a variety of ways and find their affiliation with Israel to be an important one.

A. **A number of books have been written and films made about the horrors of the Shoah.** (Anne Frank, Victor Frankl, and Elie Wiesel are three such authors.) Write about one of these accounts.

B. **Theodor Herzl proposed creation of a state of Israel in the late 1800s.** What arguments might he have given to the world community in favor of his proposal? What arguments might have been given against his proposal?

C. **Research the origins of the modern state of Israel and write a report about it.**

D. **Write about the origins and current state of Israeli-Palestinian relations.**

ACTIVITY

Vocabulary

Ashkenazim: Jews originally from Germany and Eastern Europe.

Diaspora: Spread of Jews outside of Israel. Refers especially to Jewish communities without a homeland from 70 to 1948 CE.

mitzvah: Jewish law.

Sephardim: Jews originally from Spain, Portugal, and Northern Africa.

Shoah: Murder of six million Jews under Nazism. (The term "holocaust" refers to the murder of Jews and non-Jews by the Nazis.)

Spanish Inquisition: Trials designed to convict people who undermined the Christian faith. Began in Spain in 1492 and continued intermittently until the early nineteenth century.

Talmud: Rabbinic interpretations and applications of the Torah compiled just before and after the beginning of the Common Era.

Western Wall: A wall of the temple in Jerusalem that survived after its destruction by the Romans in 70 CE.

Zionism: Movement to re-establish a Jewish homeland in Palestine.

For Review

22. What 70 CE event transformed Judaism?
23. What is the relationship between the Talmud and Torah?
24. Who were the Sephardim and the Ashkenazim?
25. What was the Spanish Inquisition?
26. What position did Saint Augustine of Hippo take regarding Jews?
27. What principal differences exist among the four major branches of modern Judaism?
28. Define Zionism and Shoah.

IV. Jewish Holy Days
Meeting God Throughout the Year

The Sabbath. The most striking characteristic about Jewish holydays is that they are typically celebrated more in the home than at synagogue. Observant Jews celebrate the weekly Sabbath (Shabbat or Shabbas) with a ritual meal on Friday evening since days are counted from sunset to sunset. Synagogue services are typically held Saturday mornings. In a sense, the Jewish Sabbath is meant to be a day-long meditation. That is, the spirit of meditation, which we will learn more about in relation to Hinduism and Buddhism, permeates the spirit of the Sabbath. It is a day to stop business as usual, to rest, to appreciate God and God's gifts, simply to *be* rather than to *do*. The prayer book of the Reform movement contains the following description of the Sabbath (quoted in Stephen J. Einstein and Lydia Kukoff, *Every Person's Guide to Judaism* [New York: UAHC Press, 1989], 8):

> *There are days*
> *when we seek things for ourselves and measure*
> *failure by*
> *what we do not gain.*
>
> *On the Sabbath*
> *we seek not to acquire but to share.*
>
> *There are days*
> *when we exploit nature as if it were a horn*
> *of plenty that can*
> *never be exhausted.*
>
> *On the Sabbath*
> *we stand in wonder before the mystery of*
> *creation.*
>
> *There are days*
> *when we act as if we cared nothing for the*
> *rights of others.*
>
> *On the Sabbath*
> *we are reminded that justice is our duty and*
> *a better world*
> *our goal.*

Rosh Hashanah and Yom Kippur—The High Holy Days. The Jewish year begins on the first day of the autumn month of *Tishri*. Rosh Hashanah, literally "the head of the year," begins ten days of reflection and renewal ending with Yom Kippur, the day of atonement. The **shofar**, a ram's horn that sounds the beginning of the new year, is the symbol most associated with Rosh Hashanah. Yom Kippur is a day of fasting and repentance for wrongdoings of the previous year. It is the holiest day of the Jewish calendar. Even if Jews do not attend synagogue services on other days, they tend to participate in services during the High Holy Days.

Sukot. If you live near a synagogue or a Jewish home, late in autumn you might notice on the property a hut-like structure covered with branches, fruits, and vegetables. This temporary dwelling is a *sukah* and represents the Jewish harvest festival Sukot. In ancient Israel, during harvest-time it was more practical to stay out in the fields rather than to return home after the day's work. Jews found both historical and religious significance in this experience of the fragility of life and of dependency upon God, reminiscent of the time when their ancestors lived in temporary dwellings on their way to the Promised Land. The festival is also known as the "Feast of Booths" or the "Feast of Tents." Sukot ends with **Simchat Torah**, when the annual reading of Torah ends and a new cycle of reading Torah begins.

Pesach. Pesach, or Passover, is a springtime festival. It commemorates the Exodus from Egypt. The central event of Pesach is a ritualized meal celebrated at home called a **seder.** The meal is solemn, festive, and elaborate. The seder is a meal of free people, not of those still in the bondage of slavery such as the Jewish ancestors experienced while in Egypt. In order to assure that the meaning of the meal is not lost, the youngest child present asks four questions focused on the one question: Why is this night different from all other nights? Seven weeks after Pesach Jews celebrate **Shavuot**, the festival of weeks. It marks both the end of spring and reception of the Ten Commandments.

Hanukah. Hanukah is a minor Jewish holiday. However, especially in America, it has taken on increased significance simply because it falls around the time of Christmas. It is the feast of the rededication of the Temple, when the Greek rulers who controlled ancient Israel were driven out and the Temple was purified. Once again, Hanukah is celebrated mostly in the home where an eight-branched candlelabrum or **menorah** is ritually lit each night for eight days. Hanukah, like Christmas, is associated with light during the darkest time of the year.

The Church Speaks

In the Old Covenant bread and wine were offered in sacrifice among the first fruits of the earth as a sign of grateful acknowledgment to the Creator. But they also received a new significance in the context of the Exodus: the unleavened bread that Israel eats every year at Passover commemorates the haste of the departure that liberated them from Egypt; the remembrance of the manna in the desert will always recall to Israel that it lives by the bread of the Word of God; their daily bread is the fruit of the promised land, the pledge of God's faithfulness to his promises. (*Catechism of the Catholic Church*, #1334)

A. Jewish holy days are typically celebrated in the home. Is this true for the holy day celebrations of your religion? What are some ways that your home life could be spiritually enriched?

B. Find out what role each of the following plays in a Jewish home: mezuzah, Kiddush cup, challah, keeping kosher.

C. Write a report on the meaning and customs associated with one of the holy days listed in the text or with one of the minor Jewish holy days not mentioned here.

ACTIVITY

Celebrating the Jewish Life Cycle

God said to Abraham, "As for you, you shall keep my covenant, you and your offspring after you throughout their generations. This is my covenant, which you shall keep, between me and you and your offspring after you: Every male among you shall be circumcised. You shall circumcise the flesh of your foreskins, and it shall be a sign of the covenant between me and you. Throughout your generations every male among you shall be circumcised when he is eight days old....So shall my covenant be in your flesh an everlasting covenant. Any uncircumcised male who is not circumcised in the flesh of his foreskin shall be cut off from his people; he has broken my covenant." (Genesis 17:9–12a, 13b)

A Young American Jewish Woman Describes Her Experience

To start off, I'll tell you that I am a Jew. Although I am an American, when people ask what I am, I say Jewish. Jews have never been able to fit into the convenient categories used by people to define nation, race, religion, and other social groups. Except for the fact that Jews obviously do not constitute a race (for race is a biological designation), Jews are not just a religious faith, even though they are that; and they are not just a nation, even though they are that too, according to the definitions of the term "nation." The problem is usually resolved by using the term "people" instead of either faith or nation. This difficulty in categorizing the Jewish people may well be part of their uniqueness.

The first words of any introduction to the Jewish daily way of life must speak of kindness (*hesed*), because we believe that Jewish religious faith and ritual observance aim, above all, to achieve a perfection of the human relationship and to create a better society. While I know that I cannot possibly live by all the laws, teachings, or guidelines dealt with by Jewish law or faith, I try my best. I was always told that if I had to summarize the Torah in one sentence, I should say, "Love your neighbor as yourself." An ethical act, an act of kindness or of charity, performed not for any ulterior motives but in the belief that this is God's will, is very much in the category of a religious act and constitutes the fulfillment of religious law. To the extent that it provides spiritual satisfaction, it is a legitimate religious experience. Every day I try to do a mitzvah, whether I hold a door open for someone, give someone a ride, or find something and try to get it back to its owner.

While growing up I never understood why all the other kids got Santa and chocolate bunnies while I only got to light candles and eat extra large crackers that definitely didn't melt in your mouth. Nevertheless, with age comes understanding. I now know what Hanukah means. It's not just the holiday when I got gifts but a holiday that is observed for eight days. It commemorates the historic victory of the Maccabeans following a three-year long struggle against the ruling Assyrian-Greek regime that conspired to impose restrictions against Jewish religious practices and values. Hanukah means dedication and refers to the rededication of the Temple to the service of God. I may not have had Santa, but looking back I think I made out better by getting gifts on eight nights.

Growing up Jewish was also confusing because holidays always fell on different dates each year. Jewish people follow a different calendar than the Gregorian calendar. One way to look at the difference is that the Jewish year follows the lunar cycle of the moon as it circles the earth. Therefore, the Jewish dates are always the same each year. The English dates are the ones that are different. Being Jewish and American has been a challenge for me, but I have come to appreciate both aspects of my life. (Blaine Spector, a college student from Philadelphia, PA.)

Circumcision. Scripture clearly states that the circumcision of infant boys signals the covenant between God and the Jewish people. For Jews, circumcision is a deeply religious event that typically takes place in the home accompanied by prayers and festivities. Scripture describes no such initiation ritual for girls, although a ceremony for the naming of infant girls serves the purpose of formally initiating girls into the Jewish community.

Bar Mitzvah and **Bat Mitzvah.** A Jewish boy becomes a bar mitzvah when he turns thirteen. That is, he is now called upon to observe the commandments. (Bar mitzvah means "son of the commandment.") Beginning in the Middle Ages, a special ceremony marking a boy's becoming a responsible adult and an adult member of the Jewish community began to take shape, which is known today as the bar mitzvah ceremony. The official ceremony can take place anytime after a boy's thirteenth birthday, and typical-

Hasidic Rabbis in Israel celebrating at a wedding while in traditional dress

ly follows a period of studying the Hebrew language and Jewish beliefs and practices. An important component of the ceremony is the young man's first public reading from the Torah scroll at a synagogue service. Except in most Orthodox synagogues, during the past century a similar ceremony began to be held for girls, called a bat (or bas) mitzvah. Especially in the United States, the day of a bar or bat mitzah has come to be the occasion for a great family celebration.

Wedding. A case could be made that living a celibate life as a monk or a nun has been the Christian ideal for much of Christian history. This is not the case for Judaism, in which marriage and family life are the ideal. A number of symbols and rituals associated with a Jewish wedding ceremony stand out. A wedding takes place under a canopy called a **chupah.** The chupah symbolizes the Jewish home that the couple is now starting. After the couple express their commitment to each other and the groom places a ring on the bride's finger, the couple shares a cup of wine to symbolize that they will now share everything in their life. The ceremony ends with the groom stepping on a glass and everyone saying *Mazel tov*—Good Luck! (Why the groom breaks a glass is not certain, but a number of meanings have been suggested.)

Death. Burials in Judaism are to take place soon after a person dies, without embalming the body or placing it on display. Judaism has developed specific practices to guide people though the grieving process when a family member or loved one dies. For instance, an initial seven-day period of mourning, called *shivah* (seven), is spent at home where friends gather to join those in mourning and recite special prayers.

ACTIVITY

Choose one event or period in the Jewish life cycle.
Find out more about it, and compare the way it is celebrated with similar events or periods in your own religion.

Judaism in the United States

In 1654, twenty-three Jews arrived in New Amsterdam. Today, New York City has the largest population of Jews of any city in the world. Nonetheless, Jews living in the United States have had to carve out a niche for themselves in an overwhelmingly Christian country, where there has been a history of discrimination against Jews and even persecution of Jews. Even today, newspapers report hate crimes against Jews.

Given the relatively small numbers of Jews in the United States, one problem that concerns the Jewish community is **assimilation.** Assimilation refers to a minority group, such as Jews, risking the loss of their identity by becoming part of the dominant community. Jews have frequently faced this dilemma, from the time of their stay in Egypt prior to the Exodus. Generally, Jews discourage converts. (Remember, Judaism is the religion of Jews.) Therefore, whenever a Jew marries a non-Jew, there is the danger of one less family sustaining the Jewish community of the future. The more Jews dismiss their customs and practices, the more likely they are to lose their Jewish identity.

If you were Jewish and felt strongly about the importance of maintaining your Jewish identity, how would you respond to the following situations.

A. Your local school wants to hold a Christmas party. As part of the festivities Santa Claus will distribute a small gift to all children.

B. You are the only Jewish family on your block. Your neighbors are planning a night for caroling. They intend to line the sidewalk in front of their houses with candles. They would like you to have candles on your sidewalk as well so that there is no break in the lights along the street.

C. Your children would like to have a Christmas tree in their house like their Christian friends have.

D. Christmas is coming. You are trying to figure out what to do on Christmas day.

ACTIVITY

Conclusion

An Ongoing Journey of a People and Their God

The encounter between Abraham and his family with God set the Jewish people on a journey that has taken them, despite constant challenges, through four millennia. Along the way they have enriched the world in numerous ways. Christians and Muslims owe a particular debt to them. Entering a new millennium, Jews continue their struggle to be faithful to the covenant and a light to the nations. Judaism continues to be the vibrant and developing faith of a small but significant portion of the world's population. Its message of ethical monotheism remains a challenge for the Jewish people and the world.

ACTIVITY

Women Rabbis

Sally Priesand became the first woman rabbi in 1972. Since then, many women have become rabbis in Reform and Reconstructionist Judaism. Most Conservative communities also welcome women to become rabbis; Orthodox communities do not. Find out the current number of women rabbis in the United States.

Re-Thinking Judaism

A. Judaism is the story of the Jewish people's relationship with God through history. In an essay or art form, describe developments that have taken place during your life in your relationship with God.

B. Find out more about one person who played an important role in Jewish history. Describe the contribution that this person made to the religion.

C. Name and explain major themes in Judaism. Describe how they are similar to or different from themes in your own religion.

D. Imagine that you are Jewish. Describe your experience of your faith to someone who is not Jewish. Include a discussion of both the comforting and challenging aspects of being Jewish.

E. Describe one characteristic of Jewish faith that you would like to incorporate into your own faith life. Explain why.

Vocabulary

assimilation: Members of a minority group taking on characteristics of the dominant culture in which they live.

chupah: Canopy used during a wedding ceremony.

menorah: Candlelabrum. A seven-branched menorah is used in the synagogue, while an eight-branched menorah is used at Chanukah.

Seder: Passover meal.

shofar: Ram's horn used to signal the new year.

For Review

29. What function does the Sabbath play for Jews?

30. What feasts mark the beginning and end of the High Holy Days in Judaism? What time of the year are they celebrated?

31. What is the origin of Sukot? What does it celebrate today? How is it celebrated?

32. What does Pesach commemorate? How is it celebrated?

33. What does Chanukah celebrate? Why has it taken on increased significance recently?

34. What serves as the initiation rites for infant boys and girls into Judaism?

35. What do *Bar* and *Bat Mitzvah* mean? What is the significance of these ceremonies?

36. Name two rituals associated with the Jewish wedding ceremony.

37. What is Shivah?

38. Why is assimilation a concern of Jews in America?

CHAPTER 3

CHRISTIANITY

Jesus' Kingdom
of God Movement

Two thousand years ago in a remote province of the Roman Empire a movement began that would transform the world ever after. The leader of the movement, a Jewish peasant named Yesue or, in Greek, Jesus, led an active public life for at most three years. He gained followers because of some marvelous things he said and even more so because of some wonderful deeds he performed. He had good news even though for many times were hard. Some came to view him as the messiah, the one who would usher in the peace and prosperity that so many longed for. Indeed, for his followers the very glory of God shone through this humble but impressive man. His message struck a chord among enough people in his community that some local leaders, believing him to be a threat, called for his death. Nevertheless, the movement continued despite—or, more surprisingly, as a result of—the execution of its leader at the hands of the Roman prefect in Jerusalem. Today, people who claim to be followers of Jesus can boast of being members of the largest religion in the world.

What was the message of Jesus? Why was it and is it so alluring? What became of this message as it spread throughout first the Jewish community, then the Roman Empire, and finally the entire world? What do people who call themselves followers of Jesus believe? What do they do? No one can claim to know the full scope of human history without knowing the story of Jesus and his continuing movement.

Overview

- Jesus–his message and Christian teachings about him–is the foundation of Christian belief and practice.

- Christianity faced five major crises that shaped its historical development.

- Christianity today exhibits worship styles, morality, and roles for women and men reflecting its various branches.

- Traditionally Protestantism was the dominant religion in the U.S. Today all branches of Christianity face issues associated with increasing secularization.

Before we begin...

A. How would you describe the central teachings of Jesus and Christianity?

B. If you had been alive during the time of Jesus, do you think you would have become a member of his movement? Why or why not? What might have appealed to you about Jesus? What might have frightened you about him?

C. Why do you think this particular religion grew into the largest of the world's religions?

What Did Jesus Teach? What Do Christians Believe?

What we know about Jesus we know primarily through four writings, the **Gospels** according to Matthew, Mark, Luke, and John. Each gospel portrays Jesus from a unique point of view. Each gospel represents a testament written to affirm faith in Jesus for a community struggling with what such faith means. Just as we cannot completely separate the historical Siddhartha Gautama from the stories affirming him as the Buddha, so we cannot step outside of the gospel accounts affirming Jesus as the **Christ** and uncover the "historically accurate," "true-to-life" Jesus. The person we meet in the gospels is the "Christ of faith," the one the gospel writers believed to be the savior of the world. In a sense, the historical Jesus lies hidden behind these portraits. However, if we want to know what this religion truly stands for, then we need to attempt to be as historically accurate about the person of Jesus as we can be. To understand him as best we can, we will examine first the teachings *of* Jesus and then secondly the teachings *about* Jesus.

I. Teachings of Jesus

Your kingdom come,
Your will be done
on earth as it is
in heaven. (Matthew 6:10)

Most scholars today agree that the message of Jesus centers around his proclaiming the coming of the **kingdom of God.** However, this particular concept is not easily defined. Essentially the term refers to the will of God, the world as God intends it to be. That being said, we can misinterpret the concept in two ways. On the one hand, we would be wrong to reduce the kingdom of God to being solely an earthly, this-world entity. Such an interpretation would be an overly *material* understanding of God's kingdom. On the other hand, we would be wrong to reduce the kingdom of God exclusively to an after-death entity, totally separate from the concerns of this world. Such an interpretation would be an overly *spiritual* understanding of God's kingdom. Neither Jesus nor the entire Jewish tradition of which he was a part separated the spiritual from the material in such a clear-cut fashion. As we will see, Christianity views Jesus himself as both human and divine; and Christians pray for the kingdom to become a reality on earth as it already is in heaven.

Being a Jew, Jesus had a Jewish sense of what the world would be like

Vocabulary

Christ: a Greek word for the Hebrew messiah, meaning "the anointed one," a king. The term "Christ" came to be applied exclusively to Jesus so that Christianity is the religion of Jesus the Christ.

gospel: The literary form of the four accounts of the life of Jesus included in the Christian Scriptures. The term literally means "good news," a description that the earliest gospel—the Gospel according to Mark—applies to itself.

if people acted as God intended them to. He was greatly disturbed that the "ways of the world" in which he lived were so different from the way God intended the world to be—the kingdom of God. He held out a vision of a new community; he wanted his movement to be a world-changing one. He invited

people regardless of their social status, ethnic background, or religion to join in this movement. In a sense, the Hebrew Bible had already described the kingdom of God in the story of creation and the garden of Eden, in the vision of the Promised Land as a place where justice and compassion would reign, and in the sermons of the prophets who constantly called Israel back to following God's ways. Jesus built on, expanded, and personified this important Jewish concept.

Reading the Hebrew Scriptures and the gospels together, we discover that for Jesus and the other saintly Jews who preceded him God reigns when people such as widows and orphans are taken care of, when the land is used to meet the needs of all members of a community rather than to increase the wealth of a greedy few, when rulers make the welfare of people their priority rather than the building of grander palaces, when those who are physically or mentally ill are treated with great care and respect, when strangers are treated kindly, when anyone who is suffering is comforted, and when the dying are given hope in eternal life. Jesus offered the hope that such a world exists in eternity, with God in heaven beyond the bounds of time. He also called people to view themselves and others as God views them and to act accordingly.

A. Describe an exclusively material interpretation of the kingdom of God.

B. Describe an exclusively spiritual interpretation of the kingdom of God.

C. What are possible problems with reducing the concept of the kingdom of God either to a material-only or a spiritual-only understanding?

ACTIVITY

The Beatitudes: A Charter for the Kingdom

If there is a "charter" for Jesus' understanding of the kingdom of God, it would be the **Beatitudes**. Both Matthew's gospel (in 5:1–12) and the Gospel of Luke list characteristics describing members of Jesus' movement. Luke has the shorter, more direct, and probably older list of beatitudes:

> Blessed are you who are poor,
> for yours is the kingdom of God.
> Blessed are you who are hungry now,
> for you will be filled.
> Blessed are you who weep now,
> for you will laugh.
> Blessed are you when people hate you, and when they exclude you,
> revile you, and defame you on account of the Son of Man. Rejoice
> in that day and leap for joy, for surely your reward is great in heav-
> en; for that is what their ancestors did to the prophets.
> But woe to you who are rich,
> for you have received your consolation.
> Woe to you who are full now,
> for you will be hungry.
> Woe to you who are laughing now,
> for you will mourn and weep. (Luke 6:20–25)

ACTIVITY

A. Read again carefully the list of "blessings and woes" from Luke 6:20–25. If someone totally unfamiliar with Jesus and with Christianity came upon this passage, would that person receive an accurate picture of Jesus and his message?

B. Based on Luke 6:20–25, what might someone unfamiliar with Jesus understand as core elements of his message?

C. Are there other dimensions to Jesus' message not contained in Luke 6:20–25 that you would want to explain to someone unfamiliar with Jesus and with Christianity? If so, what would they be? Then, look through the gospels to determine whether or not you can find support for these additional dimensions of Jesus' message.

Did Jesus Offer a Plan of Action?

If Jesus began a movement that evolved into what we know as Christianity, did he propose any program, a specific plan of action for his community? Again, the gospels provide us with clues about what it means to be a follower of Jesus. Here are four interwoven themes that suggest the types of activities Christianity stands for.

Sharing Meals. Many scholars suggest that sharing meals represents a core activity of the Jesus movement during and immediately after his lifetime. Especially back then sharing a meal was a real as well as a symbolically potent statement about how people perceived one another. Jesus himself practiced and advocated universal meal sharing. That is, he ate with anybody and everybody and called upon his followers to do the same. Of

Celebrating the Eucharist

course, this practice was most baffling when Jesus ate with tax collectors, with women driven to a life of prostitution, and with various others who were classified as sinners by the upright members of society.

Today, a central practice for most Christians is the **Eucharist**, gathering around a table and celebrating Christ in the taking of bread and wine, giving thanks, breaking of the bread, sharing of bread and wine by the community. This important Christian ritual symbolizes and makes real the central Christian teaching mentioned above, the kingdom of God. That is, in the Eucharist people are nurtured by God and reminded that no one is to go hungry in this barrier-free setting of a shared meal, which is the very image of the kingdom of God proclaimed by Jesus. (As we will see, different groups of Christians interpret the meaning of the Eucharist differently. However, all Christians accept that Jesus intended table fellowship—and all that it represents—to be a fundamental as well as a symbolically rich Christian activity.)

> One of his most characteristic activities was an open and inclusive table. "Table fellowship"—sharing a meal with somebody—had a significance in Jesus' social world that is difficult for us to imagine.

It was not a casual act, as it can be in the modern world. In a general way, sharing a meal represented mutual acceptance. More specifically, rules surrounding meals were deeply embedded in the purity system. Those rules governed not only what might be eaten and how it should be prepared, but also with whom one might eat. Refusing to share a meal was a form of social ostracism. Pharisees (and others) would not eat with somebody who was impure, and no decent person would share a meal with an outcast. The meal was a microcosm of the social system, table fellowship an embodiment of social vision. (Marcus J. Borg, Meeting Jesus Again for the First Time [HarperSanFrancisco, 1995], 55)

ACTIVITY

A. As best as you can, draw a picture of people gathered around a table sharing a meal. Then write a meditation about the symbolism of eating together, reflecting on possible implications of table fellowship and the Christian message. As part of your essay address the question: Why is universal meal-sharing, making sure that everyone is fed, a God-like activity?

B. Besides being hungry for food, people can be hungry in a number of other ways. Draw a picture or write a story, a poem, or an essay about a particular kind of hunger that meal-sharing symbolically addresses.

C. Find out how each of the following Christian churches views the Eucharist. That is, do they speak of Christ's presence in the Eucharist? How often do they celebrate the Eucharist? How often do they hold communion services? Under what form or forms is communion typically received? Who may celebrate the Eucharist and receive communion? Apart from the celebration of the Eucharist itself, do they celebrate other rites using the eucharistic elements of bread and wine?

- **Roman Catholics**
- **Eastern Catholics**
- **Lutherans**
- **Presbyterians**
- **Baptists**
- **Eastern Orthodox**

Healing. Clearly, Jesus was a healer. Indeed, healing was central to his mission and to that of his community. The earliest leaders of Jesus' movement were called **apostles**, a word meaning "those who are sent." One of the most important activities that Jesus sent the apostles out to do was healing. The many instances of healing recounted in the gospels indicate that Jesus always connected physical and spiritual healing together. For instance, Jesus would accompany physical healing with a statement such as, "Your sins are forgiven. Go and sin no more." Both healing and forgiveness are works of the kingdom; both involve restoring the human person and the human community to the way God intends them to be. For Christians, healing and forgiveness lead to salvation. The root meaning of this word is "health." The goal of the Christian life—salvation—is not separate from the means to the goal, participating in the healing of life's hurts and in the healthy restoration of the human community. A key dimension of the Christian agenda is identifying how people are hurting and seeking to ease their pain. Finally, Christians believe that God will bring all pain and suffering to an end. As we will see, this is the meaning behind another great Christian belief about Jesus—the paschal mystery.

> *The joys and hopes, the griefs and anguish of the people of our*
> *time, especially of those who are poor or afflicted, are the joys and*
> *hopes, the grief and anguish of the followers of Christ as well.*
> *(Vatican Council II,* The Church in the Modern World, *1)*

Make a list, as complete as possible, of ways that Christians participate in the healing practice of Jesus. (Remember that from a gospel perspective healing is physical as well as spiritual, personal as well as social.) Based on your list, write an essay on the following topic: Healing represents a necessary and fundamental activity of the Christian life.

ACTIVITY

Unconditional and Inclusive Love. Of course, love is not something separate from sharing meals and healing, but since it is so important a part of Jesus' message it deserves to be highlighted. In fact, according to the Gospel of John, Jesus proclaims love to be the one identifying characteristic of his followers:

> *I give you a new commandment, that you love one another. Just as*
> *I have loved you, you also should love one another. By this every-*
> *one will know that you are my disciples, if you have love for one*
> *another. (John 13:34–35)*

Here's a description of what love means given by Jesus in the section of the Gospel according to Luke following the beatitudes:

> *But I say to you that listen, Love your enemies, do good to those who hate you, bless those who curse you, pray for those who abuse you. If anyone strikes you on the cheek, offer the other also; and from anyone who takes away your coat do not withhold even your shirt. Give to everyone who begs from you; and if anyone takes away your goods, do not ask for them again. Do to others as you would have them do to you.*
>
> *If you love those who love you, what credit is that to you? For even sinners love those who love them. If you do good to those who do good to you, what credit is that to you? For even sinners do the same. If you lend to those from whom you hope to receive, what credit is that to you? Even sinners lend to sinners, to receive as much again. But love your enemies, do good, and lend, expecting nothing in return. Your reward will be great, and you will be children of the Most High; for he is kind to the ungrateful and the wicked. Be merciful, just as your Father is merciful. (Luke 6:27–36)*

This passage presents a challenging but accurate description of the Christian practice of love. As Jesus talks about it, love is both unconditional and all-inclusive. That is, true love doesn't pick and choose whom to love and when to love them. True love extends equally to those like us as well as to those unlike us—even our enemies! True love remains steadfast in good times and in bad. Jesus points out that unconditional and inclusive love is the Christian ideal because it is the way of love exhibited by a kind and merciful God. For Christians, an important way that God's love is manifest is through their own acts of love. Their love of God is not to be separated from active love of other people. Thus love is both a challenge for Christians and grounds for their being a people of hope. Even if they fail in their attempts at love, God does not. Indeed, Christianity came to recognize God as an intricate, intimate web of love, a Holy Trinity of Father, Son, and Spirit.

Justice. We have already examined the powerful message of justice found in the Jewish tradition. Jesus took up and carried on this message in his own teaching. Jesus demonstrated particular concern for those in his society who were poor and destitute. He recognized that they were the ones who obviously had the greatest need of help. Their lacking adequate food and shelter was a clear violation of God's will and a distortion of what God's reign should be like. Therefore, righting such wrongs—works of justice—is an essential component of any Christian agenda aimed at building up God's kingdom. As the world's Catholic bishops wrote in 1971, working for justice is essential to the Church's vocation and mission and "a constitutive dimension of the preaching of the gospel" (Synod of Bishops, "Justice in the World," Introduction).

Both love and justice share a common goal, transforming a society in which some people dominate others into a community of sharing and mutual giving and receiving. Use examples to describe similarities and differences between love and justice.

II. Teachings about Jesus

Incarnation. For Christians, Jesus was not merely a great prophet, an important teacher, a miracle worker, and a charismatic leader. For Christians, Jesus did not merely point to God and tell people about the wonders of God. Members of other religions could say all of these things about Jesus and not be Christian. Instead, Christians believe that Jesus is *God in the flesh.* This teaching is so central to Christianity that it is fair to say that no one can count herself or himself a Christian who does not hold this belief. The term for this fundamental Christian belief is the mystery of the **Incarnation.**

This mystery, the most hotly debated theological concept in the first few centuries of Christian history, clarifies the Christian understanding of the relationship between Jesus and God. On the one hand Jesus is totally and completely human; to say otherwise would be to deny his humanity and thus to deny the Incarnation. On the other hand Jesus is also God totally and completely; at no point does God end and Jesus begin, or Jesus end and God continue. Conflicting viewpoints on this issue were so troublesome in the early Church that the Emperor Constantine himself—not yet a baptized Christian at the time—called the

Key Themes in Christian Beliefs about Jesus

- Incarnation
- Paschal Mystery
- Trinity

Christian bishops together in the year 325 at Nicea to straighten it out. Bishops met again in 381 at Constantinople to further refine the basic beliefs of Christianity. However, the statement emerging from these two gatherings is typically called simply the **Nicene Creed.** It has remained the standard or **orthodox** teaching on the subject ever since. Here is the part of that creed, as it is recited in Roman Catholic liturgies, that articulates Christian teaching about Jesus:

> *We believe in one Lord, Jesus Christ,*
> *the only Son of God,*
> *eternally begotten of the Father,*
> *God from God, Light from Light,*
> *true God from true God,*
> *begotten, not made, one in Being with the Father.*
> *Through him all things were made.*
> *For us men and for our salvation*
> *he came down from heaven:*
> *by the power of the Holy Spirit*
> *he was born of the Virgin Mary, and became man.*

The Incarnation is a mystery upon which there could be much fruitful reflection. Christians believe that in his very being Jesus reconciles humanity and divinity—that is, the human longing for fulfillment is now achieved. In Jesus the power of God shines through the very frailties and limitations of the human condition. (For instance, are you feeling alone and worthless, as if nobody cares? In the person of Jesus, Christians find a powerful statement about how much God—the one who matters most—is with us and cares for us. Indeed, Incarnation means that God takes on flesh and therefore is one with us.) Also, because of the Incarnation, Christians claim that we have direction about how to participate in God's kingdom. (In other words, do you want to know how to participate in God's reign? You need look no further than to the words and deeds of Jesus who is human like us but also divine.) Finally, because of the Incarnation, Christians profess that we humans have "one of our own" through whom we can encounter God—Jesus Christ.

Paschal Mystery. The second great Christian belief is that the human life of Jesus—which includes his comings and goings, teachings and healings, suffering, death, resurrection, and sending of the Spirit—is the cause of salvation. Christians call this belief the paschal mystery—paschal is Greek for

Passover—because its theme mirrors so closely the theme of the Exodus in the Hebrew Scriptures. Why did Jesus live, suffer, and die? The Nicene Creed says simply that it was "for us," "for our salvation," and "for our sake." It is as if the gospel writers want to tell us in dramatic fashion, "See how much God loves us!"

As with the Incarnation, this belief about Jesus has inspired Christians for two thousand years. Christians of the Eastern Churches, whom we'll meet shortly, celebrate that they are indeed one with God because Christ has broken down the barriers between God and human beings once and for all. Evangelical Christians, whom we'll discuss later in the chapter, refer to themselves as "born again" thanks to the death and resurrection of Christ. However it is understood, to be Christian means to believe in the paschal mystery. To believe in the paschal mystery means to be a person who is ultimately filled with joy and hope, no matter what one's current state in life happens to be.

> For our sake he was crucified under Pontius Pilate;
> he suffered, died, and was buried.
> On the third day he rose again
> in fulfillment of the scriptures;
> he ascended into heaven
> and is seated at the right hand of the Father.
> (The Nicene Creed)

ACTIVITY

A. Christians believe that Christ's resurrection brought about "new life." List some characteristics of what you think this new life is meant to be like. Secondly, list some characteristics of the "old life" that the paschal mystery has overcome. Finally, write an essay describing what the paschal mystery means to you.

B. Write an essay describing ways that Christian new life is similar to or different from what other religions believe.

Trinity. Christian teaching about the Holy Trinity makes some non-Christians squeamish, especially Jews and Muslims. It affirms monotheism but can appear to be a diluted or distorted version of it. Do Christians believe in one God or three? The answer is that Christianity has never entertained anything other than monotheism. The Holy Trinity is a statement about, an explanation of, the one and only one God. Is God the God of creation, the

An iconic image of the Trinity

God who saved the Israelites from slavery and the God who harangued the Jewish people about remaining faithful to their covenant? Christians answer with an unhesitating yes. When Muslims profess that there is only one God, do Christians agree? Again the answer is an unhesitating yes. The Christian creed settled on "God the Father" as the term that most closely describes God encountered in this fashion.

However, Christianity does not stop with this understanding of God. For Christians, God is experienced in relationship. If people believe that God the Father is a remote, distant, absent God, they would be wrong. A loving father wants to share himself with his children as completely as he can. God accomplished this self-giving through the person of Jesus, his son. Christians, then, view Jesus as the Father's first-born son, an important concept in the Mediterranean cultures at the time of Jesus, who is at the same time "one in being with the Father."

Carrying this dynamic, relational view of God one step further, Christians propose that God does not become present in Jesus Christ and then return to being absent from the affairs of human lives. Instead, the Holy Spirit remains actively present in the world, especially in and among all those who show their belief in God through word and deed. This person, the Holy Spirit, is no less God than the Father and the Son are. Christianity came to understand that these three persons-in-relationship, while distinguishable, were also inseparable; a full understanding of God requires each of them. The term used to explain the "three-in-oneness" of God is the Holy Trinity.

You are likely to hear Christians talk about "three persons in one God." In the Greco-Roman world we discover words for person that mean "face" or "mask." We can think of a mask—someone's persona—as hiding who a person truly is. (Behind a smiling mask, or persona, can actually be a very sad "person.") This is not the way Christians understand the word person in the Trinity. Each person—Father, Son, and Spirit—does not hide the reality of God but rather *is God in a distinct way.* Thus Christians believe in one God present to us in three persons, the Holy Trinity—Father, Son, and Holy Spirit. A Presbyterian pastor explains the Christian teaching about the Holy Trinity this way:

You won't find the word Trinity in the Bible. Nor will you find the language of "three-in-one" or "three persons, one substance" in the Bible. It's not there. Nowhere does the Bible contain a doctrine of the Trinity. The doctrine we have today for the Trinity is the culmination of a long process spanning the first few centuries of the church....

In the end, here's what Christians came to think about the nature of God. First, they observed that God created the universe and then took care of it all. This person they called "God the Father." Next, they observed that this same God...came to us in Jesus of Nazareth, having both divine and human natures. God was "up in heaven," but God was also "down here," alongside us or with us. This person they called "God the Son," the eternal Word or Logos who was with God from the beginning, at creation itself, and who was truly God. Finally, they observed that God came to us at Pentecost and could be found in us or among us as guide and friend. Jesus referred to this God who comes to us as the "Spirit of Truth" and the "Advocate." This person they called "God the Holy Spirit." (Douglas J. Brouwer, Remembering the Faith: What Christians Believe [Grand Rapids, MI: William B. Eerdmans Publishing Co., 1999], 144-45)

ACTIVITY

Unlike Jews and Muslims, Christians—especially Catholic and Orthodox Christians—are comfortable imaging God, recognizing, however, that no image captures all that God is. (If you're Irish or American, you are probably familiar with Saint Patrick's use of the shamrock to try to explain the concept of the Trinity.)

Draw a symbolic representation of one of the following:

- **God the Father**
- **God the Son**
- **God the Holy Spirit**
- **the Holy Trinity**

Explain why you chose your image or images.

Vocabulary

Beatitudes: Characteristics of the members of Jesus' movement found in the Gospel of Matthew, chapter 5, and in the Gospel of Luke, chapter 6.

Vocabulary (continued)

Eucharist: Literally means "to give thanks." Originally a meal commemorating Jesus' last supper with his closest friends, early on it became highly ritualized and focused on bread and wine. Different Christian bodies view the eucharistic celebration and the bread and wine used in it differently.

Holy Trinity: Three persons in one God; three ways that God is present to human beings, as Father, Son, and Spirit.

incarnation: Belief that Jesus is fully divine and fully human.

kingdom of God: A key theme in the message of Jesus: God's will for individual people and for the human community; life with God on earth that reaches its fulfillment after death.

Nicene Creed: Summary of Christian beliefs formulated in 325 CE at the Council of Nicea, expanded in 381 at the Council of Constantinople.

Orthodox: That which is designated to be a true and accurate teaching, in contrast to a "heresy," which is designated to be a false and inaccurate statement about Christian beliefs.

paschal mystery: Belief that the whole life of Jesus—birth, actions, teachings, ministry, suffering, death, resurrection, ascension, sending of the Spirit—redeems humanity.

For Review

1. Name the four gospels contained in the Christian Scriptures.
2. What does the term "Christ" mean?
3. Explain the difference between an overly material and an overly spiritual understanding of Jesus' teaching about the kingdom of God.
4. What are the Beatitudes?
5. What does it mean to say that Jesus practiced universal meal sharing?
6. Who were the apostles?
7. According to Jesus, what quality characterizes his followers?
8. According to Jesus, who were the people most in need in his society?

9. What relationship exists between the Church's mission and justice as stated by the world's Catholic bishops in 1971?

10. Define the following terms: Incarnation, paschal mystery, the Holy Trinity.

III. Christian Historical Development
Five Crises

If things had not changed or developed from what existed during the first couple of decades of the Christian era, then we wouldn't have a religion—Christianity—separate from Judaism. Instead, today as we travel across the globe we find onion-shaped spires on Eastern Christian churches, unadorned meeting houses of the Puritan tradition, grand cathedrals representing the high Middle Ages in Europe, and modern auditoriums more suited to preaching and group singing than to table fellowship. Each one of these claims to be a valid expression of Christianity. How did this change occur? To get the full story, take a church history course. To get a general overview of major developments in the history of Christianity, it's helpful to understand five major crises faced by this religion and the transformations that occurred in response to these crises. For each of these crises we can identify key figures and key events.

Crisis #1: What Does It Mean to Be Christian as Opposed to Jewish?

Christianity began as a Jewish movement. Jesus himself was Jewish, as were the early leaders of the movement. However, a development began to occur that led to a change. Specifically, many non-Jews were attracted to this form of Judaism. In response to their interest, what was the Christian community to do? A key figure in resolving this crisis was a man named **Saint Paul**. A key event was a gathering of Christian leaders that took place around the year 49 known as the **Council of Jerusalem**.

A case could be made that Christianity would never have moved beyond being another expression of Judaism were it not for Saint Paul. He possessed qualities that the original apostles didn't. Paul was a Pharisee, an educated Jew. His hometown, Tarsus, was a center of Greek culture. He was also a Roman citizen. (Few people at the time were citizens; only an elite were. Even in Rome itself, most people living there were slaves. Since Paul was a Roman citizen, when he was executed for sedition in Rome he was beheaded, which was a quick and less painful death than his companion Saint Peter underwent. Treated as a common criminal like Jesus, tradition says that Peter was crucified—but upside down!)

The combination of being (a) an educated Jew, (b) familiar with high Greek culture, and (c) a Roman citizen made Paul perfectly suited for spreading the gospel message beyond the villages and countryside of Judea where Jesus and the first disciples came from. Paul and the other apostles focused their preaching in the synagogues and among the Jews of the towns they visited—after all, the message of Jesus was a Jewish message; to follow Jesus meant to be Jewish. However, so many non-Jews liked what they were hearing from these Christian preachers that the leaders of the Christian movement had to re-think their policy. Did non-Jews have to become Jewish to belong to the Christian community? For instance, did grown men need to become circumcised according to Jewish law if they wanted to confirm their belief in Jesus Christ? You can read about this controversy in a book of the Bible called the **Acts of the Apostles**, chapter 15.

At the meeting in Jerusalem mentioned above, the leaders gathered together to debate the issue declared that non-Jews *could* be full members of the Christian community without being circumcised and without following all of the dietary and other laws that Jews were called upon to follow. With that pronouncement, the Christian movement took a clear step away from being strictly a Jewish movement. It now existed as a separate, distinct, unique entity. While the split between Judaism and Christianity isn't simply the result of one decision at one meeting, it was events such as this one that resulted in the religious landscape that we have today—Jewish synagogues and Christian churches, congregations of Jews and congregations of Christians, Jews partaking of a Sabbath meal on Friday nights and Christians attending Sunday services, the Jewish religion and the Christian religion.

Crisis #2: What Does It Mean to Be Christian in the Roman Empire?

Once Christianity was cut loose from its Jewish moorings members of the movement faced new trials and tribulations. Leaders of the Roman Empire recognized Judaism to be an ancient religion and granted it legal status. Apart from Judaism, Christianity fell into a different category altogether; it became an illegal cult. So-called "mystery cults" abounded in the Roman Empire of the time. It's easy to see how the Christian community, if subjected to rumor, would be a suspect group. ("Don't Christians hold secret meetings where they eat flesh and drink blood?!") Two people who played key roles in deciding the fate of Christianity in the Roman Empire were the emperors **Nero** and **Constantine**.

During Nero's reign (54-68 CE) a great fire destroyed much of Rome. According to a historian writing a few decades after the event, rumor spread that Nero himself had set the fire. Here's what the Roman historian Tacitus reports as Nero's response to that rumor:

A. Saint Paul was not afraid to make a case for Christianity before the most educated people of his time. Read about the way he explained the Christian message to the elite of Athens in Acts 17:16–34.

1. What was the attitude of the Athenians to Paul and his message?

2. What line of reasoning did Paul use to reach the Athenians?

3. Do you think that highly educated people would be more or less drawn to Christianity? Why?

4. If you were called upon to explain basic Christian beliefs to people who are unfamiliar with Christianity, what would you say? Do you think they would hear it as "good news"? Why or why not?

B. Before becoming Christian, Saint Paul led the persecution of Christians in the name of the Jewish high priests. Acts 9:1–25 tells the story of his conversion. Read this account and describe the transformation that took place in Paul. If you were to interpret this story as symbolic of the conversion process in general, what significance would the various dimensions of the story hold?

ACTIVITY

Therefore, to squelch the rumor, Nero created scapegoats and subjected to the most refined tortures those whom the common people called "Christians," [a group] hated for their abominable crimes. Their name comes from Christ, who, during the reign of Tiberius, had been executed by the procurator Pontius Pilate. Suppressed for the moment, the deadly superstition broke out again, not only in Judea, the land which originated this evil, but also in the city of Rome, where all sorts of horrendous and shameful practices from every part of the world converge and are fervently cultivated. (quoted in John P. Meier, A Marginal Jew [New York: Doubleday, 1991], 89-90)

In other words, thanks to Nero the initial answer to the question, What does it mean to be Christian in the Roman Empire, was *persecution, torture,* and *death*. For almost the first three centuries of the Christian era, to be Christian meant to be subject to persecution. There were times when persecutions were more or less intense, but nonetheless Christians remained an outcast group for all this time. Joining the Christian community meant at least the possibility of losing one's home, of being sent to prison, and of undergoing the worst tortures the legal system of the empire could dream up. This situation continued until another emperor, Constantine, changed the status of Christians and entirely transformed the relationship between the religion and the empire.

In 313 Constantine issued a decree, the **Edict of Milan**, which granted legal status to Christianity. Actually, Christians had been growing in numbers and influence before Constantine's decree. However, with Constantine the answer to the question, What does it mean to be Christian in the Roman Empire, changed dramatically. Before him, to be Christian was to be an outcast and an outsider; after him, *not* to be Christian was to be an outsider. Before him, to get ahead in the government or the military it was best not to be Christian; after him, to get ahead in the military and the government it was important to *be* Christian. For better or for worse, the empire, "civilization," and Christianity now were intertwined.

A. Write a poem, a song, an essay, or a short story about being an outsider, about being a member of the "in-crowd," or about the contrast between the two. Would you prefer being an outsider or in the "in-crowd"? Why?

B. One theologian has suggested that when Constantine legalized Christianity he actually sucked some of the spirit out of the movement. Why do you think he would make such a claim? What was it like to be Christian before the Edict of Milan compared to afterwards?

C. Find out what you can about one of the martyrs from the first few centuries of Christianity. Write a report on him or her.

Crisis #3: What Does It Mean to Be Eastern as Opposed to Western Christian?

Emperor Constantine figures into this third crisis that Christianity faced as well. Besides making Christianity legal, he also decided to move the capital of the empire to what was then a small trading post called Byzantium, modern-day Istanbul in Turkey. He called the new capital "New Rome," but most people simply referred to it as "Constantine's City"—Constantinople. This transfer of power from west to east symbolizes tensions that existed in the Christian Church from Constantine's time and reached a crisis point in the eleventh century. The eastern half of the empire spoke Greek primarily and Greek culture dominated more so than in the West, where Latin was the common language. In the East, a number of ancient Christian centers flourished and established a theology and church practices that were adopted by the areas surrounding them. In the West one city dominated the frontiers of the empire spreading ever westward—Rome. Since barbarian tribes to the north and west were such a constant threat, Rome focused its attention more and more on Western Europe. This east-west split in language, culture, customs, and concerns eventually led to a formal split between the Western Church and the Eastern Churches—the **East-West Schism**. The year was 1054, and two key figures were Michael Cerularius and Humbert of Moyenmoutier.

The East-West Schism refers to the pope of Rome and the patriarch of Constantinople excommunicating each other, that is, each declared the

The Siege of Constantinople (painted in 1499)

other no longer members of the one true Church. Michael Cerularius was the patriarch at the time and Humbert of Moyenmoutier was the cardinal-secretary to the pope who led a delegation to Constantinople to work out differences between the two. Due to some misunderstandings, neither treated the other kindly, and the schism was on. From then on the Western Church came to call itself Catholic, while the Eastern Churches called themselves Orthodox. (Actually, even though 1054 is the date when the schism was declared, it was really the crusades that occurred a century or so after that cemented the east-west split. Crusaders from Western Europe, sent to fight Muslims, ended up sacking Constantinople and stripping its churches of everything valuable.)

Following the formal split numerous attempts were made to reconcile the Churches. There is still a Western Church, centered in Rome and under the leadership of Rome's bishop, the pope. Eventually some communities of the Eastern Churches reestablished full communion with the Roman Catholic Church while some did not. As a result, today there are **Eastern Catholic Churches**, which maintain their own unique style of worship, practices, and church governance but are in full communion with the Roman Catholic Church. There are also **Eastern Orthodox Churches**, which maintain their own unique style of worship, practices, and church governance but are not in full communion with the Roman Catholic Church. In 1965, Pope Paul VI and Patriarch Athenagoras I of Constantinople revoked the decree of excommunication that their predecessors had imposed nine hundred years earlier. While relations between the Roman Catholic Church and the Orthodox Churches have warmed considerably over the past few decades, the two groups remain officially separated and maintain separate leadership.

ORIGINAL PATRIARCHATES:
Western Church of Rome

Byzantine (8,050,000):

Albanians	Russians
Bulgarians	Ruthenians
Georgians	Romanians
Greeks	Ukrainians
Italo-Albanians	Yugoslavs
Melkite	Slovak
Hungarians	

Alexandrian (330,000):

Coptic (Egypt)	Ethiopians (Abyssinians)

Antiochene (2,700,000):

East Syrian
- Chaldean
  - Middle East
  - Europe
  - Africa
  - the Americas
- Syro-Malabarese [India]

West Syrian
- Malankarese [India]
- **Maronite worldwide**
  - mainly Lebanon
- **Syrian**
  - Syria
  - Lebanon
  - Iran
  - Egypt
  - Turkey

Jerusalem (Armenian)(150,000):

Near East	Africa
Middle East	Americas
Europe	Australia

Vocabulary

Acts of the Apostles: Book of the Bible that tells the story of the beginning of Christianity.

East-West Schism: The split between Eastern Orthodox Churches and the Western Church.

Eastern Catholic Churches: Church communities whose origins are in the Eastern Roman Empire and who are in full communion with the Roman Catholic Church.

Eastern Orthodox Churches: Church communities whose origins are in the Eastern Roman Empire and who are not in full communion with the Roman Catholic Church.

Edict of Milan: Emperor Constantine's decree making Christianity a legal religion in 313.

Patriarch of Constantinople: Head of the Byzantine Orthodox Church.

ACTIVITY

A. **A number of factors led to the East-West Schism. Research the topic and compile a list of these factors.** Then write an essay explaining the schism from either the perspective of the Orthodox Churches or the Western Catholic Church.

B. **Sharing religious perspectives and practices similar to the Orthodox and yet being in full communion with the Roman Catholic Church, Eastern Catholics occupy an interesting position within Christianity.** What do you think are some problems that might arise in terms of how Eastern Catholics are viewed by Western Catholics and by Orthodox Christians? What unique contributions do you think Eastern Catholicism can add to Christianity?

For Review

11. Why was Saint Paul well-suited to spread the Christian message to non-Jews?

12. What decisions did the Council of Jerusalem make?

13. Which part of the Christian story is told in the Acts of the Apostles?

14. Once it was no longer an expression of Judaism, what status did Christianity hold in the Roman Empire ?

15. What role did Nero and Constantine play in the fate of Christianity?

16. How did Constantine figure into the third crisis faced by Christianity?

17. What caused the Roman Church to focus its attention more and more on the western part of the empire?

18. What roles were played by Michael Cerularius and Humbert of Moyenmoutier?

19. What was the East-West Schism and when did it occur?

20. What is the difference between Eastern Orthodox and Eastern Catholic Churches?

Crisis #4: What Does It Mean to Be Catholic as Opposed to Protestant?

In a typical American city, on the same street corner there might be a Lutheran and a United Methodist church while down the street are Catholic and Baptist churches side by side. Why this duplication of space? Aren't they all Christian churches? A person who represents a key to understanding the diversity that currently exists within Western Christianity is Martin Luther. A key date is 1517.

Before Luther and the Protestant Reformation, in Western Europe there was not Catholicism as opposed to Protestantism. There was just Christianity. After Luther, this was no longer the case. Martin Luther was a German Augustinian monk, one of many people at the time who realized that the Church needed reform. He questioned some Church practices popular at the time and some theological interpretations common-

Martin Luther

ly held. In 1517 another monk, Johann Tetzel, received a commission from the pope to travel through Germany and raise money for building the great Saint Peter's Basilica in Rome by in effect selling indulgences, Martin Luther used the occasion to call for debate about this practice and others like it. According to tradition, he posted a list of his positions on these issues on the church doors in the town square of Wittenburg where he taught scripture. His list, called the "ninety-five theses," caused quite a stir. He actually sent them to his local bishop and believed that if the pope read them he would agree with Luther.

If his "ninety-five theses" had been read only by whoever happened to see them on the church door or by a few Church officials, then probably not much would have come of them. However, about seventy years earlier another German had invented the printing press. By 1517 many European towns had printing presses in operation. Thanks to this modern invention, Luther's ninety-five theses made their way across Europe. Many people found that his views resonated with their own. Others, such as Church leaders in Rome, did not respond kindly to this monk's criticizing their policies and practices. Although the pope condemned him for his teachings, for various reasons Luther avoided punishment that he might have received if it were one hundred years earlier—such as being burned at the stake!

Because of this combination of events—(a) that conditions indicated the need for Church reform, (b) that less antagonistic calls for reform were not being heeded by Church leaders, (c) that Luther posted his ninety-five theses calling for reforms, (d) that his message spread rapidly and far, and (e) that he was able to get away with it—makes 1517 the year we can call the beginning of the Protestant Reformation. By the end of the sixteenth century lines were clearly drawn between the Catholic Church and an increasing number of Christian denominations that can be labeled Protestant Churches.

What are indulgences?

The Catholic understanding of the concept "indulgences" is not exactly the same today as it was at the time of Luther and the Reformation. However, indulgences remain part of the Catholic body of teachings. Here is a capsule description of what the term means.

Catholics who perform harmful acts have available to them a sacrament, called penance or reconciliation, by which they can actually hear from a priest that God forgives their sins. However, is that the end of the matter, or is further cleansing from the residual effects of their wrongdoing necessary? This is where indulgences come in. According to standard Catholic teaching, there is a need for cleansing even after confession and forgiveness. Indeed, this cleansing can take place in this life or even after death—a condition known as purgatory, which simply means "cleansing." Personal prayers and good deeds can make amends for wrongdoing and wash away the negative residue left over from sin. However, there are also the sacrifice of Jesus and the prayers and good deeds of so many holy people past and present. These are the "treasury of the Church" that offset and make up for the harmful effects of sin by others. This treasury of merit available to Catholics seeking to make up for any harm still remaining from their sins is known as indulgences.

Is helping to build a church a type of good deed that would cleanse oneself or perhaps a loved one of any ill effects remaining from one's sins? The pope in Luther's time said yes. He invited Christians to help pay for the building of Saint Peter's Basilica in Rome. In exchange for doing this good deed, they would receive indulgences for themselves and for their loved ones in purgatory. Luther rejected this understanding of how God's grace operates and felt this practice called for public debate—thus he posted his ninety-five theses and the Protestant Reformation began.

Do research on three of the following and describe their role in the turmoil surrounding the Reformation.

- Erasmus
- John Tetzel
- Frederick of Saxony
- Emperor Charles V
- King Henry VIII of England
- Revolt of the German peasants in 1524
- John Calvin
- Huldrich Zwingli
- Menno Simons
- George Fox
- Council of Trent
- Ignatius Loyola
- Charles Borromeo

Key Distinctions between Catholic and Protestant

It's important to keep in mind that all branches of Western Christianity were shaped by the Reformation. During the four centuries after the Reformation, for many Christians being *Catholic* meant not being Protestant while being *Protestant* meant not being Catholic. Once again Luther gives us an idea of the major differences between these two forms of Christianity.

Luther put forth three propositions that clearly distinguish his views from those of Catholicism.

1. the priesthood of all believers
2. salvation comes from faith alone
3. Scripture alone is the basis of Christian teachings

1. Priesthood of All Believers. Luther called on nuns and monks to leave their convents and monasteries and to lead good Christian lives as laypersons. (He himself discontinued his life as an Augustinian monk, married a former nun, and had a number of children.) Luther maintained a belief in the need for a separate ordained ministry, but within Lutheranism the priestly identity of the ordained ministers is not as distinct from that of the non-ordained ministers as it is in Catholicism. Catholicism places great emphasis on priests who are ordained to perform certain cultic, prophetic, and shepherding functions that only they can perform—such as presiding at the celebrations of the sacraments of Eucharist, penance, and anointing of the sick; delivering the homily at liturgies; and becoming the pastor of a parish. The distinction between the priestly identity of the ordained and the priestly identity of laypeople in the Catholic Church has received more attention since changes in the Church ushered in by its

Vatican Council II in the early 1960s. While continuing to hold onto the essential difference between the ordained priesthood and the priesthood of all believers, this gathering of bishops acknowledged that all Christians share in the one priesthood of Christ by virtue of their baptism—a concept that Luther himself would have supported.

2. Salvation Through Faith Alone or Faith-Plus-Good-Works. While Protestantism asserts that faith alone brings salvation, Catholicism has traditionally proposed that faith must be demonstrated through "good works" if it is to lead to salvation. Here's an example to illustrate this distinction. If someone were to ask you, "Are you saved?" or "Do you accept Jesus as your personal Lord and Savior?" you can be sure that the one asking the question represents a particular expression of Protestantism. These questions imply an inner conversion experience, an experience of being "born again," a feeling of personal relationship with Christ. There are Protestants who would answer these questions affirmatively and without hesitation. On the other hand, in answer to the question, Are you saved, Catholics would tend to hesitate and answer, "I don't know yet. I have been baptized, I attend Mass regularly, I confess my sins to a priest when I can, and I help those in need." In other words, Catholics have a whole sacramental system of "good works" in which they are expected to participate. They are also expected to perform good deeds and to avoid sin, with the understanding that such actions make a difference in terms of their ultimate destiny. To over-simplify the matter, we can say that for Catholics faith is less an *inner experience* and more a participating in the sacraments and a living out of the Christian life. The Protestant spirit, on the other hand, affirms that no amount of good deeds can earn a person salvation. The only thing necessary for our salvation has already been accomplished—the sacrifice of Christ on the cross. Faith is our acceptance of this gift. This controversy between *faith* versus *faith-plus-good-works* has led to much theological discussion between Catholics and Protestants. Recently a group of Catholic and Lutheran theologians studying the question has stated that it finds no substantial difference between the Catholic and the Lutheran view on the matter. Leaders of the Catholic Church and of the majority of Lutheran churches have accepted these findings.

3. Scripture Alone or Scripture and Tradition. Since Luther believed that many Church leaders of his day were distorting or misinterpreting the Christian message, he went back to the beginning documents of

Christianity—the scriptures—as the one source of truth. Catholicism points out that, while the scriptures are certainly very important sources of truth, in fact they are part of something else—tradition. In other words, there was a Church before there was a fixed set of books making up the Christian Scriptures. There was tradition before the New Testament was written down, and Christian tradition continued after it. Therefore, the tradition of official Church pronouncements and the life and teachings of Christians help us to understand the truths contained in scripture. As successors of the first Christian leaders, the pope and bishops play a decisive role in defining and interpreting teachings found in scripture or tradition. Here again, there have been developments on this issue between Catholics and Protestants recently. Since Vatican Council II, Catholics have emphasized scripture more than ever before, and some Protestant churches have increased their frequency of celebrating the Eucharist—a practice strongly emphasized in the Catholic tradition.

Luther emphasized that grace, faith, and salvation are free gifts from God. We can do nothing to earn these gifts— otherwise they would not be gifts.

A. Explain the difference between receiving a gift and receiving pay- ment for work done.

B. Gift-giver or payment-receiver: Which more accurately describes your understanding of the way God relates to human beings? Why?

C. What are some implications of viewing God as a gift-giver or as a task-master?

Distinguishing among Protestant Denominations

So many Protestant denominations exist, are there common threads run- ning through them and are there ways to distinguish among them? One way to categorize Protestant Churches is to view them in terms of how strongly they repudiated certain features of the Christianity that existed at the time of the Reformation. In more positive terms, *each Protestant body emphasized ways of being faithful to Christ that differed to varying degrees from the dominant forms of living the Christian life that existed at the time of the Reformation.* The Christianity of the day placed an emphasis on externals—sacraments with their symbols and rituals, statues and stained glass windows, candles and incense, clergy as mediators of Christ, relics and other devotions to the saints. (Keep in mind that printing was fresh on the scene. Before this time the Christian message had to be communicated through these nonverbal signs since books for the general public didn't even exist.) Think of Protestantism as a movement away from the emphasis on such externals. As Protestant groups moved further and further away from these aspects of contemporary Christianity, they emphasized more and more:

- one's internal disposition, rather than performing the proper formula of each sacrament;
- reading scripture and preaching, rather than external rituals;
- personal authority, rather than placing authority in external leaders;
- simplifying church decoration, rather than the use of ornate altars, paintings, statues, and depictions of the saints;
- the person of Jesus, who is the focus of scripture, rather than Mary and the saints, who are secondary figures in scripture;
- the local church congregation, rather than the universal church.

To a great degree, Catholicism held onto the emphasis on externals that Protestantism rejected. The Protestant movement did not end in the sixteenth century. Within Protestantism, groups are continually merging with one another and separating into distinct denominations. For example, Episcopalians can be "high church"—closely resembling Catholicism—or "low church"—more Protestant in style. At last count there were more than fifteen separate groupings of the Baptist Church. Perhaps the major group that carried Christianity the furthest away from an emphasis on externals is the Religious Society of Friends, or "Quakers." Quakers don't have churches; they have meeting houses. They don't have altars, statues, stained glass windows, or paintings. They employ no set ritual during their services; instead everyone sits in silence and anyone who receives inspiration from God stands up and speaks as the Spirit moves her or him. Although there are elders, Quakers emphasize that they are all equals, a society of friends. Think of Protestantism, then, as a continuum from Episcopalians, to Lutherans and Presbyterians, to Congregationalists and Baptists, to Quakers. In a sense, each group became more "Protestant" and less "Catholic." Three popular expressions of Protestantism today are Pentecostalism, fundamentalism, and Evangelicalism, which we'll look at as a response to the next crisis faced by Christianity.

Protestant Denominations

One expert, David B. Barrett, suggests that there are 33,000 separate Christian groups. Many of them want simply to be called "Christian" rather than be associated with any larger denomination. Nonetheless, we can identify major, at times overlapping, groupings of Christian communities who are not Eastern Orthodox or Catholic.

Anglicans, Episcopalians

Lutherans

Calvinists, Presbyterians

Methodists

Baptists and Anabaptists

Congregationalists

Pentecostals and Evangelicals

ACTIVITY

A. **Find a list of Protestant denominations.** Write a report on the origins, beliefs, practices, and current membership statistics of one of them.

B. **Interview someone who is a member of a Protestant Church and report on the person's understanding of her or his church's beliefs and practices.**

C. **If you are a Christian, attend a church service of a denomination other than your own.** Write a report describing differences from and similarities with services in your own church.

D. **Look up the term "relic."** Explain the significance that relics held and continue to hold in Catholicism. What are possible positive aspects of devotional practices associated with relics? What are possible abuses associated with such practices?

Crisis #5: What Does It Mean to Be Christian in the Modern World?

Is there any question but that the modern world has challenged all religions, including the various branches of Christianity? No single event marks the beginning of "the modern world," and no one characteristic describes it. Nonetheless, it's clear that the world of the past few centuries or so is decidedly different from the world that preceded it. One characteristic that marks the modern world is an emphasis on science as the way to truth. Different Christian groups responded in varying ways to the challenges posed by science and the modern spirit. Here's a quick summary of some of those responses.

The Catholic Response to Modern Thought. The Catholic response to changes occurring in the modern world can be summed up in two events: Vatican Council I and Vatican Council II. In 1869, Vatican Council I declared that when the pope proclaims a doctrine regarding faith or morals to be infallible he is immune from making any fundamental errors. While this doctrine of **infallibility** confronts more than just those who would claim that science holds a privileged place over faith in the search for truth, nonetheless it does challenge the modern reliance on science to the exclusion of faith. It also suggests an attitude of rejection of and defiance against the dominant spirit of the modern age which wants to hold all truth claims up to the scrutiny of scientific investigation. In 1950, Pope Pius XII declared an infallible doctrine that the Blessed Mother of Jesus was assumed bodily into heaven. He based this judgment not on any scientific proof. Instead, he noted that the Catholic community had for a long time believed in the assumption of Mary and also that it was indeed "fitting" that Mary would be assumed bodily into heaven when she died.

While Vatican Council I reflected a Catholicism that wanted to hold onto the past and to hold out against the onslaught of the modern age, Vatican Council II revealed a very different attitude toward the modern world. An Italian word used to describe what Pope John XXIII had in mind when he called for the council is *aggiornamento*. It means "updating." At Vatican Council II the assembled bishops came to see the modern world not as evil but as offering developments with which the Church could be in dialogue. In fact, the Church can learn from the sciences and technological developments, just as the Church in turn has much to say to all citizens of the modern world, not just Catholics. Since this council, Catholics have been trying to figure out how best to reconcile being faithful to their religion while also being concerned about and involved in the modern world.

ACTIVITY

Write an essay defending or refuting the following statement:
• In the past few decades, Catholicism has come to be much more at home in the modern world. This has been a positive development for that religion.

Response of the Eastern Christian Churches. Many of the Eastern Christian Churches went from existing in countries predominantly ruled by Muslims to trying to survive in Communist-controlled countries. Holding onto the old ways was a political as well as a religious statement. For instance, in China where Roman Catholicism had made some inroads before Communists took control of the government, an underground church continued to practice Catholicism exactly the way it had been in the 1940s. Only in the 1990s, when greater freedom of religion was allowed, did Chinese Christianity consider newer, different forms of worship. Likewise, since the fall of Communism in the early 1990s Eastern Christian Churches have been trying to remain true to their traditions while identifying their place in the modern world and in modern Christianity.

Two Protestant Responses to the Modern World. One response within Protestantism to the modern world was the **social gospel movement**. This movement linked Christian faith with addressing the social problems caused by industrialization, the growth of cities, and the darker side of "progress" in the modern world such as rural and urban poverty. You may be familiar with the Salvation Army and with the YMCA/YWCA movements, which attempted to improve the lot of people struggling in the growing cities of the nineteenth century.

In contrast to the social gospel movement, fundamentalism and Evangelicalism are two related strands of Protestantism that take a decisive stand over against science and the modern spirit. Although it had earlier

St. Peter's Basilica in Rome

roots, fundamentalism began formally early in the twentieth century. It called for (a) belief in the divinity of Christ, (b) a strictly literal interpretation of the Bible, (c) evangelization—that is, missionary activity proclaiming Jesus as the sole savior of the world, (d) the necessity for personal conversion to Christ, and (e) belief in the second coming of Christ. These positions, considered to be the "fundamentals" of Christianity, were an attack against some key expressions of the modern spirit. For instance, a literal interpretation of scripture countered the new scientific theories of evolution; vigorously spreading the message of Jesus countered the proposition that Christianity is just another religion, neither better nor worse than any other; and personal conversion countered those advocates of the social gospel who were emphasizing social action as the primary way to bring about God's kingdom. The Evangelical movement continued to adhere to the major principles of fundamentalism but did so with a less antagonistic attitude toward the modern world and toward those who don't share their beliefs. In fact, distinguishing between the two groups is often impossible. Billy Graham is the person most prominently associated with Evangelical Christianity. He began his Evangelistic Association in 1950 and became the leading spokesperson for the movement. For decades he was a popular speaker and advised U.S. presidents. In the 1980s he even met with Pope John Paul II who called him "his brother."

> The question that comes to many minds is this: Just what must I do actually to receive Christ?...First, you must recognize that God loved you so much that He gave His Son to die on the cross....Second, you must repent of your sins....Third, you must receive Jesus Christ as Saviour and Lord....Fourth, you must confess Christ publicly. (Billy Graham, from World Aflame, quoted in Robert S. Ellwood, Jr., Words of the World's Religions [Englewood Cliffs, NJ: Prentice-Hall, 1977], 374-75)

A. Find out what you can about how each of the following viewed the role of Christianity in the modern world:

- Jane Addams
- Billy Graham
- Walter Rauschenbusch
- Dorothy Day
- Pope Pius IX
- Aleksandr Solzhenitsyn
- Pope John XXIII

B. Some Evangelical Christians find their experience of personal relationship with Christ to be an inspiration for getting involved in social issues. Write a report on Jim Wallis and Sojourners magazine, which he edits.

C. Many members of the social gospel movement also felt strongly the need for personal conversion to Christ. Do religious experiences encourage people to be actively concerned about those in need? Explain why or why not.

Answer agree, disagree, or uncertain to the following statements. Explain your answers.

1. Accepting evolution means rejecting Christianity.

2. Along with teaching the theory of evolution, schools should teach the biblical view that the world was created in seven days.

3. If it reflects the belief of most of its citizens, a particular state should be able to enact a law requiring that only the biblical version of creation is taught in science classes in public schools.

4. Analyzing scripture scientifically takes away from its sacredness as the word of God.

5. Participating in external rituals such as the sacraments is not particularly important for one's spiritual life. What is most important for a Christian is having a personal relationship with Christ.

6. If people truly believe that Christ is the savior of the world, then they should do all that they can to convert others to Christ.

7. Preparing for the next life—heaven or hell—is more important than trying to change conditions for the better in this life.

8. Most developments that have occurred in modern times are antagonistic to Christian faith.

9. If I were to list the principal values of the modern world alongside the values of Christianity, the two lists would be very different.

Vocabulary

Evangelicalism: An expression of Protestantism that emphasizes personal conversion to Christ or the experience of being "born again."

fundamentalism: In Protestantism, a movement formally begun at the beginning of the twentieth century in the U.S. but having earlier roots that advocated a literal interpretation of scripture, evangelization, and personal conversion to Christ.

infallibility: Catholic doctrine that the pope is immune from making fundamental errors when he declares a doctrine of faith or morals to be infallible.

social gospel movement: A movement begun in the latter half of the nineteenth century within Protestantism emphasizing renewing and reforming society as the primary duty of Christians.

Vatican Council I: Gathering of the Catholic bishops of the world in 1869 at which the doctrine of papal infallibility was proclaimed.

Vatican Council II: Gathering of the Catholic bishops of the world that took place from 1962-1965. It fostered a spirit of greater openness to and dialogue with the modern world as well as renewal of Catholicism itself.

For Review

21. What led Martin Luther to write his *ninety-five theses*?

22. What combination of events makes 1517 an appropriate date for the beginning of the Protestant Reformation?

23. What are indulgences?

24. What three theological propositions distinguish Luther and the reformers from traditional Catholic teaching?

25. What position did the Catholic bishops of Vatican Council II take regarding (a) priesthood and (b) scripture?

26. What did a recent Lutheran-Catholic commission conclude regarding the issue of faith and good works in relation to salvation?

27. What does it mean to say that Protestant denominations represent a movement away from certain emphases in the Christianity at the time of the Reformation? Why is the Quaker religion an extreme example of this reaction to Reformation-era Catholicism?

28. What characteristic of the modern age has had an important impact on Christianity?

29. What two events represented the Catholic Church's changing attitude toward the modern world? What was that change?

30. What political factor has strongly affected the experience of the Eastern Christian Churches in modern times?

31. Explain the difference between the social gospel movement and the Fundamentalist movement.

32. What did Billy Graham contribute to modern Christianity?

Monks and Nuns in Christian Tradition

While living as a monk is a central focus of Buddhism and also important in Hinduism, Christianity also has a tradition of monks and nuns. In Catholic and Orthodox Christianity, living the monastic life has held a special place for centuries.

Is the monastic life a waste of time? Shouldn't Christians be out there in the world actively trying to change it for the better? Interestingly, two of the most famous modern contemplatives saw their living of the monastic life as intimately connected to active involvement in the world beyond the monastery walls. Saint Thérèse of Lisieux, although she lived in a monastery from the middle of her teen years until her death in her twenties, has inspired many Catholics to make a difference in the world by lovingly doing the little things of daily life. Thomas Merton, who lived as a monk on the grounds of a monastery in Kentucky, was also famous for his writings about peace and justice issues.

A. Look up the word "contemplation." Write a brief essay about the role of contemplation in the Christian life.

B. Write an essay about either Thérèse of Lisieux or Thomas Merton.

IV. Christianity Today
Styles of Worship

On the one hand, styles of worship are decidedly different among the three Christian traditions. On the other hand, Eastern, Roman, and many Protestant churches follow a basic format in their services. Catholic, Orthodox, and Episcopal churches in particular divide their central worship service into the Liturgy of the Word and the Liturgy of the Eucharist. The Liturgy of the Word centers around a public, formal proclamation of passages from scripture, especially the gospels, followed by a homily explaining and applying their message. In most Protestant Churches, the sermon is the central focus of the service. Roman Catholic and Eastern Christian services emphasize more the Liturgy of the Eucharist than the Liturgy of the Word. Eastern Christian Churches, both Catholic and Orthodox, have continued to follow a format in their liturgy that is more or less a thousand years old. The Roman Catholic Church updated its liturgy around forty years ago so that it looks and sounds more modern than an Eastern Christian service. Around the same time many Protestant Churches also underwent a process of liturgical renewal so that their services are now closer to the Catholic style and vice versa.

If you are a Christian, attend a service in a Christian Church different from your own tradition. (Or you might tune in a religious television program featuring a service different from your own tradition.) Report on similarities and differences with your own Church's service. If you are not a Christian, attend a Christian service and report on what you observe.

ACTIVITY

Foundations for the Christian Moral Life

On the one hand, the life and teachings of Jesus contain important implications for living a moral life. On the other hand, he gave no clear-cut set of rules to follow. His pronouncements on right conduct often were radical and extreme by accepted standards. It wasn't long before some Christians softened his message, "Be perfect, therefore, as your heavenly Father is perfect" (Matthew 5:48) by adding, "but do what you can." Sometimes

Icon of St. Peter with Jesus

Christians seem to have totally turned around his message. For instance, Jesus tells Peter in no uncertain terms, "Put your sword back into its place, for all who take the sword will perish by the sword" (Matthew 26:52). After the Roman Empire adopted Christianity the cross was placed on its military standards and the Church added to its regular prayers, "Grant victory to the emperor over the barbarians"—a variation of which is still recited in Eastern Christian Churches in its prayer called the troparion (or poetic hymn) of the cross! We can, however, make some general distinctions among the three major Christian traditions regarding their approach to morality.

Eastern Christianity. For the most part, the Eastern Christian Churches adopted a medical model for the moral life. That is, they take seriously that human beings are meant to be perfect since they were created in the image of God. (In Greek, "image" is **ikon** or *icon*—a term that holds great significance for the Eastern Churches.) Sin, or wrongdoing, is a sickness that indicates how far we are from being the image of God we were intended to be. Taking steps to improve our spiritual life so that we experience more and more our union with God in Christ is the way to combat the infections—sins—still present in our person. Here's a prayer from the Byzantine Catholic Church that is said daily during their Great Fast which reflects the medical model of morality:

> *O Lord and Master of my life, grant that I may not be infected with the spirit of slothfulness and meddling, of ambition and vain talking.*
>
> *Grant instead to me your servant the spirit of purity and humility, the spirit of patience and neighborly love.*
>
> *O Lord and King, bestow upon me the grace of being aware of my sins and of not thinking evil of those of my brethren. For You are blessed forever and ever. Amen.*
>
> *(Quoted in* Shown to Be Holy, *[God With Us Publications, Pittsburgh, PA:1990], 40-41)*

Roman Catholicism. The Roman Catholic Church, on the other hand, adopted a legal model for morality. It found in the thought of the great classical philosophers the concept that there is a "**natural law**" which should regulate the behavior of all people. We discover this law—actually a set of general moral principles—by investigating human nature. If we can identify human nature—how human beings ought to act, then we can establish a set of laws or principles to guide human behavior. What instrument is available to human beings for discovering the laws of nature? Reason. Here is what the official *Catechism of the Catholic Church* says about this natural moral law: "The natural law, present in the heart of each [person] and established by reason, is universal in its precepts and its authority extends to all men" (1956).

Protestantism. One possible foundation for Christian moral teaching is surprisingly absent from our discussion so far—the Bible! Of course, both Eastern Christianity and Roman Catholicism consider scripture to be the definitive guidepost for the moral life. However, it took Protestantism to restore the Bible as its exclusive foundation for morality. For instance, if you happen to stay in a hotel in the United States, you might find in a drawer of the nightstand a copy of the Bible. Inside its cover you might read a list of problems and next to each one a suggested passage from scripture that addresses the problem. That Bible was supplied by a Protestant-affiliated group because according to the Protestant spirit the Bible holds the answers to all of life's problems. Early Protestant leaders felt that it was presumptuous of human beings to expect to arrive at truth using reason alone. The only true law is the written law, the law of God found in scripture. Human beings should use this law as their exclusive guide for living the moral life. Here is how one of the most influential early Protestant leaders states this case:

> *Accordingly (because it is necessary both for our dullness and for our arrogance), the Lord has provided us with a written law to give us a clearer witness of what was too obscure in the natural law, shake off our listlessness, and strike more vigorously our mind and memory. (John Calvin,* Institutes of the Christian Religion, *vol. 1 [Philadelphia, PA: The Westminster Press, 1960], 368)*

A. Write an essay describing sin as disease. Include in your essay a prescription for how one might cure this particular disease.

B. Read again the quote about natural law from the *Catechism of the Catholic Church.* Give a specific example of a "moral law" that might be considered an expression of the natural law. Explain why this particular "law" reflects the traditional Roman Catholic understanding of natural-law morality.

C. Defend or refute each of the following statements:

1. Human beings should rely first and foremost on their reason when determining right and wrong.

2. Human reason is an inadequate resource for determining right from wrong. Christians should use the Bible as their primary source of moral guidance.

Has Christianity Been Good News for Women?

The beginning of this chapter points out that the Gospel according to Mark refers to its account of the life and message of Jesus as *good news*, from which we get the term "gospel." Has Christianity been good news for women, or has it contributed to their oppression? As you might expect, this question cannot be answered with a simple yes or no.

Scholars studying Christian origins find some remarkable examples of equal treatment of women and men on the part of Jesus. A number of years ago one theologian even published a controversial article entitled, "Jesus Was a Feminist." Although that sounds too much like an attempt to transfer a twentieth-century label to a first-century Jewish culture, nonetheless it does suggest how much Jesus stood out from the common norms of his day in his attitude toward women. Jesus apparently had women friends, which may not sound peculiar in our day but was highly unusual then. Jesus asks a woman he meets by chance at a well to go into her town and preach his message. Here again, Jesus went against his cultural norms simply by talking to an unknown woman in a public place. Asking her to spread the message was even more an indication of Jesus' egalitarian view toward women.

The Christian Scriptures taken as a whole do not give such a clear-cut egalitarian viewpoint. Scholars suggest that there are two main reasons for this ambiguity: (a) All New Testament writings were probably written by men so that we are receiving men's points of view exclusively, and (b) Christianity gradually adapted to the cultural norms of the day. One writer describes the New Testament descriptions of women's roles in the early Church in this way:

> One must be careful not to force the New Testament evidence one way or the other. On the one hand, it does not name women as apostles or show them presiding at the Eucharist. The New Testament does not give much information about who presided at the Eucharist. On the other hand, one cannot assert dogmatically that women did not exercise leadership roles in the primitive Christian communities. The fact that some women are identified as ministers (Rom 16:1), as hosts for the local ecclesial assembly (Col 4:15), as wandering husband and wife co-workers or evangelists (Rom 16:3-5, 7; 1 Cor 16:19), as exercising prophetic roles in the assembly (1 Cor 11:5), or as "prominent among the apostles" (Rom 16:7) should make one very cautious. Nor can it be denied that as the Christian communities became more structured and inculturated toward the end of the New Testament period, they also became more restrictive in terms of what women could do. (Thomas P. Rausch, SJ, Catholicism at the Dawn of the Third Millennium [Collegeville, MN: The Liturgical Press, 1996], 216-17)

The debate within Christianity today is not about whether women or men are inferior to each other. Rather, the question centers around whether or not women and men should perform different roles. For instance, should preaching and presiding at religious services—traditional priestly functions—be restricted to men? Should the most powerful positions of leadership in the various Christian denominations be reserved for men exclusively? Should women and men perform different functions in the family and the workplace based on either scripture or nature?

A. Feminists propose that women as a group have been and continue to be oppressed in many ways. Feminists advocate that women and men should work against any oppression of people based on gender. Defend or refute the claim, "Jesus was a feminist."

B. Look up the New Testament passages listed by Fr. Rausch in the above quote and state what each one says about a role women exercised in the early Church.

C. In later New Testament writings there appear so-called "household codes," which restrict the public role of women in the Church. Read the following passages and write about the view of women presented in each one:

- Colossians 3:18–4:1
- 1 Peter 2:13–3:7
- Ephesians 5:22–6:9
- Titus 2:5–9

D. The Catholic Church does not permit women to be priests. What is the reasoning behind this position?

E. What position on women's roles in ministry do the following groups have:

- Episcopalians
- Baptists
- United Methodists
- Assemblies of God
- Fundamentalist Christians
- Orthodox Christians

Christianity in the United States of America

European domination of the Americas brought Christianity with it. In the United States, Protestantism held something of an unofficial status as the religion of the nation, at least until the mid-twentieth century. The original French and Spanish Catholic settlers were often pushed to the fringes of American society, and the later great waves of Catholic immigrants had to make their way in a Protestant-dominated culture. In the United States, if you weren't Jewish or Catholic or some other non-Protestant religion, you were essentially categorized as "Protestant."

The battle that Christianity is now waging in the United States is mostly between itself and an increasingly secularized spirit. Liberal Christians,

Catholic or Protestant, believe that finding a common ground with secular values is the best way for Christianity to have an impact on the modern world. That is, some modern trends and even some so-called secular values—such as democracy, tolerance of differences, and the separation of church and state—can enhance Christianity. Conservative Christians, Catholic or Protestant, believe that they should hold onto their "old time religion" and fight secularizing influences as best they can. For example, conservative Protestants advocate state-sponsored or organized prayer and the teaching of **creationism** in public schools, their particular understanding of Christian values serving as the basis for legislation, no work on Sundays, and often a distinct separation of the roles of women and men. Conservative Catholics generally want nuns and priests to dress in distinctive clothing, traditional devotional practices to be the centerpiece of Catholic worship, special devotion to Mary and the saints, and an emphasis on obedience to the pope. Liberal and conservative Christians often find themselves on opposing sides of hot-button issues of the day such as right to life issues, capital punishment, warfare, patriotism, health care, immigration, HIV/AIDS prevention, gay rights, foreign aid, environmentalism, how to interpret the Bible, and religion in politics.

Pentecostalism

The first Pentecost occurred in Jerusalem when the apostles were touched by the Holy Spirit and for the first time publicly preached the Christian message apart from Jesus. According to the story, the Spirit moved them to speak in strange languages; but, oddly enough, people who spoke different languages actually understood them! A spirited, emotional, enthusiastic style of Christianity continues today in Pentecostal Churches. If you attend a Pentecostal service, expect loud music, spirited singing, bodies swaying and hands clapping, and a vibrant preacher. Pentecostal Christianity was an important expression of Protestantism throughout the twentieth century in the United States and represents one of the fastest growing forms of Christianity throughout the world today.

Find out more about Pentecostalism.
What do you think accounts for the growing popularity of this style of Christianity?

ACTIVITY

A. Most people do not fit neatly into categories such as "liberal" and "conservative." However, there are clear differences across today's religious landscape. Look over the characteristics of conservative Protestants and conservative Catholics presented in the text. Do you think that conservative Catholics would feel closer to conservative Protestants than to liberal Catholics? Do you think that liberal Catholics would feel closer to liberal Protestants than to conservative Catholics? Explain.

B. Describe liberal and conservative approaches to secular trends in American society. Which approach do you believe would be better for keeping Christianity viable and true to its roots? Explain why.

C. Fundamentalist Christians want science classes to teach evolution as only one theory about the origins of life on earth. They also want "intelligent design theory" to be taught along with any other theories about the origins of the universe. Do you agree?

Conclusion
Christianity Affirms the Uniqueness of Jesus

Other religions advocate belief in God, connect that belief to love and justice, and even offer hope of life beyond death. Does anything set Christianity apart from other religions? The answer to that question is a personal one—the person of Jesus Christ. For Christians Jesus human and divine, Jesus giving his life on the cross and rising to new life, sets their religion apart from all others. Because of these beliefs about Jesus, Christians place in Jesus their hope and salvation. An Easter prayer from the Catholic tradition expresses well this belief in Jesus:

> *Risen Jesus, fill me with the joy of your Resurrection. Surround me with the radiant light of your glory. Transform all the areas of my life that are in need of your healing touch. Like Mary of Magdala, let me hear you whisper my name. Like the disciples on the road to Emmaus, help me to know you in the breaking of the bread, the holy Eucharist. With Thomas, let me touch you and cry, "My Lord and my God." Risen Jesus, cover me with the radiance of your love. Let me be your messenger of peace, joy, and love to all I meet. Amen.* (Catholic Prayers and Devotions [Liguori, MO: Liguori Publications, 1998], 15)

Eastern Rite Catholics in the U.S

From 1889 to 1914 many members of Eastern Catholic Churches came to the industrial heartland of the United States. They came from Ukraine, Poland, the Carpathian Mountains of Slovakia, and other parts of the Austro-Hungarian Empire to work in mills and factories, coal mines and railroads. Today they are members of the Albanian Catholic Church, Bulgarian Catholic Church, Croatian Catholic Church, Czech Catholic Church, Greek Catholic Church, Hungarian Catholic Church, Melkite Greek Catholic Church, Romanian Catholic Church, Ruthenian Catholic Church, Ukrainian Catholic Church, or one of the smaller Eastern Catholic Churches.

More recently, Eastern Catholics from the Middle East have migrated to the United States. They are members of the Maronite Catholic Church, Chaldean Catholic Church, Syrian Catholic Church, Armenian Catholic Church, or one of the smaller Eastern Catholic Churches. All told, there are members of more than twenty Eastern Catholic Churches in the United States today.

Vocabulary

creationism: Belief in the literal meaning of the first of the two creation stories found in the Book of Genesis, namely, that God created the universe and all creatures in it in seven days.

ikon: Greek word meaning "image." Eastern Churches place great significance on two-dimensional depictions of Jesus and the saints which they call ikons.

Liturgy of the Eucharist: A form of Christian prayer structured generally to include a thanksgiving prayer over bread and wine, the recitation of the Lord's Prayer, the exchange of a sign of peace, and the distribution of communion. The second half of a Catholic Mass.

Liturgy of the Word: A form of public Christian prayer structured generally to include readings from the Bible, a responsorial psalm, a homily, amd intercessory prayer. The first half of a Catholic Mass.

Vocabulary (continued)

natural law: Approach to morality traditionally emphasized in the Roman Church that uses human reason to investigate human nature in order to arrive at general moral principles.

secularism: Viewpoint that religion should be excluded from influencing civil governmental affairs and decision-making.

For Review

33. What are the two major parts of the Catholic Mass?

34. What do Catholic and Orthodox Christians emphasize in their worship?

35. What do Protestant Christians emphasize in their worship?

36. What model does Eastern Christianity use as the foundation for morality? What model does Roman Catholicism use as the foundation for its morality?

37. What serves as the foundation for Protestant morality?

38. How did Jesus treat women in respect to the cultural norms of his day?

39. What two factors may have led the Christian Scriptures to include statements that reflect the dominant cultural norms regarding women?

40. Around what issue does the current debate about women in the Catholic Church revolve?

41. Which religion has historically been the dominant religion in the United States?

42. What is the difference between a liberal and a conservative Christian response to secularism?

CHAPTER 4

ISLAM

Peace Through Surrender to God's Will

Across the desert sands of Arabia nature is seldom friendly. Life itself is a struggle. Out of this harsh environment emerged one of the world's greatest religious figures, someone who offered a straightforward, no-nonsense approach to addressing all of life's challenges. Indeed, the case has been made that Muhammad was the most influential person of all time, religious or otherwise. He himself didn't separate the spiritual from the social, economic, and political. He called people to surrender to God's will in every aspect of their lives. In his view he didn't start a "new" religion at all. Rather, he simply reaffirmed the religion God intended for all humanity from the time of Adam. Today nearly one out of five people is a member of this community dedicated to surrendering to God's will as it was made known through the prophet Muhammad.

Overview

■ Islam shares with Judaism and Christianity belief in God as the omnipotent creator and sustainer of the world and the source of all truth.

■ Islam is a religion as well as a community system based upon revelations to Muhammad, who is regarded as the last and greatest prophet.

■ The five pillars are specific practices that serve as the foundation for Muslim life.

■ In the Qur'an and the example of Muhammad Muslims find guidelines regulating all areas of life, such as warfare, the role of women and men, divorce, and economic matters.

■ Developments that have taken place in the modern world have created tensions within Muslim communities.

ACTIVITY

Before we begin...

Describe what Judaism and Christianity say about truth and the way to peace. Then after reading about Islam, state what you see as similarities and differences among the three religions in relation to these two concepts.

I. Islam

The Religion of Peace through Submission

Glory to you (O Lord), knowledge we have none
except what You have given us,
for You are all-knowing and all-wise. (Koran, Sura 2:32)

Remember our discussion about the great religious questions in Chapter One? Who are we? Where have we come from? Is our existence limited merely to the time from conception to death? Besides practical considerations, is there a fundamental reason why we should be concerned about the suffering of others? Left to our own devices, we humans seem to be condemned to uncertainty about the most important questions of life. A religion is of no value unless it offers a window into these great mysteries.

What does the religion of Islam offer to the discussion about seeking truth? Are we human beings left alone to search for truth using the obviously imperfect and inadequate powers that we possess? If that were our fate, Islam acknowledges that we would surely be a sorry lot. Alone, we are incapable of arriving at ultimate truth. Islam, however, is based upon the belief that human beings are not alone in the universe. Islam begins with a principle apart from which there could be no Islam— God. The all-powerful and all-knowing creator of all things is also compassionate. That is, God has not left human beings to try to make their way through life on their own. Instead, God has chosen to step into human history and speak to specific persons who alert us about what is truth and what path of life is aligned with the truth. (Actually, God does not actually "speak" directly. Instead God speaks through **angels**, bodiless creatures of light who serve as God's messengers.)

To whom has God spoken? Islam proposes that God has spoken to specific people chosen to proclaim God's message. These chosen spokespersons are called **prophets**. The word for prophet in both Arabic and Hebrew is *nabi*, which means "mouthpiece." (Muslims also distinguish between a nabi, a prophet in general, and a *rasul*, meaning messenger. A rasul is essentially a messenger with a book, such as Moses, Jesus, and Muhammad.) Prophets such as Abraham, Moses, and Jesus served the important function of being a mouthpiece for

God. God's words to the prophets have been written down and are available to people who want to know God's message. Therefore, Islam believes firmly that scriptures exist in which God's word can be found. For instance, the Hebrew Bible contains, among other things, a list of Ten Commandments given by God to the prophet Moses. Anyone who wants to follow the true way, the way of God, should follow these commandments.

What is human destiny in this worldview? For Islam, since God's decrees are available to people, they will be judged by how faithful they are to these decrees. With death comes judgment. Based on this judgment after their earthly life, either paradise or punishment—heaven or hell—awaits all people. Here we have a summary of fundamental Islamic beliefs:

1. God (God exists; God is all-powerful and the source of all truth)
2. Angels (God's messengers)
3. Prophets (specific persons who have been God's mouthpiece)
4. Scriptures (which contain God's messages)
5. God's decrees (God's directions for how people should live and act found in scriptures)
6. Judgment (heaven or hell based on fidelity to God's decrees)

> Guide us (O Lord) to the path that is straight,
> The path of those You have blessed,
> Not of those who have earned Your anger,
> nor those who have gone astray. (Koran, *Sura* 1:5–7)

ACTIVITY

Look over the six fundamental beliefs of Islam.
In terms of your understanding of Judaism and Christianity, are these two religions completely compatible with Islam? Why or why not?

Revelation: "in the heart" or "through the ear"

Within Islam, the question has been posed about the revelations received by Muhammad: Did he receive them "in his heart" or "through his ear"? That is, did Muhammad spend time meditating and while doing so discover a message from God within himself—in his heart? Or, did Muhammad actually meet a physical being apart from himself, the angel Gabriel, who spoke God's message to him—through his ear? It's hard for us of the modern age to understand what kind of distinctions people of the early Middle Ages, when Islam began, made between spiritual and physical experiences. In the end, however, to be Muslim means to believe that God is the source of all true revelation and that Muhammad received Qur'anic revelations from God.

Would it make a difference whether you understand revelation to take place in the heart or through the ear of a prophet? Explain.

Define what the word "revelation" means apart from a religious context. Then describe the religious meaning of the term. Write a short story that has as its theme revelation in some religious sense of the word.

Vocabulary

angels: Spiritual creatures who serve as God's messengers to humanity.

nabi: Arabic and Hebrew word for prophet, meaning "mouthpiece."

prophets: People who are spokespersons for God, through whom God's message is revealed.

Qur'an: Literally "recitation." God's messages revealed to Muhammad. Also written as "Koran."

revelation: In the general sense, the reception of insight or experience of ultimate reality. As understood by the religions originating in the Middle East, a communication by God to a person or people concerning ultimate reality.

For Review

1. What do Muslims propose as the only valid starting point in the search for ultimate truth?

2. According to Islam, what role do angels and prophets play in the search for truth?

3. What is the root meaning of the word nabi? What does it indicate about the role of prophets in Islam?

4. According to Islam, where can one find God's messages to human beings?

5. List the six fundamental Islamic beliefs.

6. Define revelation. Explain the difference between an understanding of revelation taking place "in the heart" or "through the ear" of a prophet.

Islam: The Straight Path

The religion is **Islam**. A member of the religion is a **Muslim**. Defining these terms is an important starting point in understanding the religion. (Note that if you read about this religion in other sources you might discover that terms are not always spelled the same way. For instance, "Muslim" may be spelled "Moslem." "Muhammad" may be spelled "Mohammed" or some other variation of the word. Each spelling is an attempt to put into English the pronunciation of an Arabic word.)

One root for the word Islam is the Arabic term ***salaam***. (You may be familiar with the Hebrew equivalent, *shalom*.) Salaam is a greeting. It wishes another person peace and well-being, similar to the English greeting "hello," which means "good health to you." According to Islam, what is peace? How does one attain peace? As you might guess from our discussion so far, the answer is that true peace comes only from surrender to God's will. Therefore, the term "Islam" can be defined as *peace through surrender to God's will*. A Muslim, then, is *one who submits to God's will*. This is the Muslim religion, pure and simple.

Can a person have peace without an experience of God? Why or why not? How important is it to believe in God to have true peace? Explain.

Is Islam the Oldest Religion? the Youngest Religion? the Only Religion?

If the questions in the above heading were part of a multiple-choice test, the answer would be: "all of the above." How can that be? If we are to know what it means to be Muslim, we must first understand how the religion perceives the unique nature of human beings. According to Islam, we humans are fundamentally different from other creatures. Horses and dogs—in fact, all animals other than humans—are "muslim" by nature insofar as they follow God's will instinctively. (They are muslim not in a formal sense but in a general sense, and thus the word here is written in lower-case m.) Human beings, on the other hand, must choose whether or not to follow God's will—that is, whether or not to be muslims.

Islam, the oldest religion. Adam, whom Muslims consider the first human being, was also the first muslim—lower-case m—because he surrendered to God's will. (Those of you familiar with the biblical Adam and Eve story know that he also refused to surrender to God's will on one fateful occasion, which caused him untold grief, but that for the most part he was a faithful muslim.) Thus Islam, the religion of submission to God's will, is the oldest of the world's religions, dating back to the first humans Adam and Eve.

Islam, the youngest religion. However, Adam and later prophets did not receive the full story about what God's will entails, or at least part of the message was forgotten, until God decided to speak to one particular prophet living in a town located in the Arabian desert near the Middle Eastern trade routes. Muhammad of Mecca began hearing the angel Gabriel speaking God's word to him in the early decades of the seventh century of the Common Era. God let it be known that this man, Muhammad, was the last in the line of prophets. The final and complete word of God can now be found written down in a book called the Qur'an, a collection of the recitations of God that Muhammad reported to anyone who would listen. Therefore, Islam is the youngest of the major religions of the world. One could not be a Muslim in the formal and complete sense— Muslim with an upper-case M—until God's final word was revealed to the prophet Muhammad. Actually, the religion of Islam in the formal sense began in a particular year, 622 CE, in a particular town, **Medina**, following a particular event—the *hijrah*, which we'll explain soon. Even after that, the community continued to learn what it means to be Muslim since

Muhammad received further revelations until he died ten years later.

Islam, the only religion. Indeed, for Muslims, Islam is the *only* true religion. Either one submits to God's will or one doesn't. Human beings can choose to follow their own path to truth, or they might seek answers from any number of idols and false gods. Both of these options are misguided and can only result in failure. Such paths would not be true religious paths. Islam, following God's will as revealed through the prophets culminating in the final prophet, Muhammad, is the only "straight path" to truth and righteousness. If God is the only source of truth, then Islam—the religion of submission to God's will—is the only authentic religion.

ACTIVITY

A. Answer yes or no to the following questions:
- Do you believe in God?
- Do you believe that people should try to follow God's will in living their lives?
- Do you personally try to do God's will as best you can?

Based on your answers, are you a muslim (lower-case m) as described in the text? Explain.

B. Write an essay in response to the following statement: If someone truly believes in God, then that person should set as his or her highest priority seeking to do God's will.

Muhammad and the Origins of Islam

Who was this man who convinced so many people that God indeed was speaking through him? He lived to be sixty-two years old, from 570 to 632 CE. Only during the last twenty or so years of his life did he act as a prophet and leader of a religious movement. Before that time he was a shepherd in his youth and a caravan driver during the prime of his life. Although not wealthy, he was a member of the dominant tribe of his hometown in a society based strongly on tribal ties. His fortunes changed for the better when he married a wealthy widow named **Khadija**. After his marriage he began to spend a good portion of his time in caves outside Mecca where he began to hear a voice speaking to him. At first he thought it was a *jinn*, one of the supernatural creatures of fire that Arabs believed inhabited desert places such as these caves. (Today *jinns* continue to be part of folklore even in the West where they are known as "genies.") Instead the voice insisted that it spoke in the name of **Allah**.

You probably already know that the Muslim name for God is Allah. What made this notion of God so revolutionary in Muhammad's time? A helpful way to understand what this

A street in modern Medina

name means is simply to think of it as an abbreviation for *Al* (the) *Illah* (God). Allah, or *Al Illah*, means "the God"—the one and only God. There is no other god. The God, Allah, is the same God who created the universe and the earth and all its inhabitants in the first place. The God who spoke to Muhammad also spoke to Abraham and to Moses. Muslims would also say that, rightly understood, the God of Muhammad is also the God of Jesus. Certainly, the world knew monotheism before Muhammad from Jews and Christians along with some other religions of the Middle East. However, at the time of Muhammad his culture was predominantly polytheistic. More specifically, each tribe had its own god or set of gods. Most people in the area viewed even Jews and Christians as belonging to separate tribes. Muhammad's monotheism downplayed such tribal boundaries and offered a different way to view people. In the big picture there is, first of all, The God. This God is not the God exclusively of Arabs or Persians or Jews or Christians, but the God of all. Therefore, everyone—regardless of tribe—is equal before God; everyone—regardless of tribe—is meant to be a submitter to God's will; everyone—regardless of tribe—is subject to the same laws and moral code since all true law has its source in the one God, Allah.

Revelations from God to Muhammad began when he was in his early forties and continued intermittently until the time of his death. At first he didn't know what to make of these revelations, but Khadija encouraged him to treat them seriously and to recite them to the people of Mecca. Muhammad himself was probably illiterate, so he wasn't out in the caves reading books by candlelight in order to manufacture these revelations. He was an upright man who spoke well but never in a fashion that equaled the words he said came from God. What was the source of these words, then?

Could they indeed have been the words of God? Those who believed they were, and a growing number of Meccans did, came to be called Muslims, since they were fashioning their lives on these messages from God revealed through the prophet. By the year 622 this group gained enough followers that it was perceived as a threat by the leaders of the town. Muhammad made arrangements with the citizens of a town north of Mecca called Yathrib (later re-named Medina). They welcomed Muslims from Mecca to come to their city where the revelations from God to Muhammad would serve as the basis for their laws governing their political, social, economic, domestic, and personal life. A large contingent of Muslims secretly left Mecca and made their way to Medina in what is known as the *hijrah* or *hegira*, meaning "flight." More importantly, Muslims mark the year 622 as the beginning of their calendar since in this year in Medina the first formal Muslim community came into existence.

Even after the Muslims left their city, the leaders of Mecca felt threatened by the growing power of the Muslims. They sent out an army to crush Muslim power in Medina, but a Muslim army of much smaller numbers defeated them. Historians debate to what degree this battle of Badr was a defensive one on the part of the Muslims. Nonetheless, eventually Muhammad and an army of Muslims entered Mecca, cleansed its central shrine of idols housed there, and established Mecca as the community's spiritual center. Until his death in 632 the Muslim community grew and became more and more consolidated under Muhammad. When he died, his friend **Abu Bakr**—one of his earliest followers who took over as his successor, announced to the crowd gathered: "If you have been worshipping Muhammad, know that Muhammad is dead. If you have been worshipping Allah, know that Allah lives forever!" Thus Islam proposes that it avoided the mistake made by Christianity—identifying the messenger (Jesus) with the one who gave the message, God.

ACTIVITY

The text gives only a sketch of this important man, Muhammad. Find out what you can about him and write a more detailed account of his life. Include in your biography key themes in his story and key contributions he made to world history.

The Most Influential Person of All Time?

A number of years ago an author put together a coffee-table book titled *The One Hundred: A Ranking of the Most Influential Persons in History* (Michael H. Hart [New York: Citadel Press, 1992]). Obviously, such a list is pure speculation and largely subjective. Nonetheless, he places Muhammad at the top of the list and makes a case as to why he belongs there. Although more people in the world profess to be Christian than Muslim, in the book Jesus comes in at number three. According to the author, Jesus shares credit for the spread of Christianity with two other persons—Saint Paul and Emperor Constantine. (By the way, Isaac Newton is listed as the second most influential person in history. If you want to know why, read the book!)

What makes Muhammad a possible candidate for being the most influential person of all time? For one thing, historically the extent and the rapidity of Muslim expansion are second to none. We think of Muhammad and Islam as emerging out of the Arab world, which is true to a degree. However, as already mentioned people in the Middle East identified themselves by tribe, not as being "Arab" or some other ethnic or racial identity. Within one hundred years of Muhammad's death, an Arab-Muslim empire extended from the section of France bordering Spain in the West to parts of India in the East. One particular battle, the **Battle of Tours** in 732, probably is responsible for preventing all or most of Europe from Muslim domination. Arabic, the language of the Qur'an and of the earliest leaders of this empire, was its official language. Christianity, on the other hand, spread mostly through an empire that already existed, the Roman Empire. Christianity adopted the language and political structures of this empire. The Muslim Empire first united tribes that traditionally had been fiercely disunited and then spread the religion, the language, the culture, and the political power far beyond the boundaries of the Arab world. (Today only a minority of Muslims are Arab.)

> By 732, Muslim Arabs controlled the Iberian peninsula (Spain and Portugal), the land of the Carthaginians (North Africa), the land of the ancient pharaohs (Egypt), the holy land of the Jews and Christians (Palestine), the land of the ancient Babylonians (Mesopotamia), the land of the once great Persian empire, the land of northwestern India, and of course their own vast land, Arabia. They had conquered more territory than the Romans and all in one century. (Steven L. Jantzen, Kenneth Neill, and Larry S. Krieger, World History: Perspectives on the Past [Lexington, MA: D. C. Heath, 1988], 177)

Religion and Politics in Islam

If you tend to think of religion as something separate from other aspects of life, then no doubt you are uncomfortable linking Islam the religion with military conquests and political power. Islam itself has never made such distinctions. If God is God, then all areas of life should be governed by God's commands. Using God's revelations as their basis, Muhammad established guidelines for spiritual practices, economic practices, punishment of wrongdoers, family life, and so forth. In so doing he established a rule of law for a society in which previously "might makes right" tended to be the overriding principle of social interaction, especially between tribes. The moral code introduced by Muhammad also bettered conditions for slaves, foreigners, women, poor people, and other outcast groups. Remember that to be Muslim means to be one who submits to God's will, no matter how wealthy or poor, how powerful or powerless. Every Muslim is to follow the strict moral code handed down by God and written in the Qur'an.

> To the few Meccans who took him seriously Muhammad preached a simple message. He said they must abandon their pagan idols and their licentious ways and repent before the one true God, Allah, lest they be condemned at the Last Judgment to eternal hellfire. From the beginning, his message was tied to a program of social reform. Prayer and belief alone were insufficient; it was necessary to trade honestly, treat women better, care for orphans, forgo usury, and abandon infanticide. (Thomas W. Lippman, Understanding Islam [New York: Meridian Books, 1995], 40.)

The Influence of Muhammad on Arab Life and Beyond

- replaced polytheism with monotheism

- replaced people's tribal identity with a universal, shared identity—being submitters to God's will

- replaced "might makes right" and tribal concerns with a strict, universal moral code—one applicable to all people

- increased equality of all levels of society

- improved the lot of the many groups of people suffering under the social system of the day

- established a community structure and system of governance that held sway over a large portion of the world's population and is still appealed to today

- began an empire that spread Islam and Arabic culture from the Atlantic Ocean to India

- made Islamic teachings the basis for all aspects of personal and social life

- was a successful spiritual as well as political and military leader

A. If you were to make a list of the most influential people (a) in all of history and (b) in today's world, would those you choose tend to be:

- political leaders
- military leaders
- religious leaders
- artists or musicians
- teachers or writers
- scientists or doctors
- other

Do you find that certain groups of people are more influential today than they tended to be in the past? (For instance, are political leaders more important today than religious leaders compared to a thousand years ago?) Explain your answers.

B. Write up pros and cons of the following statement:
Religion and politics should be kept separate.

ACTIVITY

Vocabulary

Abu Bakr: Wealthy Meccan businessman, one of earliest followers of Muhammad who served as his successor in leading the Muslim community.

Allah: Muslim name for God, meaning "The God."

Battle of Tours: (732 CE) Defeat of Muslim forces who had entered France by a Christian army, restricting Muslim control of Western Europe at the time to Spain and Portugal.

hijrah: Flight of Muslims from Mecca to Medina in 622 CE. Also called the hegira.

Islam: "Peace through surrender to God's will." Religious community dedicated to surrendering to God's will as revealed through Muhammad (570–632 CE).

jinn: In English, "genie." Creatures made of a fiery substance that inhabit in particular desert places. In Arab folklore they tend to be mischievous and troublesome to human beings. Muslims consider satan to be a jinn.

Khadija: Muhammad's first wife.

Medina: City two hundred and fifty miles north of Mecca where the first Muslim community was established in 622 CE. Burial place of Muhammad.

Muslim: In general, anyone who places highest priority on submission to God's will. In the more narrow sense, anyone who belongs to the community of people who seek to submit to God's will as revealed through the prophet Muhammad.

salaam: In Arabic, "peace." Used as a greeting similar to "hello" in Arabic-speaking countries.

For Review

7. Define the terms Islam, Muslim, and salaam.

8. Explain why Muslims view their religion as at the same time the oldest, the youngest, and the only religion?

9. What is the difference between a "muslim," written in lower-case m, and a "Muslim," written in upper-case M?

10. When did Muhammad live?

11. Who were Khadija and Abu Bakr?

12. What is the modern counterpart of the word jinn?

13. What does Allah mean?

14. What was the perspective on God held by most Arabs of Muhammad's time?

15. What impact did Muhammad's monotheism have on his society?

16. What identified a person as a Muslim during the very beginning stages of the religion?

17. Why is 622 CE recognized as year one of the Islamic calendar?

18. Why is it inaccurate to say that people in Muhammad's society viewed themselves as Arabs?

19. What impact did the Battle of Tours have on world history?

20. How was early Muslim expansion different from Christian expansion?

21. Why do Muslims see no distinction between the religious and the political dimensions of life?

22. Describe how the introduction of the Muslim moral code affected people in Muhammad's society.

II. Islam and the Religious Traditions of the Middle East

Who will turn away from the creed of Abraham
but one dull of soul?
We made him the chosen one here in the world,
and one of the best in the world to come,
(For) when his Lord said to him: "Obey," he replied:
"I submit to the Lord of all the worlds."
And Abraham left this legacy to his sons...
(Koran, Sura 2:130–132)

Children of Abraham. Islam sees itself as aligned with Judaism and Christianity. All three religions have their origins in wandering tribes, **Semites** or Semitic peoples, who inhabited the Middle East for centuries. Judaism, Christianity, and Islam are all children of Abraham, the great Semitic patriarch written about in the Hebrew, Christian, and Islamic scriptures. Abraham fathered only two sons—Ishmael and Isaac. However, from these two sons came the Arabs who became Muslim (through Ishmael) and the Jews (through Isaac). Christians, of course, trace Jesus' lineage back to Abraham as well. Thus all three religions claim Abraham as their father in faith as well as in fact.

People of the Book. The Qur'an also refers to Jews, Christians, and Muslims as **People of the Book**. That is, members of each religion consider a collection of writings to be the actual word of God. Jews believe that the Hebrew Bible is the word of God. Christians believe that the Hebrew Bible as well as their additions known as the New Testament are together the word of God. Muslims accept the Jewish and Christian Scriptures as well as the Qur'an as the word of God. Therefore, Muslims have always regarded Jews and Christians as fellow believers rather than as **infidels**, or nonbelievers. In territories ruled by Muslims, Jews and Christians were given a special title—**dhimmis**, meaning "protected people." They were not to be treated like infidels. Although the Qur'an itself warns that some Jews and some Christians are not true muslims, or followers of God's will, nonetheless it recognizes the right of members of these religions to be communities separate from the Islamic community who worship and follow God according to their own scriptures.

A Christian View of Islam

While perspectives on Islam differ among the various Christian denominations, over the past forty years the official Catholic position on the religion has recognized that Christians and Muslims, even though they have important differences, are one family in faith. For instance, the world's Catholic bishops said the following in a statement from its Vatican Council II held in the 1960s:

The Church has also a high regard for the Muslims. They worship God, who is one, living and subsistent, merciful and almighty, the Creator of heaven and earth, who has also spoken to humanity. They endeavor to submit themselves without reserve to the hidden decrees of God, just as Abraham submitted himself to God's plan, to whose faith Muslims eagerly link their own. Although not acknowledging him as God, they venerate Jesus as a prophet; his virgin Mother they also honor, and even at times devoutly invoke. Further, they await the day of judgment and the reward of God following the resurrection of the dead. For this reason they highly esteem an upright life and worship God, especially by way of prayer, alms-deeds and fasting. (*Declaration on the Relation of the Church to Non-Christian Religions*, #3)

Muhammad—The Seal of the Prophets. In the days before the printing press and FAX machines, rulers would place their official seal in wax on a letter or proclamation to indicate that it indeed originated with them. One title that Muslims give to Muhammad is **the seal of the prophets**. The title affirms that Muhammad was the greatest and the last prophet. That is, he communicated God's words so clearly and so thoroughly that additional prophets were no longer needed. Instead of looking for more prophets, people need only read the Qur'an, which contains God's final and complete message.

Write a paragraph describing the Islamic understanding of prophecy. Then suggest an image or an analogy, such as the cup of tea analogy, that would illustrate this understanding. Explain why.

ACTIVITY

Prophecy and the "cup of tea" analogy

According to Islam, Muhammad was the last prophet. How many prophets preceded him? The Qur'an names twenty-five prophets, two Arabs and the rest Jews. (If you know the Bible you would recognize many of the people identified by the Qur'an as prophets.) However, Islam does not give a complete tally about how many prophets have existed. Therefore, at least theoretically other cultures may have had prophets who received revelations from God and whose scriptures could contain God's truth as it was understood by particular people. The Qur'an states that to every people an apostle has been sent.

An analogy that describes the phenomenon of prophecy is the making of a cup of tea. Early prophets received the beginning messages from God, much as a cup of tea begins with boiling water and tea leaves. Then later prophets revealed additional messages that further clarified God's message, just as someone might sweeten tea with sugar or honey. Finally, through Muhammad, God revealed the final and complete truth, just as someone might add milk or lemon or some other flavoring to make a complete cup of tea ready for drinking.

The Qur'an and Earlier Scriptures. For Muslims, Muhammad was the last and the greatest prophet. However, he was not the only prophet. The Qur'an is the final and complete scripture. However, it is not the only scripture. The Hebrew Bible and the Christian Scriptures are also the word of God. However, from a Muslim perspective they suffer from two flaws not found in the Qur'an: (1) they are incomplete, and (2) they are distorted. For Muslims an obvious distortion that crept into the Christian Scriptures is the way Jesus' relationship with God is portrayed. According to the Qur'an, Jesus was born of the virgin Mary, he is the messiah of the Jews, and he will come again on the Last Day. However, he is not God; he never claimed to be God. The gospels, written decades after the actual events and not by eyewitnesses to the events, distorted Jesus' message. The Qur'an, on the other hand, was compiled immediately after Muhammad's death and confirmed by a number of Muhammad's closest companions who were with him from the beginning. The Qur'an clarifies a number of other distortions found in the earlier scriptures. For instance, Adam's sin is his alone and not the sin of all humanity. According to later Muslim tradition, Abraham was instructed by God to sacrifice his son **Ishmael**, not **Isaac**. Muslims point out that such distortions do not mean Jews and Christians lack authentic scriptures. However, if they wish to authenticate their scriptures they need to read them in light of God's final and undistorted revelations collected together into the Qur'an.

Adam and Eve, from a copy of the Fainama ascribed to Ja'far al-Sadiq, ca. 1550

The Qur'an: God's Greatest Gift

The foundation of Islam is the Koran (qur'an, "recitation") which is, for the pious Muslim, not the word of a prophet but the unadulterated word of God, which has become audible through Muhammad, the pure vessel, in "clear Arabic language." (Annemarie Schimmel, Islam: An Introduction [Albany: State University of New York Press, 1992], 29)

The Qur'an that we can pick up at a bookstore is actually a copy of the eternal Qur'an, written on tablets found only in heaven. The Qur'an that we can read in a book God spoke through an angel speaking in Arabic. Therefore, Arabic is the language of the angels. People who truly want to read the Qur'an should learn Arabic. Translations do not do it justice. Indeed, there are pious Muslims who have memorized every word of the Qur'an, which approximately equals in length the Christian New Testament. Any belief, any policy, or any practice that a Muslim espouses must find its justification in the Qur'an. The Qur'an is scripture, not a work of philosophy. Therefore it is not laid out in any logical format. Just as Jews and Christians debate the meaning of various passages in their scriptures, so Muslims search for the true meaning of statements from the Qur'an that might even appear to contradict themselves. Some statements address specific problems that were facing the Muslim community in quite specific circumstances, leaving Muslims of today to struggle with how to apply the message to very different circumstances. The fault does not lie in the Qur'an but in human comprehension of this God-given collection of recitations. Thus, the Muslim community has built an elaborate system using Hadith, analogy, and consensus to determine what is prescribed and what is forbidden.

The Qur'an is divided into one hundred and fourteen **suras**, the name given for the individual recitations that Muhammad pronounced as the revelations given to him. Unlike the Bible, which follows a basic chronological order, the suras of the Qur'an are arranged more or less by decreasing length. Here are some passages from the Qur'an that can give you at least a feel for this book that guides so many people throughout the world today.

> God does not wish
> injustice to the creatures of the world.
> For to God belongs all
> that is in the heavens and the earth,
> and to God do all things return. (Sura 3:108–109)

> God does not wrong any one,
> not even the equal of an atom;
> and if men do good
> He multiples it by two,
> and adds a great reward of His own. (Sura 4:40)

> The Christ, son of Mary, was but an apostle,
> and many apostles had (come and) gone before him;
> and his mother was a woman of truth.
> They both ate the (same) food (as men). (Sura 5:75)

> As for the life of this world,
> it is nothing but a frolic and frivolity.
> The final abode is the best
> for those who are pious and fear God. (Sura 6:32)

> "O My creatures, there will be no fear or regret
> For (those of) you on that day
> who believed in My revelation and submitted.
> (You will) enter the gardens, you and your spouses, and be glad."
> Golden platters and goblets will be passed around,
> and every thing the heart desires and pleases the eye
> will be there, where you will abide for ever. (Sura 43:67–71)

Vocabulary

children of Abraham: As understood by Muslims, the three religions who claim Abraham as their father in faith: Judaism, Christianity, and Islam. Abraham is an early biblical figure who demonstrated belief in one God and submission to God's will, thus one of the first identifiable "muslims."

dhimmis: Literally "protected ones." Muslim term for Jews and Christians in recognition that they are believers in the one true God.

infidels: Those who do not believe in the one true God.

Isaac: Son of Abraham and his wife Sarah whom Jews, Christians, and Muslims recognize as the ancestor of the Jewish people.

Ishmael: Son of Abraham and the servant Hagar whom Muslims recognize as the ancestor of Arab Muslims (in the Arabic form usually written as "Ismael").

People of the Book: Any religious community founded upon divinely inspired scriptures. Islam identifies in particular Jews, Christians, and Muslims by this title.

Seal of the Prophets: Muslim term applied to Muhammad affirming him as the last and the greatest prophet.

Semites: Wandering tribes of the Middle East. The term derives from the biblical figure Shem, one of Noah's sons.

suras: Chapters of the Qur'an. Each sura is a recitation Muhammad gave of a divinely inspired message he received from God through the angel Gabriel.

For Review

23. Who were the Semites?
24. What three religions consider themselves children of Abraham?
25. Why do Muslims consider members of certain religions to be "people of the book"?

26. How did Muslims view Jews and Christians who lived in territories under their political control?

27. What does it mean to say that Muhammad is the "seal of the prophets"?

28. How do Muslims view the Jewish and Christian Scriptures?

III. The Five Pillars
Foundations for Living a Life of Submission to God

When we look at primitive architecture we can identify much more readily what function each part of a structure serves. Old or new, a building's pillars, whether visible or hidden, support and uphold the entire structure. Take away one of the pillars and a building is on shaky ground. Take away a number of them and a building collapses. This is also the way it is in Islam with the five pillars, five specific practices that a devout Muslim should perform regularly. Muslims are strong in their faith to the degree that they are diligent in performing the pillars. If they slack off in doing one or two of them, their faith weakens. If they discontinue them, then their faith is likely to collapse.

The Five Pillars

1. **Profession of faith**
2. **Prayer five times a day**
3. **Giving designated alms to the poor**
4. **Month-long fasting during daylight hours of Ramadan**
5. **Pilgrimage to Mecca once a lifetime**

Profession of faith. "There is no god but God; Muhammad is God's prophet." That's the Islamic creed. Look at it closely and you will realize that within this brief sentence lie the six elements of the Islamic creed mentioned earlier: God-angels-prophets-scriptures-God's decrees-judgment. In other words, if you believe in God and in Muhammad as God's prophet, then it follows that God's message to humanity lies in the Qur'an, which contains God's decrees upon which all people will be judged. As a pillar of the Islamic faith this brief statement is not simply something to be said and believed; it is to be lived. The Arabic word for this first pillar is *shahada*. It literally means "witness," not creed. Muslims are to witness to the truth of the statement by living out all that God asks of them. That is, the Muslim creed is not a statement of belief but a commitment to a way of life. Islam does not have priests or sacraments in any formal sense. Therefore, merely affirming the shahada three times in a public setting makes one a Muslim.

Prayer Five Times a Day. If you have ever seen a Muslim perform the specified prayer ritual (known as *salat*), then you know that an important part of the ritual calls for prostration—kneeling with head bent to the ground. A devout Muslim might actually wear a sign of faith, a forehead that over a lifetime shows the wear of constantly touching the ground from practicing the prayer ritual five times daily as the pillar prescribes. Muslims can pray at any time and in any fashion. The second pillar of the faith, however, is a precise ritual. Throughout the world Muslims pray at the same times, in the same words, in the same language (Arabic), facing the same direction (the sacred shrine in the heart of Mecca), and moving through the same set of postures. If possible, Muslims gather for communal prayer at a **mosque** Fridays at noon. The ritual performed at this service is the same as that performed every other noon with the addition of a reading from the Qur'an and a sermon delivered by a leader of the community.

Whenever Muslims pray in a group, all men line up next to each other to demonstrate their equality before God. If a space cannot accommodate one line, then men form as many lines as needed. A leader might stand out from the group to make sure that the postures are performed in unison. During these designated prayer times, women stand behind the men. At a mosque, women may actually be separated from the men by a curtain or some other partition. (In 2005, a breakthrough occurred when a woman led Friday prayers in a New York mosque.)

A. Look at the prostration posture that is part of the Muslim prayer ritual. Write about how the posture is a gesture that symbolizes the core beliefs of Islam.

B. Visit a mosque, or read about one, and write a report describing what is found in it.

Giving Alms to the Poor. Most religions insist on the importance of people who are able giving assistance to people in need. How much should a wealthy Christian give to help poor people? If you ask ten different Christians and press them for a specific amount, you likely will receive ten different answers. In Islam, giving charity is not only a suggestion, it is a requirement. And the amount required to be given is exactly specified: two and one-half percent of one's wealth. To understand the nature of this third pillar of Islam (in Arabic, *zakat*) you need to put it in the context of the religion's early development. Islam encourages charitable giving in general, as do Judaism and Christianity. Islam praises charity and exhorts its followers to see to it that no one in their community is suffering needlessly. However, one difference between Islam and Christianity is that it did not begin as a movement separate from the political powers governing the territory in which it spread. From the time of the hijrah to Medina, remember, Islam *was* the governing power. Thus it had to set up a system of taxation and to subsidize social programs right from its beginnings. Not until three hundred years into its existence did Christianity become the religion of the Roman Empire. Even then there was not the complete identification between religious and political leadership as there was early on in Islam. Today in Muslim-dominated countries some governments assess the two and one-half percent as a tax. In non-Muslim countries such as the United

Prayer Rugs

As you may know, Muslim countries of the Middle East are famous for their rug work. If a devout Muslim cannot participate in prayer at a mosque, he or she may perform the ritual on a prayer rug. The rug may have the design of a mosque woven into it. Thus, a prayer rug serves as a "portable mosque" that a Muslim can step onto during prayer times.

States, Muslim communities have been searching for the best ways to maintain this important pillar of their religion.

Perspectives on wealth and sharing one's goods are both similar and different among the three religions of the Semitic tradition. In order to examine your own perspective on these similarities and differences, write a response to the following statements.

A. If Jesus had lived another twenty years and had been accepted as head of the Jewish nation, he would certainly have designated a specific amount that people would be required to give to charity.

B. Jesus was much more radical than Muhammad and Islam in what he asked of his followers. He told a rich man interested in being his follower: "Go, sell what you own, and give the money to the poor, and you will have treasure in heaven" (Mark 10:21).

C. Jews and Muslims look upon wealth and worldly possessions much more favorably than Christians do. In Judaism and Islam wealth is good, so long as you also share with people in need. From a Christian perspective, earthly riches are suspect, possibly even evil. Ideally, Christians should be poor, not rich. Jesus himself said, "How hard it will be for those who have wealth to enter the kingdom of God!...It is easier for a camel to go through the eye of a needle than for someone who is rich to enter the kingdom of God" (Mark 10:23, 25).

D. Christianity makes a much clearer distinction between earthly existence and life after death than Judaism and Islam do. This difference has implications for how each religion views material goods, earthly riches, and the role of charity.

Fasting. This fourth pillar, called *sawm*, requires Muslims to fast from any food, drink, and sexual activity during the daylight hours of the ninth month of the Islamic calendar, **Ramadan**. Since the Muslim calendar is a lunar one, months are a bit shorter than the months in the solar calendar that is in standard use throughout the globe. Also, Ramadan occurs during different seasons. Daylight, and therefore the fast, is shorter in winter months than in summer. Refraining from drink during the day, including water, is physically more taxing in the heat of summer than in winter. In

Muslim-dominated countries, those who adhere to the fast have a support system in place that helps them. In some countries a cannon blast announces the beginning and end of the fast. Employers are more understanding when workers slow their pace or spend more time in a mosque. In non-Muslim countries practicing the fast can be a greater challenge. No matter where Muslims live, doing the fast requires preparation, caution, and discipline. For instance, you know that not eating all day and then stuffing yourself at night before going to bed is unhealthy—a practice to which the Muslim fast could lead.

Islam emphasizes the great spiritual benefit that fasting achieves. However, as with all its practices, the spiritual benefits are not separated from the physical discipline involved. In our discussion of Buddhism we will look at fasting as a practice frequently advocated among the world's religions. In Islam the fast is viewed primarily as another important way of worshipping God. That is, fasting is submission to God's will. Refraining from food, drink, and sexual activity reminds Muslims that all good things are gifts from God and meant to be looked upon and enjoyed as such.

An American Muslim scholar recommends that all Americans should consider participating in a common fast, perhaps on the first day of Ramadan. In this way non-Muslims could achieve at least partial benefits of Islam's Great Fast:

- celebrating the solidarity of all people under God regardless of religion

- recognizing the importance of self-control

- appreciating the pleasures of life as gifts from God

- reminding people to share what they have with others

- setting aside time to break with routine and appreciate how our life fits into a bigger picture

Would you support a proposal to (a) hold a day of fasting (b) supported by all religious bodies (c) in conjunction with the Muslim fast? Why or why not?

The Hajj. Which city plays the most important role for the religion with which it is associated? Benares for Hindus? Jerusalem for Jews? Rome for Catholics? Certainly the case can be made that Mecca surpasses all of these as a central focus of Islam. In their daily prayers Muslims face Mecca. Muslims are also expected, if at all possible, to go on pilgrimage to Mecca, the *hajj*, at least once in their lifetime. (The word "mecca" has even entered the English language to mean a place that is the center of interest and gathering-point of a particular group of people. For instance, "Hollywood is the mecca of the movie industry.") The hajj is a pilgrimage lasting between five and ten days that occurs once a year. Muslims who participate in the hajj are not tourists but pilgrims to the holy sites. Men and women on the hajj wear simple white garments. On this occasion pilgrims set aside differences of wealth, education, nationality, and race because on the hajj all are Muslims. Only Muslims can attend the hajj, and each day's activities are clearly spelled out. The most popularly recognized scene associated with the hajj is an aerial view of the vast throng of pilgrims walking around the ancient shrine called the *ka'ba*. The word means "cube" and the shrine is called this because of its shape. It is situated in the heart of the Grand Mosque in Mecca and houses a black stone given by the angel Gabriel to Abraham and his son Ishmael who built a house to God with it on this very spot. As with the other pillars, the hajj is another specific, clearly prescribed practice by which a Muslim worships God.

A. Although non-Muslims are not permitted in Mecca, a number of Muslims have written about and filmed the events of the hajj. Write a report on the hajj, describing the activities associated with it and what experiencing the hajj means to Muslims who have done it.

B. What is the difference between being a pilgrim as opposed to being a tourist? Have you ever been on what you would consider to be a pilgrimage? Describe the experience. If you had an opportunity to go on a pilgrimage to any site in the world, where would you go? Why?

ACTIVITY

Vocabulary

hajj: Pilgrimage to Mecca required of all Muslims once in a lifetime.

ka'ba: Cube-shaped building in the center of the Grand Mosque in Mecca. Muslims pray their daily prayers facing the ka'ba.

mosque: Gathering place for Muslims to pray. Communal prayer along with a Qur'an reading and a sermon takes place in a mosque on Fridays at noon.

Ramadan: ninth month of the Islamic calendar during which Muslims fast during daylight hours.

shahada: First of Islam's five pillars; literally means "witness."

For Review

29. What function do the five pillars serve in Islam?
30. Name the five pillars.
31. What is the wording of the creed professed in the first pillar?
32. What is the literal meaning of the Arabic term for the first pillar? What does this meaning imply about the Muslim understanding of the pillar?
33. What are the specific requirements of the second pillar?
34. Name a factor that led to Islam specifying the minimum amount that Muslims should contribute to charity.
35. What are the exact requirements of the Muslim Great Fast?
36. How is being a pilgrim different from being a tourist?
37. What is the ka'ba?

The writer Edward Said describes what he calls "orientalism."
He suggests that Napoleon re-introduced many Europeans to the Arab and Middle Eastern world in particular by taking over Egypt and bringing back to France many ancient Egyptian artifacts. According to Said, since that time Westerners have certain preconceived notions about Arabs and Middle Easterners. The sum of these preconceptions he calls "orientalism." He claims that even people from the Middle East have had to address these stereotypes. On the other hand, people from the Middle East tend to have preconceived notions about the West, Western culture, and people from the West. Said calls these stereotypes "occidentalism." (Traditionally, the orient meant the East; the occident referred to the West.)

A. List associations

1. List associations that you make regarding Arab and Middle Eastern people and cultures.

2. List what you believe have been the dominant perceptions that Westerners have had about Arabs and Middle Eastern people over the past few centuries.

3. List associations that you believe people from Middle Eastern countries tend to have about people from the West.

4. List associations that you believe people from Middle Eastern countries tend to have specifically about the United States, its people and its culture.

B. Use the following questions to analyze and evaluate these associations:

1. Is there any basis for any of these preconceptions?

2. Why do you think these preconceptions came into being and continue to exist?

3. What effect might these preconceptions have on how people from different cultures view one another?

4. Have you ever felt like you were being looked at or treated as if you represented one of these preconceptions?

5. Should efforts be made to eliminate preconceptions that people from different cultures have toward one another? If so, why? How might this be done?

ACTIVITY

IV. Islam Develops
From the Seventh Century to the Modern Era

The community of all Muslims is known as the **umma**. Muslims see themselves as one community who believe in God and God's prophets and who
look to the Qur'an for guidance in all matters of life. Essentially, all members of the umma would agree with everything that has been written about
Islam in the last chapter. The two major divisions that currently exist within the umma came about because of a political controversy that took place
a few decades after the death of Muhammad. In addition to these two,
there are a number of other groups that have a different take on matters
such as how one interprets certain teachings found in the Qur'an. While
there has been animosity among these groups that has flared up and sub-
sided throughout the history of the religion, the vast majority of Muslims
recognize one another as members of the one umma.

Caliphs: Successors to the Prophet

Muhammad left a community that was rapidly expanding its political control over the Middle East while seeking to make practical decisions about
how to be faithful to God and God's law. The leaders of the community
chose one of their number, Abu Bakr, to be the first **caliph**, meaning "successor" to the prophet. The early caliphs were political and religious leaders
of Islam. The first four caliphs ruled the Islamic community until 661. Most
Muslims refer to them as the "rightly guided caliphs" since they were so
closely associated with Muhammad. However, three of these first four were
assassinated, an indication that transfer of power was not always smooth.
As successors to Muhammad, the caliphs oversaw both the religious and
political life of the community. As time went by caliphs concentrated on
political governance and relied more and more heavily on judges who were
experts in the Qur'an and its legal code to preside over religious matters.

After the first four caliphs, two dynasties ruled most of the Islamic community for the next couple centuries. In time, leaders of large areas of
Muslim-dominated territory were not generally viewed as the sole rulers
of the Islamic world. The head of the Ottoman Empire, headquartered in
Turkey, claimed the title caliph until the empire fell in the early twentieth
century. Some Muslims today propose that the worldwide community of

Muslims should return to what Muhammad intended it to be—one political and religious entity that transcends nationalities and ethnic differences.

Major Divisions within Islam: Sunnis and Shiites

The fourth caliph plays an important role in the historical development of Islam. Cousin and son-in-law to Muhammad, **Ali** was one of his first followers. When Muhammad died, leaders of the community gathered to decide who would lead them. Muhammad had no male children so dynastic succession based on blood was out of the question. On a number of occasions Muhammad had shown preference for his father-in-law, Abu Bakr, as something of a "second in command." Abu Bakr was also distinguished as being one of the earliest Muslims as well as being a pious and faith-filled man. Community leaders selected him to be the first caliph and subsequently named the next three as well. However, Ali, the fourth caliph, met with challenges. When he was assassinated in 761 a rift occurred in the Muslim community that has never been healed. The majority of Muslims proposed that caliphs should be selected by the leaders of the community and based on leadership qualities. A minority believed that Ali as blood relative of Muhammad was the rightful caliph and thus his son and future descendants alone should be recognized as leaders of Islam. Muslims who followed the *sunna*, the example and practices of Muhammad, and who based leadership on the sunna and not on blood relationship came to be known as **Sunni** Muslims. Those who countered that Ali and his descendants are the only true successors to the prophet came to be known as **Shiite** Muslims. (*Shi'a* means "party" or "supporters." Thus Shiites are "the supporters of Ali.")

As you might expect, once Sunni and Shiite Muslims became separate groups they developed differences beyond the political conflict that led to the break.
Read about these two divisions of Islam and write a report on major differences between the two. Include in your report:

- how members of these two major branches of Islam view each other
- how members of each branch view leadership of the community
- in what countries each branch dominates.

ACTIVITY

Hands, Heart, and Head: Law, Mysticism, and Philosophy in Islam

Every religion has practical, experiential, and intellectual dimensions to it. Islam is no exception. Islam developed an elaborate system of law to guide the practical decisions of its members. It also has a rich tradition of Muslims who emphasize experiencing God's presence in their lives. Finally, it has fostered the intellectual life to a degree unparalleled in human history. Here are brief descriptions of these three dimensions as manifest in Islamic tradition—the hands, heart, and head of Muslim life.

Shari'a

> *Morality for the early Muslim was thoroughly woven into the political task of founding a good and just society under the guidance of God. Throughout the history of Islam there is recognition of the central place held by the law or* Shari'a. (Ninian Smart, Religions of the West [Englewood Cliffs, NJ: Prentice Hall, 1994], 185)

It would seem to be clear how to practice being a Muslim: submit to God's will as revealed in the Qur'an and rely on qur'anic scholars to provide direction in applying the teachings of the Qur'an to various situations that arise. Islam has developed a great system of precepts and practices that together make up Islamic law. This system of law is called the **shari'a.** (As you might suspect from our earlier discussion, the term means "path," the road to the watering hole.) Of course, Islamic law scholars look to the Qur'an as the basis for their interpretations. However, during the early centuries of Islamic history sayings and stories of Muhammad as remembered by friends and followers were gathered together into what is called the **hadith.** Islamic law, therefore, functions in a fashion somewhat similar to the American legal system. In the U.S. all legal judgments must ultimately be based upon the Constitution. Interpretations of the Constitution offered by the country's founding fathers and legal pronouncements since then have set a precedent for understanding what the Constitution means. Similarly, the shari'a is based upon the Qur'an, the hadith, interpretations made throughout history, and consensus of the community. In other words, it is up to human understanding to make sense of what God meant.

Thus, Islam is a religion that emphasizes specific practices and advocates following laws that make up the shari'a. This has been the dominant approach to living as a Muslim followed by the vast majority of Muslims. However, early in Islam two other approaches blended with this mainstream approach that have enriched Islam ever since.

Sufism: Muslim Mysticism

Mysticism refers to experiencing union with ultimate reality. For monotheistic religions, it means experiencing union with God. At first this sounds like a very un-Muslim like phenomenon. That is, aren't God and human beings totally separate? In Islam, placing anything on the same plain as God is the gravest sin. However, there has been a strong tradition of Muslim mystics; and generally they have been accepted by the larger Muslim commu-

Whirling dervishes

nity as important members of the umma. Called **Sufis**, probably because they wore simple robes made of wool (in Arabic, *suf*), Muslim mystics developed elaborate systems for fostering mystical experience. Still, how can mysticism, experiencing *oneness with God*, be compatible with Islam, *submission to God*? Sufism makes the connection in this way. By faithfully engaging in mystical practices you spend all your energy surrendering your will to God so that at some point you are no longer clinging to your own will. If at some point you experience that your separate identity itself dissolves, what is left? The Sufi answer is: no longer one's personal will, only God's will; no longer oneself, only God. Thus, rather than being a contradiction to Islam, Sufism claims to be the highest expression of Islam. That is, the goal of Sufi practices is complete surrender to God's will so much so that there is no longer a distinction between oneself and God. For Sufis, surrendering to God, as called for in Islam, ultimately means absorption into God.

Sufis developed a variety of techniques meant to assist the dedicated practitioner on the way to mystical experience. One group that employs a distinctive practice is called **whirling dervishes** because they use a prolonged whirling style of dance leading to mystical experience. (A dervish is another name for a Sufi.) The Afghan poet and mystic known to the West as Rumi is credited with beginning the whirling dervishes. He began the movement in Turkey. The Sufi tradition has also produced a rich body of literature, principally brief sayings and anecdotes that when meditated upon can spark a sense of the mystical.

ACTIVITY

A. Write a report on one of the following topics related to Sufism:
   - early Sufis
   - the writings of Rumi
   - women Sufis
   - Sufi practices
   - Sufism in the United States

B. The author Idries Shah has written a number of books that contain collections of stories and sayings coming out of the Sufi tradition. Read through one of his books and write an essay about one or a few of these stories or sayings.

My heart has become confused from the world and what is in it.
Within my heart there is nothing but the Friend....
There is no real difference between the Kaaba and the idol-house
Wherever you may look, there equally is HE.
   (From the sufi Khwaja Hafiz of Shiraz, in Idries Shah, The Way of the Sufi [London: Penguin Books, 1968], 242)

O Friend,
You made me lovingly,
put me in a dress of skin and blood.
Then planted deep inside me
a seed from Your Heart.
You turned the whole world
into a sanctuary where You are
the only One.
   (Rumi: Whispers of the Beloved, *translated by Azima Melita Kolin and Maryam Mafi [London: Thorsons, 1999], 50.)*

Muslim Philosophy

Fairly early in its existence Islam bumped up against a formidable force, one which Judaism and Christianity already had to deal with. Greek philosophy proposed that in the search for truth the highest priority should be given to using the mind, human reason. Like mysticism, this position at first appears to be contradictory to the tenets of Islam. That is, the Qur'an is *the* source of truth. Its teachings do not need to make sense, follow logic, or be comprehensible to the human mind. A Muslim is to submit totally to God's will revealed in the Qur'an. However, what happened during the centuries of Islam's golden era was anything but anti-intellectual. The scholarly activity spurred on by study of the Qur'an didn't stop there. Great minds of Islam soon applied the same intellectual vigor to all areas of study. In fact, while Greek writings were generally unavailable in Europe during the time period often called the "dark ages," Muslim scholars were busy translating major Greek works into Arabic. From these Arabic translations the works of Plato and Aristotle were re-introduced to Europe.

By engaging in debate with ideas that might support or challenge Islam, Muslim scholars made major contributions to all areas of thought. Also, because the Muslim community reached from India to Western Europe it fostered a rich cross-pollination of ideas from many different cultures. Muslims revere the Qur'an as the source of truth, but they realize that they are to use their intellect to understand and apply its message.

A. Write a report on one of the following Muslim thinkers:
- Avicenna (Ibn Sina)
- Rabi'a (Rabi'a al-Adwiyya)
- al-Shafi'i
- al-Ghazali
- al-Hallaj
- Rumi

B. Identify what comprises the "hands, heart, and head" dimensions of a religion other than Islam. (For example, what kinds of commandments and practices do Judaism or Catholicism advocate? Are there groups dedicated to experiencing God directly in Judaism or Catholicism? What have been major contributions to the intellectual life made by Jewish or Catholic scholars?) Compare and contrast your findings with these dimensions as manifest in Islam.

ACTIVITY

Without the early philosophers, scientists, architects and artists of Islam, the brilliant achievements of twentieth-century science and technology would not have been possible. During a long period of intellectual and social decay in Christian Europe, Islamic peoples built a rich and distinguished civilization. While Europe went through its so-called "Dark Ages," Islamic peoples experienced a golden age of prosperity and achievement. Then when Europeans began to revive intellectual and scientific activity, it was the Muslims' previous efforts that enabled this Renaissance to succeed. During this reawakening, the immense cultural heritage from ancient Greece and the Far East reached Europe through Latin translations of Arabic books, themselves inspired by the philosophy and science of the ancients. (R. Marston Speight, God Is One: The Way of Islam *[New York: Friendship Press, 1989], 5-6)*

The Arts and Sciences in Islam

- Do you love going to algebra class? You have Muslims from the last millennium to thank for this branch of mathematics (in Arabic, al-jabr).

- Can you imagine going through life without the concept "zero"? That word (in Arabic, sifr) and the rest of our numbering system came from Muslims who developed it based on a system they adopted from India.

- Looking forward to working on a chemistry project? Rudimentary chemistry began in the pre-Christian Middle East. The ancient Greeks established many chemical theories after which Muslims greatly advanced the science, often in a pursuit known as "alchemy." Here again, Western Europe of the late Middle Ages learned its science from Arab Muslims.

- Thinking of joining the chess club? The name of the game comes from the Persian shah, meaning king. The aim of the game is checkmate, from shah mat, meaning "the king is dead." Arab Muslims learned the game when they conquered Persia and introduced it to Europe.

- Do you have a favorite, finely-decorated book that surrounds the opening letter of each chapter with stems and leaves in an elaborate design? Such decoration is called arabesque. Like Jews, Muslims do not picture God and hesitate to make images of Muhammad and other figures for fear of idolatry. Islamic art, therefore, is more decorative than pictorial. Much Muslim art centers around the written word. In addition to the arabesque style of decoration, Muslims have also perfected intricate, fancy writing styles known as calligraphy. You can see examples of Islamic decorative art in mosques, in rugs, in books, and of course in copies of the Qur'an itself.

Vocabulary

Ali: Cousin and son-in-law of Muhammad who was the fourth caliph.

caliph: Successor to Muhammad who leads the Muslim community.

hadith: Sayings of and stories about Muhammad handed down orally and then collected to help Muslims understand and apply the teachings of the Qur'an.

mysticism: An experience of union with ultimate mystery.

shari'a: Collective laws and duties of the Islamic community.

Shiite: Muslims who trace their origin back to those who believed that the caliph should be a descendant of Ali, Muhammad's cousin and son-in-law, and therefore a blood descendant of the prophet. Shiite Muslims today are mainly from Iran.

Sufis: Muslim mystics.

Sunna: Islamic customs and traditions based on the example of Muhammad.

sunni: Muslims who trace their origin back to those who believed the caliph should be chosen based on merit.

umma: The Muslim community.

whirling dervishes: Sufis who use a whirling dance as a means to achieve mystical experience.

For Review

38. Who were the caliphs and what role did they play in Islam?
39. What is the umma? What led to the two major divisions within the umma?
40. What three things form the basis of the shari'a?
41. What is mysticism?
42. What is Sufism? Explain why Sufis conclude that mysticism is compatible with Islam.

43. Who began the whirling dervishes? What technique do they employ in their pursuit of mystical experience?

44. Upon what basis could a case be made that Islam appears at first to be anti-intellectual?

45. Name two contributions Islam made to the intellectual life during its early centuries.

V. Islam in the Modern World

True or false: "All people on the earth are members of different nationalities and ethnic groups. Therefore, it is only natural that the world should be divided into distinct and separate nation states…"? Actually this notion represents a fairly recent perspective, and it is one that Islam traditionally rejects. Separate nation states are a creation of the modern world. As you recall, for centuries Muslim dynasties held political control of portions of Europe, Africa, and Asia. One change that marked the end of the Middle Ages and the emergence of modern times in Europe was the demise of the Holy Roman Empire and the birth of separate, independent nations. Then for over a century—essentially the nineteenth—European nations battled over and divided up formerly Muslim-controlled territories. During the twentieth century, as Africans and Asians regained control of their lands, Muslims struggled with being true to their religion while also carving out a place in the world community of nations.

ACTIVITY

A. Find maps from various periods in history. Describe how political boundaries changed over time. Note especially when particular nations identified as separate entities came into existence in Europe, Africa, and the Middle East.

B. Write a report on one of the following topics:

- Early Muslim expansion
- The Battle of Tours in 732
- Islam in Spain and Portugal
- Islam in Pakistan and India
- Islam in Eastern Europe

Two Positions. One important figure who addressed the challenge to Islam brought on by the modern world order was a Muslim Turkish leader named **Ataturk**. In 1923 Turkey became a modern republic. Ataturk proposed the idea that Turkey should be a completely secular state, abandoning the idea of a trans-national Muslim community under the leadership of a spiritual-political figure, a caliph. His idea was that Islam should serve as a *moral* force in a nation rather than as a formal political force. Many Muslims rejected this idea. They viewed the establishment of secular governments and separate nations within the Islamic community as giving in to Western ways. A number of movements under the heading **Islamic revivalism** have proposed political arrangements that would more closely mirror the early days of the Muslim movement. One person who personified Islamic revivalism to the world was the Iranian **Ayatollah Khomeini**. (An ayatollah is a Shiite religious leader.) In 1979 his followers ousted a very westernized leader, the Shah of Iran, and established an Iranian government run essentially by Muslim religious leaders and based solely on Islamic principles. Today much of the conflict and controversy that exists in the Muslim community worldwide centers around this issue:

- Was Ataturk correct? Should Muslims accommodate themselves to the political realities that emerged out of the modern West, particularly the separation of politics and religion?

- Were Ayatollah Khomeini and Islamic revivalists correct? Should Islamic teachings, principles, and religious leaders dictate governmental laws, policies, and actions?

- How much latitude should be given to human interpretation of Shari'a?

To further complicate the matter, Islamic revivalists are often very conservative in their interpretation of Islamic teachings. For this reason they are often called **Islamic fundamentalists**. For example, one of the first changes to take place after the 1979 **Iranian Revolution** was the requirement that when in public all women had to wear veils covering their faces. More liberal-minded Muslims interpret Islamic teachings on this matter less restrictively. When the fundamentalist Islamic group known as the Taliban ruled Afghanistan, they banned Western movies and music in the country. Houses where people violated this rule would be seen strewn with black video tape to remind others that severe punishment awaited those who violated this perceived affront to Islam. Fundamentalists in Islam—or in any religion for that matter—fear that any loosening up of traditional beliefs and practices diminishes their religion. As a result they consider "modern" values to be an attack on their religious values and therefore need to be opposed; wherever possible laws and community practices should conform to a strict and conservative standard.

A. Write a report on one of the following topics:
- Ataturk
- the Iranian Revolution
- Islamic Fundamentalism
- Wahhabism (or Wahabism)
- the Taliban regime in Afghanistan

B. Write an essay based on the following imaginary scenario. You are the parent of three girls ages 10, 13, and 15 living in a traditional Muslim country. Recently your two older children have been sneaking off with friends to watch teen-oriented movies made in the United States and listening to rock music. Now they are asking to wear clothes reflecting Western-style dress and want to go out on dates. They are also complaining that they no longer want to attend classes at the mosque where they are learning to read the Qur'an in Arabic. What would you do? Defend your response.

C. Describe religious fundamentalism as it occurs within the Jewish, Protestant, Catholic, and Islamic communities. Explain what each group would view as the major problems facing the world, the source of those problems, and their cure.

Jihad: The Struggle to Remain Faithful to God

Can you imagine actually dedicating your life to surrendering to God's will? That would be quite a struggle. Islam has a word for this struggle—*jihad*. Some Muslims consider it a sixth pillar of their religion. Actually it is better understood as a quality to be applied to each of the five pillars. The primary understanding of jihad is a personal one. All Muslims must look within themselves to determine what struggles they face and how they are succeeding or failing in those struggles. Secondly, jihad applies as well to the Muslim community as a whole. Here the concept becomes more controversial because it involves relations between Muslim communities and other groups.

A Muslim at prayer

Often mistranslated as "holy war," jihad raises the question of the place of violence in Islam. For instance, does the Qur'an forbid or condone violence? Clearly, the Qur'an does not condemn violence. Recall from our earlier discussion, however, that the very word Islam indicates that it is a religion of peace. Remember also that for Muslims true peace comes only from submission to God's will. So long as individuals or communities do not submit to God's will, conflicts will arise. Therefore, most Muslims would agree that at times violence may be called for in attempting to resolve these conflicts. Beyond this over-arching position on violence, it is important to clarify some misconceptions about Islam and warfare.

1) Muhammad and the early Muslim community did engage in violence both in defending itself as well as in gaining political dominance over an increasing amount of territory. Conquering territory, however, did not mean that the religion was "spread by the sword," as it has been depicted in some history books. Granted, many people in conquered lands did become Muslim; but they did so for a variety of reasons. (One scholar estimates that it took two hundred years before even the majority of people in conquered lands became Muslim.) Many people in countries under Muslim control did not become Muslim. For instance, there continue to be groups of Christians in Egypt and Iraq as well as in other countries that pre-date Muslim conquest of those areas. In Spain for centuries Jews, Christians, and Muslims lived together peacefully and fruitfully under Muslim governance. Remember that Islam is, by most accounts, the fastest growing religion in the world today. As in its earliest days, people now are turning to Islam not because they are forced to but because they find truth in it that speaks to them.

2) Islam reduced and greatly restricted the violence present in the Arab world at the time of Muhammad. Resources were extremely scarce in the

world in which Islam was born. Defending tribal rights against other tribes was commonplace. Even raiding passing caravans was an acceptable occupation. After Islam, violence was restricted to one goal—defending the Muslim community from idolatry.

3) Christianity has a much bloodier history than Islam. During the **Crusades** and the **Inquisition** people who called themselves Christian practiced a level of violence far surpassing what Muslims of their day engaged in.

4) Not every Muslim group that appeals to the term "jihad" is engaged in holy war. When Napoleon took control of Egypt in 1798 it began over a century during which Muslim-dominated territories came to be subjugated to European powers. As Muslims have tried to regain power and decide upon their place in the world community that is true to their religious beliefs, some Muslims have advocated violence and have called their violence an expression of jihad. However, actual attitudes toward violence within the Muslim community today are as diverse as attitudes toward violence in the Christian community.

5) Recently, the increase in Western power and influence in Muslim-ruled countries has challenged Muslims to make political, economic, and cultural decisions that balance fidelity to their beliefs and traditions with responding to the system and values dominant in the world. Some Muslims proposed that accommodation with Western ways did not constitute being unfaithful to Islam. Others believed that Western power, Western influence, and Western ways were to be rejected and that Muslims should hold on forcefully to their social and religious beliefs and practices. For a number of decades spanning most of the twentieth century, a few Muslims in this latter group advocated the use of violence to enhance and preserve Muslim power and their understanding of a Muslim way of life. Americans encountered this advocacy of violence most tragically on September 11, 2001. Unfortunately, for many Americans, Islam will forever be associated most closely with the terrorist attacks of September 11, 2001, perpetrated by a small, fringe group who claimed to act in the name of Islam.

A. Keeping in mind that members of a particular religion can disagree about controversial topics, find out what you can about the perspectives on peace, violence, and warfare held by each of the major religions studied during this course. Where possible, compare original teachings on these subjects in the religion with later practices. Write a report on your findings.

B. Write a report on one of the following:

- the crusades or the Spanish Inquisition
- treatment of Jews under Muslim domination compared to Christian domination
- uses of the word "jihad" by various groups today
- a conflict situation in the world today where religion plays a part in the conflict

C. Defend or refute the following statements:

- Violence in the name of just causes is acceptable.
- Violence should only be employed for religious purposes.
- Only religious leaders, not political ones, should determine whether or not using violence is acceptable or not in particular circumstances.
- Religions have generally been a force for peace in the world.
- Religious conflict has either instigated or accompanied most of the world's violent conflicts.

Women in Islam

One commentator on Islam gives the religion the following mixed review in regard to its impact on women:

> The Koran ratified the traditional roles of men and women in society: men hunting and trading while women keep house, men strong and free, women somehow tainted by the reproductive process God created, dependent upon men, available for use upon demand. Still, the Koran's dictates on women's legal status (as opposed to their social status) were quite advanced for their time, and Islamic law gives women some rights more liberating than those found in Western legal codes. (Thomas W. Lippman, Understanding Islam [New York: Meridian, 1995], 97)

In other words, Islam began in a culture dominated by men and in which men's and women's roles were clearly separate. Therefore, the Qur'an is addressed primarily to men. During prescribed prayer, for instance, men line up first. Women stay behind the men. Why? For one thing, women have the children to care for and perhaps have to leave to attend to other domestic duties. Also (from a male point of view) if men tried to pray behind women they might easily be distracted. In addition, as the author points out in the above quote, due to certain bodily functions women in this culture were considered to be "unclean" at times and thus should be restricted to the back of the mosque. Therefore, while both men and women are called upon to be Muslim, they are to be Muslim in somewhat different ways.

The place of women in the world's religions has been an important and fascinating area of study recently. While we can't cover the topic in any comprehensive way here, we can note at least four points regarding women and Islam.

1) Indications are that Islam improved conditions for women in Arab society. Many Muslim historians propose that Islam introduced unprecedented freedoms for Arab women, although the historical record is unclear about the status of women in pre-Islamic Arabia.

2) The Qur'an, other foundational writings, and early practices of Islam do reflect the male-dominated worldview in existence in Arabia during the seventh century.

3) It is difficult to separate practices based on a religion from cultural practices. That is to say, not every custom found in a Muslim-dominated society is a "Muslim" practice. (In similar fashion, in many Christian-dominated countries brides wear white wedding gowns. However, it would be wrong to say that this is a "Christian" practice.) For instance, the common practice of Muslim women covering their faces in public is not specifically required in the Qur'an.

4) As has been the case wherever formal religious practices are more a male domain, Muslim women have found ways to express themselves and pursue spirituality unique to them. Especially in recent decades in response to the worldwide feminist movement, many Muslim women have consciously set about to identify what it means to be a Muslim woman, even one with feminist leanings.

A. Write a report on women in Islam, focusing on the key aspects of the religion that affect women today.

B. Write a response to the following statements as if they were made by a Muslim woman.

1. "Because I wear the traditional Muslim garb while at work, I am treated more for my effectiveness on the job than in terms of my looks."

2. "I am happy to take greater responsibility for home and the children. My husband works hard outside of the home to provide for us. This is a sensible and natural arrangement."

3. "I go out in public alone as little as possible. It is better if I am accompanied by other family members or women friends so that I can avoid trouble or the appearance of trouble."

4. "During formal prayer times, men should take the lead and concentrate more on performing the prostrations correctly. Women have other responsibilities and other ways of expressing their faith."

C. The feminist movement has had an impact on every religion. Look for how Muslim feminists critique aspects of their religion. Describe issues related to Islamic beliefs and practices that feminists address.

Muslims in the United States

Discussion about religions in the United States typically centers around the waves of immigrants from different national and religious backgrounds who made their way to the country in search of fortune and the opportunity to practice their religion freely. A few Muslims did arrive on America's shores as early as Christian Europeans did. Some Muslims, mostly young men seeking work, also came to the United States during the second half of the nineteenth century. However, until fairly recently Muslims did not make major contributions to the religious landscape of the United States. The story of Islam in the United States can be divided into three chapters: (1) African-American Muslims, (2) Muslim immigrants, and (3) converts to Islam.

Islam and the Black Experience in America. Clear evidence suggests that a number of the Africans forced to come to America as slaves were Muslims. (Undoubtedly other Africans who were enslaved came to America as Christians or as practitioners of some form of tribal religion.) Some historians estimate that as many as twenty percent of African slaves were originally Muslim. Most of these slaves and former slaves, for various reasons, ended up joining the "white man's religion"—Christianity. Therefore, today the majority of African-Americans are Christians. Nonetheless, indications are that some Muslim slaves managed to hold onto their religion, if only in secret. Here's one account indicating the existence of a Muslim slave tradition:

> A number of families now living on the coast of Georgia are said to be descendants of slaves, some of them reportedly Muslim. Best known, perhaps, is one Bilali Mahomet, who was probably taken into slavery around 1725. His Bilali Diary, written in a West African Arabic script, is now located in the rare books library of the University of Georgia. Grant records from South Carolina contain reports of slaves who refused to eat pork and who prayed to a god named Allah. For many African American Muslims today, the presence of these Muslims in early American history, and their achievements both before being taken into slavery and while in bondage, have added a great deal to the sense of pride in being Muslim and of sharing in the long struggle for freedom that has characterized the black experience in America from its earliest days. (Jane I. Smith, Islam in America [New York: Columbia University Press, 1999], 77)

For many, African-American Muslims represent the most visible presence of Islam in the United States. And among African-American Muslims the group that has made the greatest impact on United States society is the organization founded in the 1930s by **Elijah Muhammad**. Not all African-Americans who are or were Muslim are members of this particular organization; however, many are. This religious movement, most widely known as the **Nation of Islam** or simply as Black Muslims, began in Detroit, Michigan. A salesman named Wallace D. Fard was at the time preaching that blacks in the United States were originally Muslim and descendants of the original human race. Through their experience of enslavement African-Americans lost sight of their noble heritage. If blacks would renounce Christianity, the "slave religion," and adopt Islam they would regain their identity as the original noble race which was stripped from them when they were forced to leave Africa. A man named Elijah Poole found truth in Fard's message and gained enough followers that he opened a meeting hall that he called a temple. The original name adopted by the group says much about how they viewed themselves: The Lost-Found Nation of Islam in the Wilderness of North America. Elijah Poole took the name Elijah Muhammad to mark his conversion to Islam. Some converts simply changed their name to "X" until they could settle upon an appropriate Muslim name. Although it espoused Islam, Elijah Muhammad's group emphasized some teachings that clearly ran counter to traditional Islam. Perhaps most significant of these was his teaching that white people are devils and inherently inferior to black people. (If you recall, traditional Islam believes in the equality of all people before God.)

In 1947 a man named Malcolm Little, at the time jailed in a Massachusetts prison, converted to the Nation of Islam and took the name **Malcolm X**. At the age of six he had seen his home burned to the ground by members of the Ku Klux Klan, so he had experienced firsthand whites as being the "devils" that the religion preached. When released from prison in 1952 he became the leading spokesperson for the Nation of Islam. Eventually, however, he came to question some of Elijah Muhammad's personal practices as well as some of his teachings. He was removed from his position in the Nation of Islam and went on the hajj to Mecca. That experience changed him tremendously. On the hajj he saw people of all races worshipping together as Muslims. He saw the need to link concerns of blacks in the United States more closely with the international community of Islam. A few months later, in 1965, Malcolm X was shot and killed.

In 1975 Elijah Muhammad died and was succeeded by his son, Wallace. Wallace, known as **Warith Deen Mohammed**, had been a friend of Malcolm X and also questioned some of his father's teachings. Under his leadership, the Nation of Islam became associated with the international community of Islam and not a separatist group. He renamed the Nation of Islam "The World Community of Al-Islam in the West," welcomed whites and others in its services, and called for respect for the United States Constitution and United States citizenship. Meanwhile, another leader of the Nation of Islam named Louis

Farrakhan kept the name of the organization and maintained a stance closer to Elijah Muhammad's. After years of going their separate ways, Warith Deen Mohammed and Louis Farrakhan publicly reconciled with each other in February 2000. A newspaper account of the event referred to an earlier occasion that led up to this reconciliation:

> Since recovering from prostate cancer and complications caused by treatment, Farrakhan, 66, has sought to distance himself from the inflammatory racial rhetoric that for years characterized his leadership. In December, he declared he was a new man with a new message. Standing alongside Catholic priests, Jewish rabbis and Muslim clerics at a news conference here, he called on all people of the world to "try to end the cycle of violence and the cycle of hatred." He also pledged to "spend the rest of my days working to uplift a fallen humanity. Regardless of their color, their race or their creed." (William Claiborne, "Farrakhan reunites two rival factions" [Philadelphia Inquirer, February 26, 2000], A-3)

ACTIVITY

A. Read more about the Black Muslim movement and then write an essay responding to one of the following questions:

1. If you were in Malcolm X's situation—an African-American man in prison during the 1940s—would you join the Black Muslims? Why or why not? What would be the appeal of the movement?

2. If you were a white Christian minister invited to debate Elijah Muhammad during the 1950s, what criticisms of his positions on social and religious matters would you make? How do you think he would respond to your criticisms?

3. Was the change of direction brought about by Warith Deen Mohammed a rejection of the movement's ideals or an outgrowth of them? Explain.

B. Write a report on one of the following men, describing the appeal that Islam had for him:

- Malcolm X
- Kareem Abdul Jabaar
- Muhammad Ali
- Louis Farrakhan

Immigrants and Converts. In the mid-1960s immigration laws of the United States changed, making it possible for more people from different countries to become citizens. As a result, during the past forty years many Muslims of different nationalities came to the United States. Unlike the typical immigrant of earlier times, these Muslim immigrants were more often well-educated and not driven exclusively by poverty. Many of them were students and professional people. Even so, they faced certain challenges that earlier immigrants also faced, namely, how to remain faithful to their religion and their cultural heritage while also adapting to their adopted country. At least initially these Muslim immigrants often sought out and associated with members of their particular nationality. However, as Muslims entered the mainstream of life in the United States more and more, converts from both the Anglo and the Hispanic population joined their religion. While Christianity remains the dominant religion in the United States, best estimates indicate that Muslims now outnumber the Jewish population in the country. As a result, many people are currently carving out an identity for themselves that combines being a resident of the United States with being Muslim.

A. **A number of Islamic organizations exist whose goal is to offer advice to Muslims about how to live out their religion in the United States.** Search the Internet for such organizations. Report on some of the information and recommendations they provide.

B. **Make two lists, as long as possible, stating:**

1. What can Muslims offer the United States?

2. What can the United States offer Muslims?

ACTIVITY

Conclusion
A Religion of Faith and Submission

Nearly one out of five people in the world today accepts that God's word was revealed through the prophet Muhammad, making Islam the world's second largest religion. This worldwide community of Muslims looks to the Qur'an, the example of the prophet, and its own history to ascertain how to live faithfully God's will. Members of this religion affirm that the only path that truly leads to lasting peace is submission to God's will. The clarity and directness of fundamental Islamic beliefs—there is one God whose message is for everyone—has led vast numbers of people worldwide to join the religion of Islam, the community of Muslims.

Vocabulary

Ataturk: Elected first president of the modern state of Turkey in 1924.

Ayatollah Khomeini: Muslim religious leader who in 1979 guided Iran from being a highly Westernized nation to being a nation governed by strict Islamic laws and practices.

crusades: During the Middle Ages a series of invasions of the Middle East by Christian European knights intended to take control of the Holy Land from Muslims.

Elijah Muhammad: Founder of the Nation of Islam, also known as the Black Muslim Movement.

Inquisition: A practice carried out by Christian leaders in certain countries and in certain times whereby non-Christians would be punished, killed, or forced to convert to Christianity.

Iranian Revolution: Establishment in 1979 of a government in Iran based upon Islamic teachings and overseen by Muslim religious leaders.

Vocabulary (continued)

Islamic Fundamentalism: Belief that individual Muslims and Muslim nations should adhere to traditional Islamic principles and practices and should resist modernizing trends.

Islamic Revivalism: Belief that governments in Muslim-dominated countries should establish laws and policies based on Islamic teachings.

jihad: The personal and communal struggle to follow and defend God's will; sometimes translated as "holy war."

Louis Farrakhan: Black Muslim leader who, upon Elijah Muhammad's death, continued a more militant expression of the movement than that of Warith Deen Mohammed's. Early in 2000 these two leaders reconciled.

Malcolm X: Convert to the Nation of Islam who became its leading spokesperson until he left the movement in the mid-1960s.

Nation of Islam: Movement begun in Detroit, Michigan, in the 1930s that linked Islam with black separatism in the United States.

Warith Deen Mohammed: Son of Elijah Muhammad who upon his father's death became leader of the Nation of Islam and linked the movement more closely to the international Muslim community.

For Review

46. What two conflicting positions exist within the Muslim community regarding response to the modern world?
47. What contribution did Ayatollah Khomeini make to modern-day Islam?
48. How do Muslim fundamentalists view modern values?
49. What are the two meanings of the term "jihad"?
50. What is the Muslim attitude toward violence?

51. What do the Crusades and the Inquisition indicate about the actual practice of violence by Christians as opposed to Muslims?

52. How did Islam affect the position of women in Arab society?

53. What was the major change that occurred after Warith Deen Mohammed became leader of the Nation of Islam?

54. What realization did Malcolm X come to during his experience of the hajj?

55. What important event in the history of the Nation of Islam occurred in the year 2000?

56. What challenge have recent Muslim immigrants to the United States faced that earlier immigrants also faced?

CHAPTER 5

HINDUISM
One Reality with Many Faces

Along the banks of an Indian river, scantily dressed old men wait their turn to cleanse themselves by bathing in its waters. Cows decorated with sacred symbols roam the pathways of an Indian village while street merchants display an array of statues of Hindu gods. In finely decorated temples monks perform the daily rituals honoring their god. Elsewhere students sit cross-legged and in complete stillness as they chant in unison with their teacher. Meanwhile, townspeople carry a life-size statue of a goddess covered with garlands on its way to the local river where it will be laid to rest. In time a new statue will be fashioned for next year's festival in her honor. In homes across India family members bow before a statue of their ancestral god before heading off to school or work.

Hinduism, the traditional religion of India, manifests itself in each of these and in many other ways. The religion is not so much a part of Indian life as it is Indian life itself. For over thirty-five hundred years Hinduism has been the lifeblood of the vast majority of people living on the sub-continent India. Its beliefs and practices are both primitive and modern at the same time. Indeed, a journey into this religion is a journey into the human subconscious itself.

Overview

- The Aryan invasion of northeastern India ushers in a period of religious development that shapes Hinduism thereafter.

- Key Hindu concepts describe a monistic worldview.

- Hindus practice various forms of yoga to experience union with the godhead.

- Many gods and a variety of practices continue to mark Hinduism today.

Before we begin...

A. **If you are religious, name ten beliefs and/or practices from your religion that nurture your spiritual life.** For three of these, explain how they make a difference in your life. (If you can't think of ten such beliefs or practices, describe what you think would nourish you spiritually.)

B. **Explain what you think is the relationship between religious practices and beliefs.** Use examples to illustrate that relationship.

I. Hindu Origins and Scriptures

Hinduism is unique among the major religions of the world. It has no founder. It has no dogma. It has no central authority, no pope, and no ecclesiastical council to decide what Hindus must or must not believe. The result is a bewildering, glorious medley of competing philosophies, disparate religious practices, and divergent lifestyles...Like an amoeba, Hinduism constantly varies its shape. (Dianne Morgan, The Best Guide to Eastern Philosophy and Religion [Los Angeles, CA: Renaissance Books, 2001], 14)

A Religion with No Founder

No one person founded Hinduism. For every other major religion that we study we can identify someone whose life and teachings serve as its foundation. (In the case of Judaism, we can name a series of persons who shaped the religion, in particular Abraham and Moses.) For religions other than Hinduism, the life and teachings of certain persons serve as the standard by which to understand them. (For example, a Confucianist looks to the life and teachings of Confucius to decide how to live. A Christian appeals to the life and teachings of Jesus to justify beliefs and practices.) Hinduism, on the

A statue of Shiva meditating

other hand, resembles a series of rivers, all of which flow into a vast ocean. Sometimes the currents of one river appear to run in a totally opposite direction from another. For instance, at one time followers of the goddess **Kali** practiced human sacrifice. They called themselves **Thugs**, from which we get the English word. Another group that branched off from Hinduism is the **Jains**, who at first went about naked and swept the ground in front of them so that they would harm no other living creature—not even an insect. Around three million Jains still contribute to the religious landscape of India.

Since it has no founder, no precise starting point, and in fact no definitive scriptures, Hinduism is a vast array of beliefs and practices found in

India over the expanse of its history. Over time, Hinduism also incorporated the worldviews of new religious movements, such as Buddhism and Islam. As a result of this vibrant mix of religious traditions, it is possible to claim that Hinduism advocates belief either in one god or in many gods, in a personal god or in an impersonal godhead. Despite its multiplicity of beliefs, certain basic concepts underlie the many manifestations of Hinduism past and present. In fact, these fundamental concepts make the great diversity found in Hinduism possible. Coming to an understanding of these concepts will be the primary goal of this chapter.

The Aryan Invasions of India

Even though Hinduism has no founder, one series of events greatly shaped Indian religious life ever after. Beginning perhaps as early as 1700 BCE, nomadic tribes from the Middle East and Eastern Europe made their way into the north of India. With their advanced weapons—including horses and chariots—they easily conquered the people already settled in the area. The conquering tribes, known to history as **Aryans**, brought with them their own gods, religious practices, and language—**Sanskrit**. Historians refer to these Aryans as Indo-European since they ranged from Europe to the Indian sub-continent. As we will see, many Sanskrit words are similar to words in European languages such as Latin. When Adolph Hitler and Nazism gained control of Germany in the 1930s, Hitler perpetrated a myth that Germanic people were descendants of a "noble Aryan race." However, there is no historic basis to support such a claim.

Although Aryan gods replaced or blended in with the gods of the conquered Indian people, it is not accurate to say that Hinduism is the religion of the Aryans. Rather, elements of Aryanism merged with native religions to spark a period of religious development that has helped make India one of the most spiritually rich areas of the world ever since. That religious development is most evident in a series of writings that comprise the Hindu scriptures.

Before naming the Hindu scriptures, it is important to situate these sacred writings in Hindu spirituality. For the religions we have studied to date, scriptures are central and essential. (Could there be Islam without the Qur'an?) Hinduism, along with its offshoot Buddhism, emphasizes *practices* more than beliefs such as those laid out in scriptures. Both Hinduism and Buddhism offer a variety of techniques aimed at deepening human consciousness. An elite group of Hindus and Buddhists achieve a level of consciousness not typically experienced during most people's lives. They learn these techniques from others who came before them and who also found success in achieving such consciousness. In Hinduism, the spiritual giants willing to guide others in their spiritual quest are called **gurus**. Since Hinduism and Buddhism rely on experience rather than on beliefs, scriptures themselves play a secondary role in both of these religions. As we will see, this is true for Buddhism even more than for Hinduism.

Hinduism has a long tradition of spiritual guides and teachers called gurus. The word literally means "heavy" because a guru, who is widely recognized as having attained a deep level of spirituality, is heavy with religious insight and experience. Generally, someone who is a guru today was once a student of an earlier guru, who was a student of a guru before that, stretching back to the early days of Hinduism.

■ Find out more about the role of gurus in Hinduism and write a report on gurus in general or on one particular guru.

■ Does any group of people serve a similar function in your religious tradition? Explain possible similarities and differences.

A. Have you ever experienced an awareness that is deeper and more profound than you typically experience in your day-to-day life? If so, describe the circumstances surrounding the experience. What practices might help you deepen your consciousness?

B. Some people refer to a "deepened" level of consciousness when speaking about spiritual experience; others use the term "heightened" level of consciousness. Are these terms the same? What difference is implied by each?

ACTIVITY

The Hymn of Creation in the Rig-Veda

The following passage demonstrates a level of philosophical insight that we would not expect from a primitive civilization. How is this passage similar to and different from the account of creation found in your religious tradition?

There was neither non-existence nor existence then; there was neither the realm of space nor the sky which is beyond. What stirred? Where? In whose protection? Was there water, bottomless deep? There was neither death nor immortality then. There was no distinguishing sign of night nor of day. That one breathed, windless, by its own impulse. Other than that there was nothing beyond. Darkness was hidden by darkness in the beginning; with no distinguishing sign, all this was water. The life force that was covered with emptiness, that one arose through the power of heat. Desire came upon that one in the beginning; that was the first seed of mind....Where this creation has arisen—perhaps it formed itself, or perhaps it did not—the one who looks down on it, in the highest heaven, only he knows—or perhaps he does not know.

(Rig-Veda 10.129, quoted in Robert E. Van Voorst, *Anthology of World Scriptures* [Belmont, CA: Wadsworth Publishing Company, 1994], 31)

The Vedas: Seeing into the Sacred

Sometime after 1700 BCE, Aryan priests composed stories about their gods and formalized directions for sacred rituals. Together these compositions are known as the Vedas. The Sanskrit means "seeing" and is related to Latin *video*, "to see." (That is, the Vedas helped the priests see into the realm of the sacred.) The Vedas were not scriptures for everyone. Instead, they were the secret domain of the priestly caste in Hindu society. In fact, when westerners came to India and heard about these secret scriptures, they could find no written copies of them. In the 1780s, one Western scholar convinced a Hindu priest to write down the oldest and most cherished of the Vedas— the Rig-Veda. The priest was able to do so completely from memory. Following him, other priests from other parts of India also wrote down the Vedas. Surprisingly, each one wrote the exact same words.

One reason that the priests had memorized and left unchanged these over three thousand year old scriptures was that the Vedas were composed in classical Sanskrit, which had died out as the language of the people many years before. For centuries, therefore, priests recited the Vedas as if the mere utterance of them was a sacred act, while they had no idea about what the Vedas meant. It was as if a Chinese rock band mimicked English rock and roll songs without knowing what they were singing. Thanks to modern scholarship, we now know that the Vedas represent a highly developed spirituality that existed in Aryan-Indian culture at least thirty-five hundred years ago.

The Upanishads: Sitting before the Master

The Upanishads are writings composed around 500 BCE by Hindu priests to accompany the Vedas. The word means "sitting near." In this case, the Upanishads refer to insights gained from sitting before the master-teacher,

The Analogy of Salt in Water

One of the most famous passages from the Upanishads describes a conversation between a father and his son. The father uses a number of analogies to explain to his son that a hidden essence underlies everything, even though we typically can't see it. Here he uses the image of salt in water. (This particular translator refers to the underlying essence as "the Self.") If you were to try to explain the concept of an invisible essence hidden within all reality, what analogy would you use?

"Please, Father, tell me more about this Self."
"Yes, dear one, I will." Uddalaka said.
"Place this salt in water and bring it here
Tomorrow morning." The boy did.
"Where is that salt?" his father asked.

"I do not see it."
"Sip here. How does it taste?"
"Salty, Father."
"And here? And there?"
"I taste salt everywhere."

"It is everywhere, though we see it not.
Just so, dear one, the Self is everywhere,
Within all things, although we see him not."

(Chandogya Upanishad, translated by Eknath Easwaran, *The Upanishads* [Tomales, CA: Nilgiri Press, 1987], 186–87)

One of the most influential figures of the twentieth century was the Indian non-violent activist Mahatma Gandhi, whose picture hung above the desk in Martin Luther King, Jr.'s office. Gandhi stated that he found inspiration for his belief in nonviolence in the words of the *Bhagavad Gita* and also in the Christian Beatitudes.

the Vedas. While the Vedas describe many gods and priestly rituals, the Upanishads are more focused philosophical commentaries on the Vedas. The most advanced fundamental principles of Hinduism, such as belief in a universal life force underlying all reality, are expressed in the Upanishads.

The Bhagavad Gita: Song of the Lord

Many ancient cultures have grand epic poems describing the exploits of their gods and heroes. India is no exception. One of two great Indian epics is the Mahabharata. (The other is the Ramayana.) It tells of a war between two factions of a family who claim the throne of an ancient Indian kingdom. Epics, often stories of journeys or battles, appeal both to educated and

The Path to God

In this passage Krishna tells Arjuna that complete devotion to him leads to the joy and freedom that all humans seek. Is this message echoed in your own religious tradition? Explain.

> *I pervade the entire universe in my unmanifested form. All creatures find their existence in me, but I am not limited by them.... Those who worship other gods with faith and devotion also worship me....I am the object of all worship, its enjoyer and Lord....*
>
> *Whatever I am offered in devotion with a pure heart—a leaf, a flower, fruit, or water—I partake of that love offering. Whatever you do, make it an offering to me—the food you eat, the sacrifices you make, the help you give, even your suffering.*

(The *Bhagavad Gita*, translated by Eknath Easwaran [Tomales, CA: Nilgiri Press, 1985], 132, 134-35) unschooled people. Therefore, perhaps the most popular and most well-known of Hindu scriptures is a section of the Mahabharata called the Bhagavad Gita. The epic shows signs of originating around 500 BCE, but additions were probably made as late as 500 CE.

The Bhagavad Gita, literally "sung by the lord," is advice given by the Hindu god **Krishna** who serves as the charioteer of the warrior Arjuna. Arjuna is filled with doubts and misgivings as he prepares to battle his friends and cousins. Krishna uses the opportunity to explain the nature of reality and the place of human beings in that reality. The Gita mentions all the fundamental beliefs of Hinduism that we are about to explore.

One offshoot of the Aryan invasions of India is the caste system. Unlike the caste system known as feudalism in medieval Europe, the caste system—although outlawed for many years—still holds sway in India, especially in rural areas. For centuries the caste system maintained Indian social order.

Research and write a report on the four castes of traditional Indian society as well as the "out-castes." Then answer the following questions:

1. What was the highest Indian caste? What does this suggest about the importance of spirituality in Indian life?

2. What role did the caste system play in Hindu religious life?

3. Feudalism maintained the economic and social life of medieval Europe. Did feudalism also play a role in medieval religious life? Explain.

4. Are there remnants of a "caste system" in our society today?

5. Are there "outcastes" in our society today? If so, how is their place in society similar to or different from the out-castes of India?

6. How did Mahatma Gandhi view Indian outcastes?

ACTIVITY

For Review

1. For what practice were the Thugs noted?
2. How did Jains express their belief in the sacredness of all life?
3. What occurred around 1700 BCE that dramatically shaped Hinduism?
4. What was the language of the Aryans?
5. In the twentieth century, which group claimed to be descendants of the Aryans?
6. What does it mean to say that Hinduism emphasizes practices rather than beliefs?
7. What is a guru?
8. What is the literal meaning of Vedas? How does this meaning help explain the way Hindu priests viewed the Vedas?
9. What is the relationship between the Upanishads and the Vedas?
10. Who are Krishna and Arjuna in the Bhagavad Gita?

II. Basic Hindu Beliefs
A Journey into the Heart of Reality

Throughout history, to the present day, there is found among different peoples a certain awareness of a hidden power, which lies behind the course of nature and the events of human life....Thus, in Hinduism people explore the divine mystery and express it both in the limitless riches of myth and the accurately defined insights of philosophy. They seek release from the trials of the present life by ascetical practices, profound meditation and recourse to God in confidence and love. (Vatican Council II, "Declaration on the Relation of the Church to Non-Christian Religions," #2)

The Path of Desire

Pleasure. For religion scholar Huston Smith, the starting point for understanding Hindu spiritual insight is how the religion addresses these two questions: What do people want, and how do they attempt to get it? Hinduism recognizes that people seek happiness. Some people believe that the more they have, the happier they'll be. The lure of "getting and accumulating" is great. Hinduism labels this belief the "path of desire." On a basic, elementary level people seek happiness through pleasure—physical, sensual pleasure. In other words, they believe that the sensual pleasures of eating, drinking, sex, and physical comforts are the best way to achieve happiness.

What does Hinduism have to say about such pleasure-seeking? Essentially, its message is threefold:
- If you honestly believe it is right for you, it's okay to follow this path.
- In pursuing this path, follow basic morality.
- In the end, you will discover that this path leaves you unsatisfied.

A. **How is Hinduism's perspective on physical, sensual pleasure similar to or different from the perspective communicated to you by your religion?**

B. **Along with most religions, Hinduism reminds us that "pleasure" is not the same as "joy."** Describe at least three differences between pleasure and joy, then write an essay about why this distinction is or is not important.

ACTIVITY

Worldly Success. Many people seek happiness through worldly success, such as through wealth, fame, or power. ("If only I won that million-dollar lottery, I would be happy." "If only we won the championship, I'd be happy." "If only I could do whatever I want, I would be happy.") Hinduism recognizes that worldly success is another expression of the path of desire in that it represents another form of getting and accumulating. Hinduism's response to those who seek happiness in this way echoes its message regarding pleasure:

- If you honestly believe it is right for you, it's okay to follow this path.
- In pursuing this path, follow basic morality.
- In the end, you will discover that this path leaves you unsatisfied.

A. If you are religious, how does your religion view worldly success compared to Hinduism's view of it?

B. In the 1950s, religion scholar Huston Smith suggested that many more Americans seek happiness through wealth, fame, or power than through pleasure. Do you believe that his assessment is true of American culture today? Why or why not?

C. Some time ago a tongue-in-cheek bumper sticker read: "The one who dies with the most toys wins." What would Hinduism's response to this statement be?

The Path of Renunciation

Duty. Have you ever felt an urge to contribute to your community, school, family, or group of friends? Did you ever think that you'd like to make a positive difference in the world during your lifetime? Hinduism recognizes that people often come to a realization that "getting" is not the only way to happiness. Sometimes "letting go" brings happiness on a deeper level. Probably the most universal expression of letting go of one's own wants and desires for the good of others is parenthood. Statistics consistently reveal that the vast majority of Americans want to have children. Becoming a parent means signing up to be responsible for another human being for twenty years of your life or longer. In its early stages, being a parent means getting up at three in the morning to change dirty diapers when all you want to do is sleep. And most parents agree that caring for a sixteen-year-old is no easier.

Hinduism views this path to happiness as going in a different direction from the path of desire since it represents *renunciation* of what would appear to bring happiness. Hinduism has much to say about duty. (Members of each caste had their particular duties. Men and women had designated duties depending on their stage in life.) However, Hinduism warns that properly carrying out one's duty and contributing to society still does not bring ultimate happiness. Only a complete letting go brings complete happiness. This ultimate goal, which Hinduism calls **moksha**, is the only goal that truly satisfies the human spirit. The major focus of the Hindu religion, therefore, is how to attain this goal.

A. Define renunciation. Use examples to describe the role that renunciation plays in your religious tradition.

B. Traditional Hindu society identified four stages in the life cycle for men:

- the student stage

- the homeowner stage

- retirement

- the sannyasin stage

Do these stages correspond to the typical life cycle for American men? What similarities and differences exist?

C. Women in traditional Hindu society had their own duties spelled out. Typical of most traditional societies, a woman's duty was primarily to take care of her husband, her family, and her home. An extreme expression of carrying out this duty was the practice of sati, whereby a wife was expected to throw herself onto her husband's burning funeral pyre so that she could continue to serve him in the next life.

Was being a homemaker ever considered the ideal expression of "women's work" in American society? Is there such a thing as "women's work" in our society today? Explain.

ACTIVITY

Achieving True Happiness: Key Hindu Concepts

They live in wisdom who see themselves in all and all in them, who have renounced every selfish desire and sense craving tormenting the heart. (Bhagavad Gita 2.55)

"Moksha" means liberation, joy, and union. It represents a totally different way of experiencing ourselves and our relationship to everything else. However, moksha can only be understood if we examine the meaning of a number of other Hindu concepts. We will use the Sanskrit terms because they are not easily translated into English. These concepts come from a worldview that is foreign to most of us. Therefore, understanding them may be a struggle. However, since they represent how a large portion of the world's population perceives reality, the struggle is worth it. The first term we need to understand is **Brahman**.

Sometimes Brahman is defined simply as "god" or "the godhead," as if the term means essentially what monotheistic religions mean by god. The definition would be acceptable, except that we need to ask the question: Is there also "not god" somewhere? Monotheistic religions believe that there is God, on the one hand, and then everything else, which is not God. By way of contrast, Hinduism proposes that Brahman encompasses all that is. Therefore, all is Brahman; there is no "not Brahman." The belief that "all is one" is known as *monism*. Monotheistic religions tend to emphasize God as *creator* of everything. Hinduism views Brahman not so much as creator of everything but as *manifest* through everything. As such, Brahman is being itself, which shines through each individual being. Brahman is unmanifested oneness but manifests itself in the diversity of all that is—the salt that is invisible but unmistakably present in salt water.

Speaking of Brahman, the Unspeakable

When asked, "Who or what is Brahman," a wise Hindu might reply: "neti, neti," meaning, "not this, not that." If anything, Brahman is best expressed in a sound rather than in words—Om, the sound of wind and fire.

Where does the human person fit in this concept, Brahman? To answer that question, it is necessary to address other questions: Is there a limit to each person? Where and when does a person begin? Where or when does a person end? Hinduism recognizes that there is a manifest dimension to human beings—that which can be perceived by the senses. On the one hand, each person is his or her body and individual personality. However, Hinduism proposes that there is also a dimension to each person that is not visible to our senses and not knowable by our intellect as we typically employ it.

A Hindu priest making an offering

Does this notion sound like what Westerners refer to as the "soul"? Here again, the question must be asked: Is there "no soul" somewhere? If, as Hinduism proposes, all is Brahman, then each person is a manifestation of Brahman. Peel away all that is separate and distinct about a person and what remains? Brahman. Therefore, the essence of each person is Brahman—the same Brahman that is the essence of everything in the universe. The Sanskrit term for this invisible essence of each person is **atman**. The fundamental belief of Hinduism is: *atman is Brahman*. In the Upanishads, the wise father Uddalaka tries every way possible to explain to his son this relationship between his son's true "self" and Brahman. The father constantly repeats the refrain: *Tat tvam asi*—"Thou art that." You are Brahman. Ultimately, there is no place where the internal essence of a person ends and something else begins. The inner self, atman, extends beyond the limitations of time and space, just as Brahman does.

But, honestly, isn't each person unique? Are people really like drops of water in the ocean, indistinguishable from every other drop? Isn't each person instead like a grain of sand, different and distinct from every other grain? Three other concepts help explain how Hinduism addresses these questions: **samsara, jiva**, and **maya**.

One Hindu teaching about which you probably are already familiar is that of reincarnation, called in Hinduism samsara. Reincarnation refers to the transmigration of souls. You may be a seventeen-year-old American boy or a thirty-year-old Latina woman right now, but you existed in other forms in previous lifetimes. And, unless you attain moksha, you will be born again into another life form after you die. The spiritual dimension or "soul" that is uniquely you is jiva. Even your soul is a manifestation of atman, which is eternal and changeless (Brahman). Since individual souls, jivas, are specific to individual persons, they are limited.

Only by peeling away even this layer can a person experience true liberation, pure atman/Brahman.

You might ask, if I am in essence identifiable and indistinguishable from ultimate reality itself, why am I not aware of it? Hinduism answers this question in one word: maya. Sanskrit maya is related to English "magic." Magicians are adept at creating illusions, tricking us into believing that a hat appears to be empty even though it actually contains a rabbit. In similar fashion, our senses and our intellect, which are limited, are programmed to see only a limited amount of true reality. We are conditioned to focus on the physical and on what is distinctive. Our usual state of consciousness plays tricks on us, just as a magician does. If our eyes were truly opened, we would be able to see behind the surface of the person next to us and realize that he or she is a manifestation of the godhead, Brahman, as we all are. On the surface, each snowflake is unique. Below the surface, each snowflake is water. Hinduism proclaims that it makes all the difference in the world when we recognize the common essence that all beings share.

Maya, therefore, refers to appearances. It reminds us that we normally perceive only the surface of things, not their true essence. You are your body and your unique personality. You are also a unique spirit. But do you end there? Hinduism says that, in fact, you are endless. You are infinite and eternal. ("Infinite" means without end; "eternal" means outside of the constraints of time.) Only by focusing on your true essence, atman, will you experience the truth that Atman is Brahman. This experience of *liberation* from your limited self, of *union* with the all-pervasive Self, and of *joy* that comes only from identification with all beings, is moksha. *Tat tvam asi*: Thou art that.

ACTIVITY

A. Explain the difference between "monism" and "monotheism."

B. Restate in your own words the meaning of the following terms. Then use the terms to explain the way Hinduism views reality.

- moksha
- samsara
- Brahman
- jiva
- atman
- maya

C. Describe similarities and differences between these Hindu concepts and concepts or beliefs found in your own religion.

Vocabulary

atman: Brahman manifest in an individual person.

Brahman: All encompassing reality; the godhead.

jiva: A person's distinctive spiritual dimension or soul.

maya: Appearances, illusion.

moksha: Salvation, liberation, absorption into the godhead; the ultimate goal in Hinduism.

samsara: Reincarnation.

sannyasin: literally "one who neither loves nor hates anything;" the final stage in a person's life when he (or rarely she) leaves all social ties and prepares for death.

sati: The practice of wives killing themselves upon the death of their husband to continue serving him in the next life.

For Review

11. What are the two expressions of the path of desire identified by Hindus?

12. What threefold message does Hinduism give about following the path of desire?

13. Give an example to illustrate the appeal of duty.

14. What is the ultimate goal for Hindus?

15. What is Brahman? How is monism different from monotheism?

16. What is atman? What is the relationship between atman and Brahman?

17. How is jiva different from atman?

18. What is samsara?

19. What English word is related to maya? What role do the senses and the intellect play in regard to maya?

20. What is the relationship between maya and Brahman?

III. Yoga
Paths to the Goal

All paths, Arjuna, lead to me. (Bhagavad Gita 4.12)

These fundamental Hindu beliefs lead to a dilemma. If "all is Brahman," then aren't we already Brahman? Is there any point in striving to attain that which we already are? Hinduism proposes that the problem is ignorance, and we need to take steps to wash away the ignorance that clouds our vision. For example, imagine that you own a television set with an old-fashioned rabbit-ear antenna. Your TV picks up three or four stations, and to varying degrees they're all fuzzy and subject to interference whenever a plane passes by or someone moves in the room. Then you sign up for a cable service. All of a sudden you have one hundred stations to choose from, and all of them have perfect reception. Where were all of those stations before your cable service? They were there, but you were unaware of them. You needed some fine tuning—a power boost—in your television so that you could experience what previously was either fuzzy or you didn't even know existed. The Hindu word for such fine tuning and energizing is *yoga*. Without practicing some form of yoga, you are like a television set with a rabbit-ear antenna. Yoga is your cable service.

Yoga means union, discipline, or path. It is related to English "yoke," that which connects a horse or an ox to a cart. Yoga is the path that one takes to moksha. It requires discipline. Hinduism does not limit the means to the goal to only one path. In fact, each person must discover the path that is right for him or her. (And, of course, if one path fails, there are other lifetimes in which to pursue the goal.) Hinduism has a history of toleration of other religions since it views all religions also as paths to the same goal. Also, traditionally each caste had its own path to follow. If members of a

A number of religions began as attempts to consolidate all religions. One such religion began in India around 1500 CE and is known as Sikhism. At the time, Hinduism and Islam were competing for control of parts of India. Eventually Sikhism became a religion all its own with its own gurus and scripture. In the mid-1800s in Iran the Baha'i faith began, also advocating the oneness of all religions. Read about one of these religions and report on its history and beliefs.

lower caste faithfully carried out their duties, they were destined by the laws of **karma** to move up to the next level upon rebirth. Even though there are potentially as many types of yoga as there are yogis—people who practice yoga, Hindu history records four major forms corresponding to four different personality types.

A modern-day yoga practitioner

The Yoga of Knowledge. Are you a studious person? Is your idea of a good time sitting at a desk reading a dense book seeking answers to the great questions of the universe? Perhaps knowledge-seeking is the path for you. Hinduism calls the discipline of study and the search for understanding and wisdom **jnana yoga**. The goal of jnana yoga is not to accumulate knowledge but, as with all yogas, to achieve awareness of Brahman. Jnana yoga means working through the pursuit of knowledge to gain this awareness, which at first glance the human intellect seems incapable of achieving.

The Yoga of Action. The path of action is found in *karma yoga*. Karma itself is an important concept in Hinduism. It means "action." The principle of karma is that actions have consequences; whatever you do for good or ill comes back to you. Just as Hinduism recognizes the interconnectedness of all beings, it also accepts the interconnectedness of all actions, even extending over lifetimes. For example, walking through the halls and saying a kind word to another student has a ripple effect—eventually this good action will come back to you. On the other hand, walking through the halls and knocking off somebody's glasses creates "bad karma." (After such an act, don't be surprised if you are born blind in your next lifetime, Hinduism says.)

If you are more of an active, "hands on" person, then karma yoga is for you. If you were in a religion class and the teacher announced that stu-

Karma yoga is selfless action, a virtue strongly advocated in Christianity as well. Hinduism carries the meaning of "self-less" to its ultimate conclusion: If we give ourselves totally in service to others, we ultimately move beyond "self" to Brahman.

dents could either spend the next hour in class or spend the time visiting at a nearby nursing home, are you the first to volunteer to visit the older people? Then **karma yoga** is right for you. Right action means helping others not because it benefits you in any way but simply to be of service, to give oneself to others. Karma yoga, therefore, is selfless action.

The Yoga of Devotion. Perhaps you are an especially sensitive, emotional person who is overwhelmed at the realization of God's love. Sometimes you feel God's loving presence so strongly that you want to sing or dance. **Bhakti yoga**, the path of love and devotion, is for you. A practitioner of bhakti yoga focuses on one manifestation of god. Giving complete devotion to this god, a devotee seeks the joy that comes from complete surrender and union. In the Bhagavad Gita, Krishna describes bhakti yoga when he says: "Those who worship me and meditate on me constantly, without any other thought, I will provide for all their needs" (9.22).

This emotional form of yoga does not require a high level of intellectual prowess. A devotee can chant the name of a god while working in fields or vineyards. Offerings can be made to and from work, at a home shrine and also at a local temple. Therefore, bhakti yoga is one of the more popular expressions of Hinduism, especially among the lower classes in India.

> There is merit in studying the scriptures, in selfless service, austerity, and giving, But the practice of meditation carries you beyond all these to the supreme abode of the highest Lord. (Bhagavad Gita, 8.28)

Raja Yoga—the Royal Path. The three types of yoga already mentioned are all indirect paths. Through study, through service to people, or through devotion to an image of a god, a yogi achieves awareness of Brahman and of union with Brahman. The type of yoga that most Westerners associate with Hinduism falls under the category raja yoga. Raja means "royal." (An Indian maharaja is a "great king.") Raja yoga is the most direct path one can take toward experiencing union with Brahman. It follows steps and stages, moving ever inward. The first thing that a practitioner of raja yoga must attend to is behavior. There are certain behaviors that help a person achieve moksha and other behaviors that must be avoided. In addition to behavior, a yogi also must be attentive to his or her body. After all, one's body can be either a friend or a foe when spending long hours in meditation as raja yoga requires. In fact, the Hindu tradition has developed an elaborate system of postures, stretching exercises, and breathing techniques that bring about greater body control. The physical dimension of raja yoga is known as **hatha yoga**. Hatha yoga exercises have become so popular in the West that many people take "yoga" to mean "hatha yoga" exclusively. For instance, if a nearby YMCA offers yoga classes, it means the stretching and breathing techniques of hatha yoga, not dancing before an image of a god or doing good works. Of themselves, hatha yoga techniques have health benefits. For Hinduism, they are one stage in a process of turning inward.

In addition to gaining control over behavior and body, a yogi also seeks control of the mind. To do so a yogi spends hours each day in meditation. Typically, he or she sits in the famous **lotus position**, which enables a person to relax the lower body but maintain the energy flow through the upper body needed for meditation. There are many forms of meditation. Raja yoga employs **mantra** meditation, concentration on a word, phrase, or image. Eventually, constant attention to the mantra brings about the sensation that the meditator and the object of meditation are no longer separate. This initial breakthrough out of consciousness of separateness and into consciousness of union eventually leads to a sense of being absorbed into oneness itself. The goal of moksha has been achieved. After this breakthrough, a yogi perceives self, others, and reality differently.

A. Write a report on one type of yoga.

B. Which type of yoga might each of the following be practicing:
   1. A group of people sing the praises of Lord Krishna while dancing to a drum beat.
   2. A monk pores over the scriptures seeking insight.
   3. Nuns take food and clothing to people dying on the streets.
   4. An old man sits in meditation while concentrating on the sacred word, "Om."

C. Describe practices in another religion that are similar to each of the types of yoga.

D. According to hatha yoga, it is important to be physically fit if we are to journey inward spiritually. Do you believe that physical training should be part of a spiritual program? Why or why not? Is there evidence of concern for the body in your own religion's spiritual disciplines?

E. Is the Hindu principle karma similar to or different from any principles in your own religious tradition? Explain.

ACTIVITY

The Eight Stages of Raja Yoga

1. Avoid injury, lying, stealing, sensuality, greed

2. Observe cleanliness, contentment, self-control, study, meditation

3. Control and condition the body

4. Breathe properly

5. Look inward

6. Concentrate on a mantra

7. Experience separateness dissolving

8. Experience union

[Hatha] Yoga is probably the world's most perfect form of exercise. It cultivates cardiovascular health, and musculoskeletal strength and flexibility, without the painful and damaging side effects of high-impact aerobics. It tunes up every organ system—respiratory, digestive, reproductive, endocrine, lymphatic, and nervous. It cultivates the body's capacity to relax and dramatically reduces the negative effects of stress. With regular yoga practice, we breathe better. We sleep better. We digest our food better. We feel better. (Steve Cope. Yoga and the Quest for the True Self *[NY: Bantom Books, 1999], page xi)*

Vocabulary

karma: The cosmic law of cause and effect.

lotus position: Sitting crossed-legged and upright; the posture deemed best suited for meditation in Hinduism.

mantra: A word or phrase concentrated on during meditation.

For Review

21. What role does yoga play in Hinduism?
22. What attitude toward other religions is typical of Hinduism?
23. What do Hindus call the path of knowledge?
24. What is the principle of karma?
25. What types of practices could be included in karma yoga?
26. What type of personality would find bhakti yoga appealing? Why?
27. What is hatha yoga?
28. Why is raja yoga considered the most direct path in Hinduism?
29. What is a mantra and how does it function?
30. What ultimate experience is the goal of raja yoga?

IV. Hindu Beliefs and Practices Today

It is impossible and inaccurate to limit Hinduism to one set of beliefs and practices. However, a large number of Indians (and especially in the past fifty years many non-Indians as well) engage in practices representative of Hindu spiritual life. One of the most striking characteristics of Hinduism is the plethora of gods and goddesses worshipped by Hindus. Who are these gods, and how do they fit into the worldview described in the key Hindu concepts described above?

The Pantheon of Hindu Gods: Polytheistic Monism

Brahman is not a god. As the reality underlying all beings, Brahman is beyond classification and characterization. It is incorrect to speak of Brahman either as he, she, or it. Any such designation limits Brahman, and Brahman is limitless. Nonetheless, Brahman is manifest in endless ways. Brahman is creator and destroyer, the giver of life and its taker. Hinduism has a god for each of these aspects of Brahman.

When the question is asked, how many Hindu gods are there, the answer usually given is 330 million. The number is staggering, and it is meant to be. If Brahman is infinite, then there should be infinite manifestations of Brahman. The many gods of Hinduism are readily apparent in the temples, marketplaces, and homes of India. Hinduism, then, is **polytheistic**—characterized by a belief in many gods. However, if that term isn't qualified it can be misleading. Along with its polytheism, Hinduism also is the monism that we have already discussed. Together, belief in Brahman combined with belief in many gods makes Hinduism *polytheistic monism*.

You will not find a list of 330 million Hindu gods anywhere. However, there are certain gods who are particularly popular throughout India. There is, in fact, something of a Hindu trinity of most significant gods: Brahma, Vishnu, and Shiva. Not to be confused with Brahman, Brahma is the creator god. Of the Hindu trinity he has the fewest devotees. Vishnu is savior and preserver. Hindus often worship Vishnu manifest in one of his **avatars** (or manifestations). Krishna, for instance, is Vishnu in human form. As saviors, Buddha and Christ can be counted among the incarnations of Vishnu. Shiva is the destroyer god and perhaps most popular of the trinity. Shiva as destroyer should not be viewed in a negative light. Remember: much needs to be destroyed on the way to liberation. (Think about that first week of school when students must "destroy" the complacency that set in during their time off if they are to get in shape for the year.)

Gods and goddesses are often manifest in a variety of forms, and many stories tell of their exploits. In the tales about them they can appear like comic book heroes, and in fact there are comic book-like pamphlets available featuring a number of Hindu gods and goddesses. In addition to appearing in different forms, the most important gods also have families as well as animals associated with them. Shiva, for instance, is married to a goddess who can be both motherly (as Parvati) and destructive (as Kali). The bull is Shiva's animal. One of Shiva's sons, the elephant-headed and child-like Ganesha, brings good fortune and removes obsta-

Detail from a temple to Sri Sathya Sai Baba

cles. As such, he is perhaps the most popular of all Hindu gods.

Each depiction of a god is filled with symbolism. Gods often have multiple arms so that they can hold numerous symbols or communicate through hand gestures. One representation of Shiva, as Lord of the Dance, has the god holding a drum since creation began with a drum beat—an ancient representation of a "big bang theory" of creation. In another hand he holds the fires of destruction. In yet another representation, Shiva is clearly half male and half female since he destroys all that separates us from one another.

A. **If someone asked you, What is the Hindu understanding of god, how would you answer her?**

B. Write a report on one of the Hindu gods.

ACTIVITY

Hindu Worship

Generally, Hindus do not practice regular communal worship. Most worship takes place in the home where devout Hindus have a shrine to the family god. Family members perform **puja**, making an offering to the god at least in the morning and at dusk. (In a sense, saying "good morning" and "good night" to god.) Hindu temples serve as shrines to a god where priests also perform puja to an image of a god. Different parts of India celebrate festivals honoring gods according to local custom. Pilgrimages to holy places, such as to the Ganges River, are also common in Hinduism.

Research one of the Hindu festivals, such as Divali or Holi, or a Hindu holy site, such as Benares, and write a report on it.

Hindu Ethical Teachings

The root of Hindu ethical behavior is the level of awareness that a person possesses. Shiva, Lord of the Dance, dances upon an undersized, squatting person. This undeveloped person represents ignorance, which Shiva stamps out. If people treat others badly, it is because they lack awareness of the interconnectedness of all beings. Thus, an important Hindu ethical principle is **ahimsa**—nonviolence. Ahimsa extends respectful treatment beyond the human realm to all living creatures. Cows may be particularly sacred in Hinduism, but all living creatures—seen rightly—are sacred and deserve to be treated with reverence. Mahatma Gandhi was the greatest advocate of ahimsa in the modern world.

Hindu ethical behavior is based upon **dharma.** Dharma means "support." Hinduism proposes that the laws of dharma support the universe and keep everything in order. Even the gods are subject to this order. Society should be structured so that it reflects dharma, and people should live according to dharma as well. Living according to dharma means doing one's duty. Traditionally, the duty, or dharma, of a laborer was different from the duty of a member of the ruling class so that: "By devotion to one's own particular duty, everyone can attain perfection" (Bhagavad Gita, 18.45).

The classical Greeks had a similar notion that shaped Western ethical thinking. According to the Greeks, the cosmos, society, and individual persons should follow universal principles based upon the very nature of things. Natural laws governed the way people should act in their family life, in their business life, and so forth. Violating these principles disrupted the natural order. Likewise, Hinduism considers dharma to be the natural order of things and warns against disrupting that order.

Write a position paper on the following topic: Dharma—Fatalism or Freedom?

In Hinduism, Are There Heaven and Hell?

Hinduism has many images for states that resemble what might be called heaven and hell. However, since ultimately all is Brahman, it would be presumptuous to believe that an individual could end up apart from Brahman. Hell, eternal separation from God, has no place in the monistic worldview of Hinduism. If heaven means a state of union with God and complete bliss, then heaven is included in the Hindu worldview. However, for Hinduism bliss comes not from any form of self-fulfillment but from self-annihilation.

Hinduism in Western Society

Hinduism has left its mark on Western society not so much by gaining converts to the religion itself but by introducing practices that have become popular among many Westerners. We have already described hatha yoga, which is now practiced by professional football teams, movie stars, and others to promote physical health. Two other movements originating in Hinduism were introduced into the United States during the 1960s and continue to be part of America's religious landscape today. Partially, Hindu practices became particularly popular when the use of mind–altering drugs such as LSD were popular. Some Western young people came to realize that Hinduism offered ways to deepen consciousness without the negative side effects of drugs.

Transcendental Meditation. Toward the end of the 1960s, the Beatles began to write songs whose lyrics were more profound than typical rock and roll songs. Beatles' songs spoke of getting beyond the "wall of illusion" and of a reality that was "within you and without you," making us all one. Members of the band wrote some of their most creative songs while practicing meditation and studying with a guru in India. Maharishi Mahesh Yogi, who influenced in particular George Harrison of the singing group, had studied in the United States and was familiar with Western culture. He realized that the West was far advanced over the East when it came to science and technology. However, Maharishi saw India as far advanced spiritually compared to the West. Attempting to reduce Hindu practice to its purest form for Westerners, he decided upon one word: meditation. He proposed a simple form of mantra meditation to be performed twice daily for twenty minutes. He called his practice **transcendental meditation**, or simply TM.

From the late-1960s on, many Westerners practiced TM; and the Maharishi even opened a university in the United States. Scientific studies found that meditation produced definite positive benefits, countering the stress-filled lifestyles of so many people.

ISKCON, The International Society of Krishna Consciousness. In the late-1960s, a Hindu teacher named A.C. Bhaktivedanta Swami Prabhupada made his way to the counter-cultural haven of Greenwich Village, New York City. He, too, saw a spiritual hunger among the youth of the United States. He introduced a form of bhakti yoga to Americans and opened temples where people could spend their time chanting and dancing in praise of Krishna. He proposed that the way to overcome self-consciousness was through "Krishna consciousness." The way to become absorbed in Krishna was to spend every waking minute focused on Krishna. The use of prayer beads and a simple chant repeating praises to Krishna helped the practitioner achieve total Krishna consciousness: "Hare Krishna, Hare Krishna, Krishna Krishna, Hare Hare…." The magazine of the movement was called *Back to Godhead*, since its bhakti yoga practices were designed to bring people back to the god-consciousness that they were intended to have. The "Hare Krishna Movement," as it is popularly known, has a large temple in West Virginia and communities in a number of major cities in the United States.

Write a report on one of the following modern Hindu teachers:

- Sri Ramakrishna (1836–86)
- Swami Vivekananda (1863–1902)
- Rabindranath Tagore (1861–1941)
- Sri Aurobindo (1872–1950)
- Mahatma Gandhi (1869–1948)
- Ma Anandamayi (1896–1982)
- Paramahansa Yogananda (1893–1952)
- Swami Muktananda (1908–83)
- Maharishi Mahesh Yogi (b. 1911)
- Sri Chimmoy (b. 1931)
- Deepak Chopra (b. 1947)
- Baba Ram Dass (Richard Alpert)(b. 1931)

ACTIVITY

A. Name at least three impressions that you had of Hinduism before studying the religion.

B. How have your impressions changed or been reinforced by learning about it?

C. Learn about and practice some form of meditation or yoga. Describe the experience.

D. Create a visual presentation on Hindu images of god. Show the presentation to your class. If possible, include Indian music as background.

E. Write an essay describing ways that your study of Hinduism has challenged or deepened your own spirituality.

F. Read through portions of one of the Hindu scriptures. Comment on five passages that you find thought-provoking.

G. Draw a symbolic representation of the journey inward advocated by Hinduism.

Conclusion:
Hinduism Offers Many Paths for the Inward Journey

Behind its many gods and the vast array of religious activities, Hinduism has a very sophisticated understanding of the place of the human person in the universe. The Hindu worldview is ancient and primitive and yet as modern as today's quantum physics. More important, over time Hinduism has refined a variety of practices that can help the spiritual searcher journey inward. Many of these practices, such as meditation and hatha yoga, can be adapted to other religions. Finally, Hinduism reminds all of us that behind the appearances of separation and isolation there is a common life force in which we all share.

Vocabulary

ahimsa: Nonviolence applied to humans and nonhumans.

dharma: The order that exists in the universe; on a personal level, doing one's duty as it reflects this order.

polytheism: Belief in many gods.

puja: Worship of an image of god.

transcendental meditation: Hindu meditation program introduced to the West by Maharishi Mahesh Yogi.

For Review

31. What does it mean to say that Hinduism is polytheistic monism?
32. Which gods make up the Hindu trinity?
33. What is an avatar?
34. Who is the elephant-headed god of good-fortune?
35. What do the drum and fire represent in the hands of Shiva, Lord of the Dance?
36. Define puja.
37. What function do Hindu temples typically serve?
38. What is ahimsa?
39. What should be the relationship between personal dharma and cosmic dharma?
40. What are TM and ISKCON? When were they first introduced into the United States?
41. In Hinduism, is there a concept equivalent to the Christian notion of hell? Why or why not?

CHAPTER 6

BUDDHISM

Wisdom and Compassion of the Awakened One

To learn about Buddhism, don't forget what you've learned about Hinduism. An Indian prince, immersed in the Hinduism of his day, began Buddhism. In a sense, Buddhism is a Hindu reform movement—much like Lutheranism in Christian history. Just as Lutheranism remained Christian and shares essentials with other Christian groups, so Buddhism held onto the essentials of the Hindu worldview. The man who became known as the Buddha wanted to purify and simplify the religious quest to its most basic elements. Naturally, he began with what he knew—the various expressions of religious inquiry swirling around India at the time. However, the Buddha didn't want to hear about other people's understanding of truth; he wanted direct experience of truth itself. He didn't want to go through the motions of religious activity; he wanted to enter into that other realm hidden behind our everyday consciousness. Determined to find the truth, he set out on a journey that led to a profound spiritual awakening. His simple teachings and the practices he advocated spread rapidly and helped shape the religious landscape of the entire Far East. In recent times, many people from other parts of the world have found that what the Buddha taught helps them in their own spiritual quest. Often they adopt Buddhist practices without renouncing their own religion. Knowledge of the human story would indeed be incomplete without taking seriously the young prince who refused to settle for material or even spiritual riches and offered humanity a way into what he called simply being awake.

Overview

■ The life of the Buddha models the fundamental Buddhist worldview.

■ The teachings of the Buddha offer an antidote to human suffering.

■ Schools of Buddhism apply the Buddha's teachings in diverse ways.

Before We Begin...

Complete the following sentence in at least five ways:

• Being awake means…

As you study Buddhism, compare your statements to the Buddha's understanding of being awake. Then write an essay describing possible ways that the Buddha's teachings and practices could help you "wake up."

I. The Life of the Buddha
A Journey into Enlightenment

From time to time there appears in this world one who has seen the truth, a fully awakened one, blessed by the truth, abounding in happiness, a teacher of wisdom and goodness, a buddha. He, by himself, thoroughly knows and sees this universe, and knowing it, he makes his knowledge known to others. The truth, lovely in its origin, lovely in its progress, lovely in its consummation, he proclaims. A new life he makes known, in all its fullness. (Tevigga Sutta, in The Buddha Speaks, edited by Anne Bancroft [Boston, MA: Shambala Publications, 2000], 81)

A Mix of History and Myth

Buddhism begins with one person's heroic efforts to know the truth, his experience of the truth, and then his journeys to alert others about how they too can experience the truth. We know the broad outline of this man's life. However, typical of the old stories of heroic figures, what we know of the Buddha blends history (the facts) with myth (the profound meaning that lies behind the facts).

His name was Siddhartha, born the son of a king and queen who ruled the Sakya kingdom in a section of northern India that today is Nepal. Standard dates for his life span are 563 to 483 BCE, meaning that he lived to be eighty. Siddhartha is also known by his family or clan name, Gautama (or Gotama). From the moment of his birth, Siddhartha stood out as an exceptional human being. A wise old seer arrived at the palace one day and relayed the joyful news that the infant Siddhartha

A statue of the Buddha

was indeed destined for greatness; he would become either a great king or a great spiritual guide. Then the seer added a caution that caused the king to shudder: Prince Siddhartha would become a great ruler unless he encountered sickness, old age, and death.

Siddhartha's father wanted his son to rule after him, to make the Sakyas the most powerful kingdom in the land. He didn't want his son to renounce his kingship and follow a spiritual path when he grew up. The king determined to shield his son from sickness, old age, and death as best he could. To do so, he built a great pleasure garden to surround the palace. Siddhartha was to encounter no unpleasantness; all his wants were to be met. Siddhartha grew up in this sheltered world, married, and at the age of twenty-nine bore a son. Nonetheless, he felt a restlessness within himself, calling him to discover more of the world than he had encountered until then. He told his servant that he would set out into the world beyond the palace walls to find out for himself what exists there.

Once away from his pleasure gardens, Siddhartha soon happened upon people who suffered from disease and sickness. Unaccustomed to such sights, he was overcome with sadness and confusion. When he encountered old people—wrinkled, bent over, missing teeth, unsteady on their feet—Siddhartha became even more distressed. His servant had no choice but to tell Siddhartha that sickness and old age await us all. Then when Siddhartha saw the cold, lifeless body of a dead person about to be burned like scraps of wood, he broke down and realized that his life so far had been a sham, a deception. He decided that he needed to enter into this world of suffering, old age, and death if he were to be an authentic human being. He exchanged his princely garb with the tattered robes of a monk living a life of poverty. Following his encounter with these **four passing sights**—sickness, old age, death, and poverty—Siddhartha set out on a spiritual journey that would transform him into the Buddha and make him one of the most important religious figures of all time.

ACTIVITY

Write an essay explaining why you think experiencing sickness, old age, and death would start someone on a spiritual quest. In your essay address the question: Is true spirituality possible without a realization of sickness, old age, and death?

Asceticism and the Middle Way

> The way of perfection passes by way of the Cross. There is no holiness without renunciation and spiritual battle. Spiritual progress entails the ascesis and mortification that gradually lead to living in the peace and joy of the Beatitudes. (Catechism of the Catholic Church, #2015)

Siddhartha began his spiritual quest following a path that others of his time who went to extremes also followed. For six years he engaged in ascetical practices. His life became the exact opposite of his earlier life when he basked in every earthly delight. Asceticism means practicing self-denial for religious or spiritual purposes. The word's Greek origins suggest the rigors that athletes put themselves through in order to gain mastery over their bodies. Siddhartha went to extremes in his practice of asceticism. He joined a group of ascetics who lived off of the land, ate only the berries and grasses that grew in the wild, and built no protection from the elements. So extreme was Siddhartha in his asceticism that the other ascetics came to look upon him as their guru. Statues of the ascetic Siddhartha depict him as little more than a skeleton covered with skin.

Then one day Siddhartha heard a sound coming from a passing barge on a nearby river. A man was tuning his lute in order to play music. Siddhartha heard the man remark, "If the string is too loose, it will not play; if it is too tight, it will break." Siddhartha asked himself, "With my asceticism, have I tightened my string too much? Is there another way?" He drank from the river and, when a young girl on her way to leave food at a nearby shrine offered him her bowl of rice, Siddhartha ate proper food for the first time in five years. His companion ascetics viewed this act by Siddhartha as a rejection of his spiritual quest and renounced him as their mentor. Siddhartha, however, invited them to join him on a new path. He called it "the middle way." He realized that his early life of self-indulgence had made him weak and lazy. On the other hand, his extreme asceticism had caused him to focus too much on himself and on his body. Both extreme self-indulgence and extreme self-denial were forms of attachment and therefore ineffective means to enlightenment. Instead, a life of balance and harmony was best for making oneself a fit vessel for travelling the spiritual path. Siddhartha explained this approach in these words:

> Let me tell you about the middle path. Dressing in rough and dirty garments, letting your hair grow matted, abstaining from eating any meat or fish, does not cleanse the one who is deluded. Mortifying the flesh through excessive hardship does not lead to a triumph over the senses. All self-inflicted suffering is useless as long as the feeling of self is dominant.
>
> You should lose your involvement with yourself and then eat and drink naturally, according to the needs of your body. Attachment to your appetites—whether you deprive or indulge them—can lead to slavery, but satisfying the needs of daily life is not wrong. Indeed, to keep a body in good health is a duty, for otherwise the mind will not stay strong and clear.
>
> This is the middle path.
>
> (Discourse II, in The Buddha Speaks, pages 44-45)

List forms of asceticism practiced in your own or another religious tradition, then answer the following questions. Explain your answers.

- Do you find that asceticism has increased or diminished in importance in the religious tradition you selected?

- Do you believe that there is a place for asceticism in spiritual development?

- Can there be a danger to emphasizing asceticism?

- How does today's culture look upon asceticism?

ACTIVITY

Attaining Buddhahood: One Who Woke Up

Buddha's rejection of extreme asceticism did not diminish his resolve to enter fully into life's mystery and to unlock its secrets. When he arrived at a park in a town he was passing through he determined to sit under a particular tree, now called the "bo" tree or "bodhi" tree—the tree of enlightenment—until he attained his goal. For Buddhists, this sitting represents the central event in human history. "Sitting" in this case means sitting in meditation. Some accounts suggest that Siddhartha sat for forty-nine days; others indicate that the entire process happened during the course of one astonishing night in the spring of his thirty-fifth year. Before achieving his goal, Siddhartha faced temptations from **Mara**, a demon-like creature who tempted Siddhartha first with sensual pleasures, then with angry threats, and lastly as Siddhartha's very self. Siddhartha met each temptation and grew stronger in his resolve.

Finally, it happened. What "it" refers to cannot be described in words. Words belong to the world of appearances and rationality. What happened to Siddhartha was beyond words and rational explanations. He himself described what took place as "waking up." (Buddha means "the awakened one.") The suggestion is that prior to this time Siddhartha had lived in darkness, asleep. What he had previously perceived as real was actually a dream. For the first time, he was fully awake. Further explanations of his experience typically center around the nature of the self.

Other Titles for the Buddha

Most commonly given the title "the Buddha," Siddhartha Gautama is also known as:

■ Sakyamuni (or Shakyamuni), seer of the Sakya clan, and

■ Tathagata, the "thus-perfected one," referring to his condition of perfection after his enlightenment.

Since Buddha is a title, it also applies to other enlightened beings besides Prince Siddhartha. In time, some Buddhist traditions viewed Buddhas as gods. Many centuries after Siddhartha lived, some Chinese artists depicted the Buddha as a fat, jolly fellow. They were attempting to illustrate the happiness and contentment that comes with buddhahood. The laughing Buddha has come to be one of his most popular representations in the modern world.

Siddhartha woke up to the realization that his self had no real substance or permanence. Everything that anyone might identify as the self is actually empty. Far from being a negative or depressing realization, Siddhartha was filled with great joy at the emptiness underlying all beings. A cup that is filled with one particular liquid cannot take in anything else. However, an empty cup can be filled in infinite ways. Siddhartha's awakening into the infinite and eternal marks him as the Buddha, the awakened one. Buddhism is founded upon this simple but wonderful event.

> *One evening, soon after the Buddha's enlightenment, a man named Dona was walking down a rural road in northern India when he saw the Buddha walking toward him. Dona knew nothing about the Buddha but was nevertheless struck by the radiance surrounding this individual. I've never seen a mortal being look so joyful and serene, he thought, so when the Buddha came close enough to converse, Dona couldn't resist asking, "Are you, by any chance, a spirit?"*
>
> *"No," said the Buddha.*
> *"Then are you an angel?" asked Dona.*
> *"No," said the Buddha.*
> *"Are you, perhaps, a god?" asked Dona.*
> *"No," said the Buddha.*
> *"Well, what are you?" asked Dona.*
> *The Buddha replied, "I am awake."*

(Jack Maguire, Essential Buddhism [New York: Pocket Books, 2001], 1-2)

Jesus also encountered temptations prior to beginning his public life. Read the gospel accounts of the temptations of Jesus. Compare them to the temptations of Siddhartha. What realization did Jesus come to following his time in the desert compared to Siddhartha's realization?

ACTIVITY

Enlightenment Brings Compassion

The most popular image of the Buddha represents him sitting in serene meditation. His ears are elongated since, as a prince, he had worn expensive earrings. A clump of hair suggests both a crown and an expansion of his mind representing his enlightened state. He wears a hint of a smile, as if he knows something wonderful that others of us don't. After his successful journey inward, Siddhartha was drawn to remain engrossed in the tranquil peace resulting from his enlightenment. However, his enlightenment deepened his awareness of the interconnectedness of all beings. Enlightenment is not a solitary satisfaction. Rather, it leads to compassion. Indeed, upon awakening Siddhartha exclaimed:

> Wonder of wonders! All living beings are truly enlightened and shine with wisdom and virtue. But because their minds have become deluded and turned inward to the self, they fail to understand this. (Kegun Sutra, in The Buddha Speaks, 14)

Compassion means "to suffer with." It accurately describes the next and final phase in Siddhartha's journey. The sufferings that burdened people moved him. He realized that he had a message that he could share with others who wished to make the journey that he himself had made. After all, he too had spent the first thirty-five years of his life asleep and unaware. During the time prior to his awakening he was in a sense a "Buddha in waiting." Isn't everyone else a potential Buddha as well? Drawn by compassion, he dedicated the rest of his life—over forty years—to teaching the simple truths about the practices leading to enlightenment. At the age of eighty, Siddhartha died of food poisoning when a man with whom he was staying inadvertently served him food that had gone bad.

ACTIVITY

A. **The Buddha is known for the virtues of wisdom and compassion.** Define each word and explain the relationship between the two. Describe the role that wisdom and compassion play in your own religious tradition.

B. **Read other accounts of the life of the Buddha.** Name at least two other events that are reported to have occurred during his lifetime. Explain a possible meaning contained in each story.

Vocabulary

asceticism: Self-denial for religious purposes or for spiritual enrichment.

four passing sights: Sickness, old age, death, poverty; what Siddhartha encountered instigating his spiritual quest.

mara: The embodiment of evil.

For Review

1. What does it mean to say that the story of the Buddha blends fact with myth?

2. What nationality was the Buddha? When did he live?

3. What prediction was made about Siddhartha when he was born? How did his father react to this prediction?

4. What are the four passing sights?

5. What is asceticism? How long did Siddhartha practice asceticism?

6. What incident led Siddhartha to reject extreme asceticism?

7. What is the middle way?

8. Describe the circumstances surrounding Siddhartha's enlightenment.

9. What does "buddha" literally mean?

10. What did Siddhartha decide to do after his enlightenment?

11. How did Siddhartha die?

II. Teachings of the Buddha

Buddhism in its various forms testifies to the essential inadequacy of this changing world. It proposes a way of life by which people can, with confidence and trust, attain a state of perfect liberation and reach supreme illumination either through their own efforts or with divine help. (Vatican Council II, Declaration on the Relation of the Church to Non-Christian Religions, #2)

What the Buddha Did NOT Teach: Religion

One of the most famous stories attributed to the Buddha is the parable of a man shot with a poisoned arrow. While traveling through a forest, a man is shot with a poisoned arrow. A crowd gathers, wanting to help. Before he allows a surgeon to remove the arrow and administer healing medicines, however, the man insists on asking: "Who shot me? Was it a friend or foe? Was the person tall or short, dark or light-skinned? To what caste did the person belong? Was I shot in anger or by accident?" Before he can complete his questions, the man dies. Commenting on the story, the Buddha pointed out that the man is asking the wrong questions. The right question is much more direct and to the point: "Is there an antidote to this poison?"

This parable hints at what the Buddha taught and also at what the Buddha did not teach. Religions often begin with "the god question." Is there a god who created the world? Was creation—the world's and my own—a matter of chance or an act of love? For the Buddha, such questions are unanswerable and therefore useless. We know that we are shot with a poisoned arrow; the "poison" of mortality is even now working its way through our bodies. We should not concern ourselves with the source of the poison (god or gods, purposeful action or fate), but with seeking a cure for the poison.

Siddhartha spoke little about the god question. The case can be made that he was either an atheist, an agnostic, or a theist. As we will see, different schools of Buddhism take opposing positions on the god question. The most we can say about the Buddha himself is that he concerned himself little with the question. In fact, he had a skepticism about most of the elements that we typically associate with religion. For instance, is performing religious ritual beneficial? Upon seeing a brahmin priest preparing a ritual fire, the Buddha said to him: "You should not imagine, brahman, that insight comes by merely laying sticks on a fire. You should trust to the truth that is within you to

A page from the Diamond Sutra, printed in the 9th year of Xiantong Era of the Tang Dynasty

enrich your spiritual life and not to external rituals" (Samyutta Nikaya, in *The Buddha Speaks*, 83). What about miracles? The Buddha said, "I detest and will not undertake the so-called miracles of magic power and divination. I and my followers attract non-believers only by the miracle of truth" (Digha Nikaya, in *The Buddha Speaks*, 83). Is there a set of dogmatic teachings that one should accept? "Never think that I believe I should set out a 'system of teaching' to help people understand the way….the truth can't be cut up into pieces and arranged in a system" (Diamond Sutra, in *The Buddha Speaks*, 83). Are there authority figures whom we should follow—the Buddha himself, perhaps? "Accept my words only when you have examined them for yourselves; do not accept them simply because of the reverence you have for me" (Majjhima Nikaya, in *The Buddha Speaks*, 84). What about the question of an afterlife? "Vaccha, the idea that I would exist or not exist after death—such ideas lead to dense jungles and arid deserts, to entanglements as though caught by thorns. They bring about anger, delusion, and argument and they do not bring about peace, knowledge, or wisdom leading to enlightenment. I do not take up any of these ideas" (Digha Nikaya, in *The Buddha Speaks*, 89).

Statements such as these suggest that the Buddha wanted little to do with religion. He wanted people to try his program, which he found from personal experience leads to truth. The truth of which he spoke cannot be described or dissected, only experienced. He feared that "religion" could serve as a substitute for actually experiencing enlightenment and for working toward enlightenment by relying on one's own effort. Paradoxically, Buddhism, based on the life and teachings of the Buddha, became one of the world's great religions.

Siddhartha cautioned against the misuse of elements commonly associated with religion: belief in God, rituals, scriptures, authority figures, and philosophical principles. Give an example of how each one of these aspects of religion could be misused or misinterpreted. Give an example of how each one of these could be properly understood or used.

Buddhism is no more atheistic than it is theistic or pantheistic. The charge of atheism can hardly be laid at the door of a Teacher who could declare of the universe, or cosmos, in its wholeness (or thusness): "There is an unborn, an unoriginated, an unmade, an uncompounded. Were there not, O mendicants, there would be no escape from the world of the born, the originated, the made and the compounded." (Nancy Wilson Ross, *Buddhism: A Way of Life and Thought* [New York: Vintage Books, 1980], 30)

What the Buddha Taught: The Four Noble Truths

You should know that, like a doctor, you should find the right medicine for an illness. It is as a doctor that I observed the ailments of the world. (Mahaparinirvana Sutra, in The Buddha Speaks, *132)*

The Buddha's teachings do not follow a religious or philosophical model of speaking about truth. Instead, he comes at truth more pragmatically. His summary of truth reflects what we could call a medical model. That is, he makes a case for identifying the ailment from which all humanity suffers, he uncovers the cause of the suffering, and then he offers a cure. The teachings of Buddha the physician can be summed up in the **Four Noble Truths**:

- **Life is suffering.**

- **Suffering is caused by selfish craving.**

- **By ending selfish craving we end suffering.**

- **We achieve this goal by following the Eightfold Path.**

Some Westerners have found the Buddha's starting point to be discomforting: "Life is suffering." The word used literally means "dissatisfaction." Buddhists would say that this starting point is both realistic and necessary.

For instance, if you know anyone who has attended an Alcoholics Anonymous meeting, the organization that has done the most to help people overcome problems associated with alcoholism, you know that the first step toward a cure is to admit that one has a problem. People with drinking problems who make excuses or refuse to admit that they suffer from alcoholism will not take the steps necessary to overcome the problem. The Buddha himself started on his spiritual journey only after he encountered the sickness, old age, and death that plagues all humanity.

The second of the Four Noble Truths is also perplexing. Our cravings and our desires make us human. Without them, wouldn't we go through life much like Mr. Spock in the old "Star Trek" series, being completely unemotional and detached? The Buddha appears to make a subtle distinction about the delights of the world. He recognizes the pleasant experiences of life as good. The way we respond to them, however, makes all the difference. The word for the second Noble Truth literally means "grasping." The Buddha speaks against a grasping and possessive attitude. If we try to hold onto sweet sounds, lovely forms, and the pleasures of touch and taste and smell we will find disappointment. Instead, we should view them as "passing wonders." Seeing a rose and simply appreciating its beauty is a different experience from seeing a rose and wanting to possess it and keep it unchanged forever.

The Buddha told a story about a man whose young son gets lost in a forest. When the father finds the boy's shredded shirt, he concludes that his son is dead and spends his time grieving. In fact, bandits had captured the boy. Five years later, the son escapes and, now a teenager, returns to his father's house. The father, believing that his son died, refuses to welcome his son and chases him away. Grasping at one thing prevents us from appreciating other things. According to the second Noble Truth, the truth is not a matter of grasping.

The third noble truth is a statement of hope. We *can* overcome suffering and dissatisfaction. Why? Because we can overcome our grasping attitude. Part of the Buddha's insight is that our self is a "passing wonder" as much as the things outside of ourselves. We are like foam floating on the surface of a stream. Another image the Buddha used to explain this concept is that of music. We are not the lute that plays music. We are the music. The lute may stay the same, but each time music plays it is unique.

Another story from the Buddhist tradition speaks to this attitude that Buddhism seeks to cultivate. One day, a ferocious tiger bounds into a

The Eightfold Path

- right views

- right intention

- right speech

- right action

- right livelihood

- right effort

- right mindfulness

- right concentration

monk's hut. The monk runs out of his hut and through the jungle chased by the tiger. When he comes to a cliff, he finds he has no choice but to jump. He grabs onto a vine halfway down. The relentless tiger, however, peers hungrily over the top of the cliff. The monk looks down and, lo and behold, sees another equally ferocious looking tiger below. To make matters even worse, the monk notices that a mouse is above him chewing away at the vine upon which he is hanging. At that moment, the monk notices some wild strawberries growing out of the cliff beside him. He reaches over, takes one of the strawberries, eats it, and exclaims, "Ah, how delicious!"

The Eightfold Path: The Buddha's Prescription for Becoming Awake

The road to truth and joy is the **Eightfold Path**, Buddha's prescription for humanity's common disease and the fourth of the Four Noble Truths. The Eightfold Path has an all-inclusive sense to it. That is, once we accept that suffering and dissatisfaction are our lot in life and that we can overcome them, then we should dedicate all aspects of our lives to attaining that goal. The components of the path can be divided into thinking, acting, and meditating. The Eightfold Path as a medical prescription can be summed up in the following way:

1. First you must see clearly what is wrong.

2. Next you must decide that you want to be cured.

3. You must speak and

4. speak so as to aim at being cured.

5. Your livelihood must not conflict with your therapy.

6. That therapy must go forward at the "staying speed," that is, the critical velocity that can be sustained.

7. You must think about it incessantly and

8. learn how to contemplate with the deep mind.

(Nancy Wilson Ross, *Buddhism: A Way of Life and Thought* [New York: Vintage Books, 1980], 24-25)

ACTIVITY

A. If you are religious, how would you describe your religion's perspective on suffering?

B. Another word used to describe the first of the Noble Truths is "frustration." An image often used is that of a wheelcart that has one broken axle. Draw an image that would symbolize for you the meaning of the first Noble Truth.

C. An author on Buddhism tells about a tribe that captures monkeys by making traps filled with treats. A trap has an opening small enough for a monkey to put its hand in to reach for the treats, but not large enough for a monkey to remove its hand filled with them. Only by letting go of the treats can the monkey escape. Explain the message of this story in light of the Four Noble Truths. Can the story be applied to your own life in any way? If so, how?

D. Describe one way that you could incorporate each of the elements of the Eightfold Path into your own spiritual life.

A Buddhist View of Reality

Even though the Buddha himself laid out no systematic philosophy, there are certain beliefs that underscore the Buddhist worldview. Many of these beliefs reflect or build upon the Hinduism that existed during the Buddha's lifetime. For instance, the Buddha accepted reincarnation as a part of human reality but de-emphasized the need to work up through the levels of the caste system. After all, he himself was not of the brahmin caste; by birth he was supposed to concern himself with worldly affairs. Buddhism also accepted the Hindu concept dharma but applied it to the teachings of the Buddha, particularly his Four Noble Truths.

Since the truth to which the Buddha was awakened lies beyond the comprehension of our everyday consciousness, Buddhist concepts are typically stated in negative terms. That doesn't mean that Buddhism has a negative view of life but that any view of life that can be expressed in words is inadequate. A poem about a tree, no matter how beautiful, is never as beautiful as a tree itself. Talking about love is not nearly as wonderful as the actual experience of being in love. If you think about it, we often define concepts by stating what they are not. For example, happiness means not being sad. Staying still means not moving. The difference with Buddhist concepts is that they refer to realities that are not part of our ordinary consciousness.

> It is a defect in language that words suggest permanent realities and people do not see through this deception. (Prajnaparamita, in The Buddha Speaks, 105)

Words can help us enter into and appreciate reality. Buddhism cautions that words can also mask reality. Give examples to illustrate this Buddhist principle.

Anatman/Anatta—"No self." You recall from Hinduism the term atman, recognition of Brahman within the self. Buddhism holds as a fundamental principle that there is nothing that can be specifically identified as "self." To push people to realize that there is nothing substantial to which "self" refers, Buddhists use the term *anatman* (Sanskrit) or *anatta* (Pali). Buddhism has a history of questioning what makes up the self. For instance, in one exchange a monk points out that a chariot is not axles, wheels, or a cart. A chariot is not even all of these components together. Rather, "chariot" is simply a convenient way of speaking about a bundle of things bunched together. (Buddhists call them "bundles" because they are like burdens that we carry, preventing us from seeing beyond them.) Likewise, a person's self is not his or her hair, body, sensations, preconceived notions, or consciousness. Since we cannot reduce the self to any specific reality, then it is more accurate to speak of no self: anatman. ("An" = not; "atman" = self.) Again, it is important to remember that the Buddha found great joy and peace when he came to this realization. That is, his experience of no self was not pessimistic or morose but rather blissful. If the thought of having no self saddens you, Buddhists would point out that it is because you are not awake but are clinging to a shadow reality. You are in fact bigger and grander than anything you might identify as self.

> The ego changes with every second that goes by; yesterday's ego, today's ego...they're not the same. Our body changes, our cells change too. When you take a bath, for example, all the dead cells of your skin are washed away. Our brain, our mind changes; that of the adult is not the same as it was in the child.
>
> So where does the ego exist? It is one with the cosmos. It is not only the body, the mind, but it is God, Buddha, the fundamental cosmic force. (Taisen Deshimaru, Questions to a Zen Master [New York: E.P. Dutton, 1985], 13)

Nirvana—"To Be Extinguished." Long before there was a rock band by the name, Buddhism (and Hinduism) named the goal of human existence **nirvana**. Like anatman, it names what it is not rather than what it is. Nirvana means "to be extinguished"—what used to be a flame has now gone out. What becomes extinguished when nirvana is reached is any sort of grasping, including grasping onto oneself as a separate entity. Buddhist nirvana is akin to Hindu moksha. By overcoming identification with our ego, we enter into compassionate communion with the entire universe. While it means extinction, nirvana is actually an opening up, an expansion: "The image should not be the drop of water which merges into the ocean and is lost but rather the ocean which enters into the drop" (Nancy Wilson Ross, *Buddhism*, 30).

A Buddhist term related to nirvana is *sunyatta (shunyatta)*, meaning "emptiness." Sunyatta reflects the relationship between maya and Brahman found in Hinduism. Forms capture our imagination. Behind all forms there is emptiness of forms. However, this emptiness "informs" all reality. Therefore, sunyatta also refers to the interconnectedness of all beings.

Buddhist Ethics. While Buddhism began with monks who followed an intense regimen of spiritual disciplines, it soon established five basic ethical precepts that monks and laypeople alike should follow. In *Touching Peace* (Berkeley, CA: Parallax Press, 1992) the modern Vietnamese monk Thich Nhat Hanh words the precepts in the form of vows.

1. **Avoid causing harm to other sentient beings.**

   Aware of the suffering caused by the destruction of life, I vow to cultivate compassion and learn ways to protect the lives of people, animals, and plants. I am determined not to kill, not to let others kill, and not to condone any act of killing in the world, in my thinking and in my way of life.

2. **Avoid taking anything that is not freely given.**

   Aware of the suffering caused by exploitation, social injustice, stealing, and oppression, I vow to cultivate loving kindness and learn the ways of working for the well-being of people, animals, and plants. I vow to practice generosity by sharing my time, energy, and material resources with those who are in real need....

3. **Avoid sexual misconduct.**

   Aware of the suffering caused by sexual misconduct, I vow to cultivate responsibility and learn ways to protect the safety and integrity of individuals, couples, families, and society. I am determined not to engage in sexual relations without love and a long-term commitment. To preserve the happiness of myself and others, I am determined to respect my commitments and the commitments of others....

4. **Avoid untruthfulness.**

   Aware of the suffering caused by unmindful speech and the inability to listen to others, I vow to cultivate loving speech and deep listening in order to bring joy and happiness to others and relieve others of their suffering. Knowing that words can create happiness or suffering, I vow to learn to speak truthfully, with words that inspire self-confidence, joy, and hope....

5. **Avoid clouding the mind with drugs.**

   Aware of the suffering caused by unmindful consumption, I vow to cultivate good health, both physical and mental, for myself, my family, and my society by practicing mindful eating, drinking, and consuming. I vow to ingest only items that preserve peace, well-being, and joy in my body, in my consciousness, and in the collective body and consciousness of my family and society. I am deter-

mined not to use alcohol or any other intoxicant or to ingest foods or other items that contain toxins, such as certain TV programs, magazines, books, films, and conversations....

Heaven and Hell, Gods and Demons. As Buddhism spread, it accumulated a variety of beliefs and images beyond the direct focus of the Buddha himself. Most Buddhist temples and shrines house statues of fierce looking demons and also kindly figures ready to help people in their spiritual journey. It's hard to decipher

An ancient samurai warrior in armor

whether such figures are viewed as separate realities or as what we would call today psychological states. The following story from the Zen Buddhist tradition suggests that heaven and hell are not "places" but mental states.

> A big, tough samurai once went to see a little monk. In a voice accustomed to meeting with obedience, the samuai said, "Monk, teach me about heaven and hell."
>
> The monk looked up at this mighty warrior and replied in a voice of utter contempt, "Teach you about heaven and hell? I couldn't teach you about anything. You're filthy. You stink. Your sword is rusty. You're a disgrace to the samurai class! Get out of my sight!"
>
> The samurai was speechless with rage. His muscles bulged. His face got red.
>
> He swung his sword high above his head, preparing to slay the monk.
>
> "That is hell," the monk said softly.
>
> The samurai froze. Suddenly he was overwhelmed by the compassion of this tiny, defenseless man who had just risked death to give this teaching. As he slowly lowered his sword, he was filled with gratitude and wonder.
>
> "That is heaven," the monk said softly. (Jack Maguire, Essential Buddhism, 27)

A. Find out more about the following Buddhist concepts and write a report on one of them:

- Anatman
- Nirvana
- Sunyatta
- Dharma
- The Five Precepts
- Mara
- Images of gods and demons

B. If a group in your neighborhood circulated a petition listing the five vows of Buddhism asking everyone to follow them, would you sign the petition? Why or why not? Expand on one of the precepts, giving examples of how it could be applied in today's world.

Vocabulary

nirvana: Extinguishment; the goal of Buddhism; enlightenment.

sunyatta: Emptiness; the impermanence and interconnectedness of all beings.

For Review

12. What does the story of the man shot with a poisoned arrow say about Siddhartha's view of religious questions?
13. What did Siddhartha say about reliance on ritual or authority figures or belief in an afterlife?
14. Explain the Four Noble Truths as a prescription for human suffering.
15. Name two concepts that Siddhartha accepted from Hinduism.
16. Define the terms anatman, nirvana, and sunyatta.
17. Name the five basic ethical precepts of Buddhism.

III. Buddhist Sects
Their Origins, Beliefs, and Practices

Buddhism began as a movement for monks, men who imitated the Buddha seeking enlightenment. Unlike Hinduism of the time, which reserved seeking nirvana for the higher castes, the Buddha believed that people did not have to make their way through many lifetimes until they became Brahmins in order to dedicate themselves to experiencing nirvana. Instead, members of any caste could follow the middle way and the Eightfold Path. At first, the Buddha refused to allow women to be monks. His stepmother pleaded with him to be able to join the community of monks, but the Buddha refused. However, after his stepmother and some other noble women shaved their heads, dressed as monks, and walked miles over difficult terrain to ask him again, the Buddha admitted women into his community. Today there are both men and women monks in most branches of Buddhism. In some cases, married people with families have also lived as monks.

As Buddhism spread, it needed to consider the question of the role of those who wished to be guided by the teachings of the Buddha but did not live the monastic life. Development of different branches of Buddhism addressed this question in different ways. Even specifics about how to work toward enlightenment soon became a matter of debate within the community. Initially, two major schools of Buddhism emerged. In time, the one school subdivided into a variety of branches.

Syncretism: The Merging of Religions

Religions are not static entities. They change over time and take on new characteristics as they spread to new cultures. For instance, Catholicism emphasizes uniformity, universality, and structure. Nonetheless, Catholic services in an Irish community, an African community, and a Hispanic community are often decidedly different. The process of a religion changing as it merges with various cultures is known as **syncretism**. Since the Buddha's teachings were not systematic or even written down, the Buddhist movement was particularly open to syncretism. Also, Buddhism spread beyond India, itself a very diverse area, to the entire Far East. The cultures to which it spread influenced Buddhism even as Buddhism became the dominant religion in every culture east and south of India.

Buddhist Scriptures

This chapter includes many passages from a book titled *The Buddha Speaks*, suggesting that the sayings are historically verifiable as the words of the Buddha himself. During his over forty-year teaching career, no doubt the Buddha had much to say. However, his teachings were not written down for centuries. (That fact is appropriate, given the Buddha's emphasis on personal experience rather than the written word as the source of truth.) The oldest collection of Buddhist writings are the **Tripitika**, meaning the "three baskets." They are written in Pali, a popular derivation of Sanskrit, and composed about five hundred years after his lifetime. However, there are other writings in various languages identified as containing teachings of the Buddha. Buddhists themselves tend not to be so concerned about which writings can be directly traced to the historical Buddha. Instead, they are concerned about whether or not they express the truth or lead to the truth as the Buddha understood it. As a result, many Buddhists consider some writings originally composed in Chinese or another language to be part of their scriptures. This less precise understanding of what constitutes scripture contributes to the variety of expressions of Buddhism throughout the Far East.

ACTIVITY

A. The following Christian practices were adopted and adapted from pre-Christian sources. Find out the origins of each.

- Christmas trees
- Advent wreaths
- Halloween
- Priestly vestments for bishops, priests, and deacons

B. Describe how Buddhists view their scriptures compared to the way Jews, Christians, and Muslims view theirs.

The Two Major Vehicles

Is the Buddha more a divine savior of humanity, or a human being who should serve as a model for other human beings? Should Buddhist beliefs and practices be restricted to those specifically enunciated in the Buddhist scriptures, or can Buddhists add other beliefs and practices that they deem to be in the spirit of the Buddha? These two questions led to the first major division within Buddhism. Generally, Buddhists accepted differences among themselves without hostility. For instance, there was no period of warfare such as the wars that accompanied the split between Catholics and Protestants in Christian history. There were a series of councils during which representatives from different schools of Buddhism tried to hammer out their differences. Today, although admitting to a common belief in the Buddha and his teachings, branches of Buddhism take those teachings in some surprisingly different directions.

Theravada Buddhism: The Wisdom of the Elders

Theravada Buddhists answer the two questions posed above in a conservative way. They insist that Siddhartha Gautama was a human being, not a god. He attained Buddhahood through meditative practices and living the life of a monk. It is important to emphasize the Buddha's humanity. If he were a god, he couldn't serve as a model for mere human beings. The goal of Theravada Buddhism is for monks to follow strictly the Eightfold Path and other disciplines associated with a monk's life. The ideal is to become enlightened, as Siddhartha did, and from this position of being enlightened to teach and guide others. These enlightened members of the Theravada community are known as *arhats*. This way of living Buddhism adheres to the way the community of monks lived during the time of Siddhartha Gautama. Thus, followers of this type of Buddhism call their expression of it Theravada Buddhism, since Theravada means "wisdom of the elders."

What is the focus of the regimen of meditation practiced by Theravada monks? Central to their meditation is the **Triple Gem**: *Buddha, dharma, sangha*. Monks focus on the Buddha as a human being who attained buddhahood, just as they are human beings seeking buddhahood. They can attain enlightenment or buddhahood by adhering to the teachings of the Buddha—the dharma. Other monks past and present have followed the practices described in the dharma and have become enlightened. This community of monks is called the sangha.

What is the role of laypeople in Theravada Buddhism? The monks are clearly the heart and soul of Theravada. Laypeople, however, gain merit simply by being around the monks, who remind everyone else of the true nature of human life. Laypeople may also receive specific teachings from monks and thus grow in wisdom. Theravada monks do not eat after noon. They depend upon the generosity of laypeople in the community to fill their begging bowls with food for the day. (Strictly speaking, the monks do not beg; they simply accept what they are given. If a day goes by when they receive no offerings, then they do not eat that day.)

Being a monk is so central to this branch of Buddhism that all young boys spend some time as a monk. It might be for a weekend at the local monastery, or it might be for a longer period of time. For some, it is the commitment of a lifetime. A ritual exists to mark a young boy's entrance into a monastery. In imitation of Siddhartha during his princely youth, the boy is dressed in fine clothes. Then he ceremoniously parades to the local monastery where a monk shaves his head, replaces his fine clothes with the simple robe of a monk, and gives him a begging bowl and perhaps an umbrella in order not to draw attention to himself as he is walking about.

Vocabulary

arhat: A monk who has attained enlightenment.

sangha: The community of Buddhist monks.

syncretism: A combination or fusion of different religions or systems of belief.

Tripitika: "Three Baskets" of the Pali Buddhist scriptures.

Triple Gem: Buddha, dharma, sangha; also called the Three Jewels or Three Treasures.

For Review

18. How did women come to be accepted as Buddhist monks?
19. Define syncretism. Why was Buddhism open to syncretism?
20. What test did Buddhists tend to use to identify what texts were to be recognized as scriptures?
21. What are the Tripitika?
22. How does Theravada Buddhism look upon the Buddha?
23. Who is the ideal for the Theravada Buddhist community?
24. What is the Triple Gem?

Mahayana Buddhism: The Big Raft

Mahayana Buddhists answer the two above questions in a liberal way. Siddhartha Gautama was the Buddha during one lifetime. However, the Buddha came from and entered nirvana, which is beyond historical constraints. If the Buddha is the compassionate one as he demonstrated so forcefully during his life, then surely he continues to be a compassionate presence for all time and in all places. The compassionate Buddha is not only Siddhartha Gautama of history but is also a divine being. People can pray to the Buddha and invoke his help. Both monks and laypeople can experience the compassion of the divine Buddha.

Mahayana Buddhists recognize that they are interpreting the Buddha in ways that Siddhartha himself did not advocate. However, they claim that beliefs and practices should not be confined just to what the Buddha specifically taught. As long as they lead to the goal that the Buddha held out for all people, then beliefs and practices are acceptable. Mahayana Buddhists mention an analogy that the Buddha himself used when pressed about his teachings. The Buddha picked up a handful of leaves and asked the questioner, "Where are there more leaves, in my hands or in the forest?" Mahayana Buddhists suggest that Siddhartha Gautama was reminding us that sources of truth are much more plentiful than that which comes directly from him.

Mahayana means "big raft" or "great vehicle." (Early on, Mahayanists referred to Theravada as Hinayana Buddhism, which means "little raft," but that term can be understood in a pejorative sense.) The image of a raft suggests the crossing of a river, in this case from the shore of our everyday consciousness to the other shore experienced by the Buddha upon his awakening. While crossing the river, Mahayana is a big raft in a variety of ways. For one thing, it makes room for new ideas beyond the original teachings of the Buddha. For another, it places both monks and laypeople on more equal footing than Theravada does. Thirdly, it approaches the journey to enlightenment in a unique way. Mahayanists believe that we should not travel alone to the other shore and then look back upon the suffering of others. Instead, we should take time in our river crossing to help others climb on board. Therefore, the Mahayana ideal is the *bodhisattva*, a being moved by compassion to delay solitary enlightenment in order to help others. The term bodhisattva can be applied both to deities who represent compassion and to human beings who exhibit compas-

The Two Vehicles of Buddhism

Theravada	Mahayana
■ conservative	■ liberal
■ Buddha is human, a model	■ Buddha is divine, to whom we can pray
■ arhat is the ideal	■ bodhisattva is the ideal
■ emphasizes meditation	■ emphasizes prayer and meditation
■ emphasizes wisdom	■ emphasized compassion
■ monks are the focal point	■ both monks and laypeople can participate
■ spread south to Sri Lanka, Thailand, Cambodia, and Burma	■ spread north to China, Korea, Japan, Tibet, Afghanistan, Vietnam, and Indonesia

sionate living. Fouthly, historically Mahayana has been a big raft in the sense of welcoming syncretism. As Mahayana spread, it adopted beliefs and practices of the religions and cultures in which it found itself. This openness to syncretism resulted in the rich diversity found in Buddhism today. Finally, Mahayana is a big raft because it spawned a number of different expressions of Buddhism. Three of those types of Buddhism are Zen, Pure Land, and Tantric Buddhism.

ACTIVITY

A. **Write a report on either Theravada or Mahayana Buddhism.**

B. **Write a report on the story of Buddhism in one particular country.**

For Review

25. Name three ways that Mahayana Buddhism is a "big raft."

26. What is a bodhisattva?

27. How is the Buddha viewed in Mahayana Buddhism?

Zen: "Self Power" Buddhism

The Buddha was known to have been able to come up with just the right example or story to help those seriously interested in pursuing the truth. For instance, one day a large crowd gathered to hear his words of wisdom. Gautama looked out at the sea of anxious faces eager to absorb his teachings. Wondering what words to say, he instead looked down and saw a flower growing by his feet. Without saying a word, he lifted the flower for all to see. At that moment, one person experienced enlightenment.

Zen Buddhism finds inspiration in this famous "flower sermon" of the

Entrance to a Japanese garden

Buddha. Although it comes out of the Mahayana tradition, Zen resembles more closely the purity and simplicity of Theravada Buddhism. The founder of Zen was the Indian Buddhist monk Bodhidharma who traveled from the west into China. Buddhism had already found a home in China. One ruler prided himself on amassing a great collection of Buddhist texts, on building a large monastery filled with monks practicing Buddhism, and on educating all of his subjects about Buddhist teachings. When the ruler heard about the wise monk Bodhidharma, he sent emissaries to invite Bodhidharma to his palace. Bodhidharma went to the palace and heard all that the ruler had done for Buddhism. Accounts differ at this point, but legend has it that Bodhidharma refused to congratulate the ruler and actually condemned him for placing such emphasis on the external trappings of Buddhism. Instead, he walked out of the palace and made his way to a cave where he sat in meditation facing a wall for nine years.

These two stories illustrate what became key characteristics of Zen Buddhism. (1) For one thing, Zen emphasizes **simplicity**. Words and concepts can complicate matters, making it more difficult to see the reality in front of our face—such as a flower. Zen speaks of developing a "beginner's mind," capable of seeing things freshly. Zen tradition contains many stories of monks who, when asked about the nature of Zen, say something as simple as, "When you eat, eat. When you work, work. When you sleep, sleep. This is Zen."

(2) Zen emphasizes **nature**. A written form originating with Zen is haiku poetry, which seeks to express the immediacy of an experience of nature. For instance, one haiku humorously reminds us of our relationship with the rest of nature in words roughly translated as: "Borrowing my house from insects/I slept." Zen, associated most strongly with China and Japan, no doubt enhanced its nature-centeredness from its encounter with Taoism, which we'll study in the next chapter. A Zen garden doesn't require a splash of color; simple variations of green are sufficient. Water dripping from a bamboo shoot onto a rock reflects Zen more than a rushing waterfall.

(3) Zen emphasizes **direct experience**. Bodhidharma didn't want the Chinese ruler to know *about* Buddhism, he wanted him to *know* Buddhism. A major practice of Zen is *zazen*, or "sitting meditation." Long hours engaged in zazen help Zen practitioners live all of life meditatively. Drinking tea meditatively, in Zen fashion, may appear to be the same as drinking tea at any other time. However, the degree to which we enter into the present moment, savoring without distraction what we are doing right now, makes a vast difference in our being awake. Walking can be "walking meditation." Cooking a meal or cleaning a bathroom can lead to enlightenment as much as any activity can. Meditation and living meditatively prepares a person for *satori*, a sudden flash of enlightenment. It might come while pruning a rose bush, watching a sunset, or simply going about daily chores. The flash of enlightenment changes one's perspective about oneself and everything that one does. Basho, the Zen monk who originated the haiku form, describes satori in his most famous poem. One translation reads: "An old pond./A frog jumps in./Plop!" All of Zen is based upon the realization that our mind is an old pond awaiting the transforming leap of a frog to makes all things new.

> *The goal of meditation, therefore, is not relaxation, but to relax, to slow down sufficiently to silence the chatter and empty the clutter of our everyday minds. The purpose of this silencing, this emptying, is to make room in our minds…to more directly hear the voice of God calling in our minds and hearts. (M. Scott Peck,* A World Waiting to Be Born *[New York: Bantam Books,1993], 89)*

(4) Zen emphasizes **discipline**. In Japan, Zen became particularly popular among the Samurai, or warrior class. The discipline of attentiveness fostered by Zen appealed to this group whose lives depended upon their concentration on the task at hand. The martial arts in Japan are associated with Zen, as they are with Taoism in China. Although Zen wouldn't use such dualistic language, martial arts are in a sense a form of bodily meditation to accompany mental meditation. Zen discipline requires great effort. However, its goal is to come to a point where actions are done effortlessly. Think about riding a bike. First attempts require concentrating on all the separate aspects involved in bike riding: feet on the pedals, hands firmly holding on but ready to brake, eyes on the road. Discipline and practice lead to riding a bike effortlessly. Tai chi and other martial arts seek to develop, through discipline, effortless action in people. Zen's beginner's mind is effortless thinking, achieved through the discipline of meditation.

Zen has developed a great repertoire of activities to assist the practitioner in achieving satori or in simply living life more awake. There is Zen archery and fencing, Zen gardening and painting, the Zen tea ceremony, and of course haiku poetry. One interesting meditation technique is the use of **koans**. A koan is a paradoxical statement used in Zen meditation. A paradox is an apparent contradiction. An example of a paradox from the Christian tradition is the saying from Jesus, "The first shall be last and the last shall be first." Initially, the statement appears to contradict itself; it appears to be unjust nonsense. (Imagine if you were first in line for tickets to a concert and the ticket salesperson came out and said this!) However, those who penetrate this statement of Jesus can find sense to it that runs deeper than our ordinary consciousness can comprehend.

Koans are mind-boggling questions given by a Zen master to a student. The student is to meditate on the statement and return the next day with an answer. If the master finds the answer unacceptable—that is, not coming from an enlightened mind—then he or she might ignore the student, slap the student on the cheek, or use some other method to let the student know that he or she must continue to explore its meaning. Two of the most famous koans are: "You have heard the sound of two hands clapping. What is the sound of one hand clapping?" and "What did your face look like before your parents were born?"

A. Haiku are three-line poems of 5, 7, and 5 syllables per line. They are simple description but also often contain a slight twist that causes us to see things differently. (For instance, "Since my house burned down/I now own a better view/of the rising moon.") Compose a haiku that you believe reflects the spirit of Zen.

B. Write a report on one technique associated with Zen.

C. Books have been written with titles such as "Zen Running" and "Zen Skiing." Describe what you think a Zen approach to some activity would be.

D. Look through the gospels and find at least three other examples of Jesus' use of paradox in his teaching.

Pure Land: "Other Power" Buddhism

The thirteenth-century Japanese Buddhist monk Shinran did not begin Pure Land Buddhism, but he carried it to its natural conclusion. Shinran was engaged in a rigorous program aimed at gaining enlightenment. Chinese and Japanese Buddhism had developed a variety of methods for seeking enlightenment. For instance, a group known as the "marathon monks" ran long distances, up to seventy-five miles a day, for a period of one hundred days. Successful completion guaranteed enlightenment. Monks at one Japanese monastery spent time in the waters of a nearby waterfall every morning to help them "wake up." Shinran had almost completed a one hundred-day program of chanting while walking around a Buddha statue when he came to a profound insight. "Who do I think I am that I believe I can attain enlightenment through my own efforts? I am relying on the very instrument that I am trying to overcome—the 'self'! I am nobody, nothing. I am completely powerless to achieve the goal I seek."

At that moment of utter despair Shinran was filled with an overwhelmingly comforting feeling. He realized that while relying on "self power" was futile, there was an "other" who filled the void and held complete power over human destiny. This other was the Buddha whose name was chanted and in whom people placed their trust. **Amida Buddha** (or Amitabha Buddha), the Buddha of Divine Light, resided in a paradise in the west. One who had complete faith in Amida Buddha would, upon death, be brought to the Pure Land where he or she would live with Amida Buddha forever. Shinran left his monastery and married. He went into exile, but his ideas became very popular among the common people with whom he lived. Today, Pure Land Buddhism is the largest sect in Japan.

Pure Land Buddhism represents an unusual twist in the story of Buddhism. It seems to run counter to so many principles that Siddhartha Gautama himself rejected. Pure Land Buddhists would counter that their beliefs in fact reflect the very heart of Gautama's teachings. Gautama became the Buddha when he realized that there was no separate self. Pure Land takes this realization and renounces any form of self-reliance. This leads to a realization of and reliance on "other power," the power of the divine Amida Buddha. Living as a monk is not necessary. Laypeople can celebrate their faith and trust in Amida Buddha through prayers and intercessions. Pure Land religious services can seem very much like a Protestant Christian service, with prayers and communal singing.

> *There ne'er was a country so brightened with gladness*
> *As the Land of the Pure there far off to the West.*
> *There stands Amitabha with shining adornments.*
> *He makes all things ready for the Eternal Feast…*
> (from "The White Lotus Ode," quoted in Jack Maguire, Essential Buddhism, 56)

A. Find out more about Pure Land (Shin) Buddhism. Compare it to elements in your own religion.

B. If you had to choose, would you join Zen or Pure Land Buddhism? Why?

ACTIVITY

Tantric Buddhism

Tanrism, or Vajrayana Buddhism, is viewed either as part of the Mahayana tradition or as a third branch altogether— the "diamond" vehicle. It is practiced predominantly in Tibet. An important aspect of Tibetan Buddhism is the **lama**, a translation of the Sanskrit "guru." Lamas are teachers who possess secret knowledge. They pass this knowledge on in secret to their students and also decide whether a student is worthy or capable to receive the truth. Some lamas are considered reincarnations of previous lamas

Mandala. Adibuddha Vairochana, surrounded by four Adibuddhas and four Bodhisattvas

who, although enlightened, chose to return to earth out of compassion. For instance, the most famous and most important lama today, the Dalai Lama, is the latest in a long line of incarnations.

Tibetan Buddhism employs visualization techniques, such as imagining oneself as already a buddha. Circular images, called **mandalas**, assist in this meditation. Numerous gods and demons make up Tibetan religious imagery, and there are elaborate rituals available to invoke the aid of the gods. Avalokiteshvara, a bodhisattva, serves as an object of popular religious devotion and also as a model for living a compassionate life.

In 1959 China invaded Tibet, destroying most of its monasteries, killing many monks and nuns, and sending many Tibetans into exile. Since that time Tibetan Buddhism has become more popular and well-known in Europe and America.

Conclusion
Guidance for Becoming Awake

Siddhartha Gautama the Buddha refused to settle for half measures or short cuts. Once he faced head-on what being human entailed, he determined to give his all to unravel its secrets. He did come to the truth, which brought him great joy. Drawn by compassion to share his joy, he encapsulated his message into the bare essentials of Four Noble Truths. Although he did not advocate a system that he would consider a "religion," members of his community soon included religious elements into the Buddhist movement. The Buddha's life and teachings are an inspiration to everyone who senses that there can be more to life. The Buddha's message is, "Awake! Look within! You are the Buddha."

Vocabulary

Amida Buddha: (Japanese) Transcendent Buddha of Divine Light who rules the western Paradise (also Amita or Amitabha).

bodhisattva: A compassionate being; one who delays enlightenment to help others.

koan: Paradoxical question used in Zen meditation.

mandala: Circular image used for meditation or visualization.

satori: (Japanese) A sudden flash of enlightenment.

For Review

28. Describe the flower sermon of the Buddha.
29. What does the story of Bodhidharma say about Zen attitudes?
30. Name the four characteristics of Zen.
31. Give an example of a koan. What role do koans play in Zen Buddhism?
32. What realization did Shinran come to that changed his life?
33. Who is Amida Buddha?

34. What does "Pure Land" refer to?

35. What role do lamas play in Tibetan Buddhism?

36. Who is the Dalai Lama?

37. What is a mandala?

38. What 1959 event led to a transformation of Tibetan Buddhism?

ACTIVITY

A. **What would you say serves as the basis for moral behavior in Buddhism?** How is this foundation for morality similar to or different from that of other religions?

B. **If there is one quality that Buddhism has to offer people in Western society, what is it?** What could people do to cultivate this quality?

C. **Describe similarities and differences among the following:** Jesus, Muhammad, Siddhartha Gautama.

D. **Draw an image that would represent one branch of Buddhism.** Explain the image you chose.

CHAPTER 7

CONFUCIANISM and TAOISM

The Chinese Search for Harmony

In 1988, seventy-five Nobel prize winners assembled in Paris to discuss issues facing the twenty-first century. They concluded that, "If mankind is to survive, it must go back 25 centuries in time to tap the wisdom of Confucius." After the Bible, the most frequently translated work just might be a short collection of ancient Chinese verse called the Tao Te Ching, the pivotal document of Taoism. Despite attacks from modernism and over fifty years of a Communist government aggressively seeking to stamp them out, Confucianism and Taoism still influence Chinese life. Why does there remain such an interest in two religious traditions whose roots go back over twenty-five hundred years? Is there something in these religions of China that can speak to us who live in the modern West? In this chapter we will look at the religious landscape of China and search for insights that it can offer us.

Overview

■ From its earliest period, harmony and ancestor worship have been two themes that permeate religious activity in China.

■ Confucianism emphasizes morality as the means by which to create social harmony.

■ Taoism emphasizes living naturally as the way by which to achieve personal and social harmony.

Before we begin...

How would you rate your personal state of harmony? How would you rate the state of harmony currently existing in your society and in the world? What is the relationship among personal, societal, and global levels of harmony? What would you recommend as ways to foster greater harmony?

I. Folk Religion
Popular Beliefs and Practices

Besides sacramental liturgy and sacramentals, catechesis must take into account the forms of piety and popular devotions among the faithful. The religious sense of the Christian people has always found expression in various forms of piety surrounding the Church's sacramental life, such as the veneration of relics, visits to sanctuaries, pilgrimages, processions, the stations of the cross, religious dances, the rosary, medals, etc. (Catechism of the Catholic Church, #1674)

There is scarcely any proper use of material things which cannot be thus directed toward the sanctification of men and the praise of God. (Catechism of the Catholic Church, #1670)

Religion in China has certain characteristics that distinguish it from most Westerners' view of religion. For one thing, religions are much less structured than, say, Judaism or Christianity is. As a result, many religious practices can be classified either as Taoist or as Confucianist or as both. Traditionally, Chinese and Japanese people often considered themselves to be Taoist, Confucianist, and Buddhist at the same time. On occasion, they might include "Christian" among the ways they designated their religion. Westerners tend to be **denominationalist** in their religious identity. That is, if people are Christian, then they can't be Jewish. An Episcopalian cannot be a Baptist or a Muslim. Denominationalist thinking has to be set aside if we are to understand the Chinese religious landscape.

Secondly, for centuries Chinese culture included a vast array of practices loosely labeled "religious." Many of these practices resemble what Westerners might think of more as superstition or magic than religion. However, they do reflect beliefs expressed in the major religious traditions of China. It's difficult to make an exact distinction between certain beliefs and practices and label them, say, "true Taoism" and refer to other beliefs and practices as a corruption of Taoism. The religions of China operate on multiple levels.

Finally, China has a long history of what we might call **folk religion**. As the name implies, folk religion refers to beliefs and practices popular among "the folks"–the common people. It is sometimes also known as popular religion or popular piety. Elements of folk religion typically carry an unofficial or semi-official status. For instance, imagine that during a Catholic Mass, rather than actively participating in the Mass, someone is off to the side lighting a candle and praying before a statue of a saint. Mass is the official "liturgy" going on; lighting a vigil candle is an example of popular piety. Another example of Catholic popular piety: Every Catholic knows that if you lose something, saying a prayer to Saint Anthony can help you find it. No church authority officially mandates such prayer, but it is nonetheless a popular practice among Catholics. Two areas of popular religion present in Chinese culture from its earliest times are harmony with nature and ancestor worship.

List examples of beliefs or practices that might fit under the category "folk religion" in religious traditions other than the Chinese religious tradition.

ACTIVITY

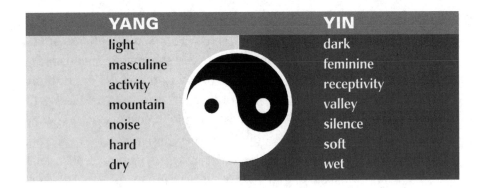

YANG	YIN
light	dark
masculine	feminine
activity	receptivity
mountain	valley
noise	silence
hard	soft
dry	wet

Yang-Yin: The Search for Harmony

Stores in your local mall that sell necklaces and other trinkets probably feature something displaying the yang-yin symbol. The symbol predates formation of the two Chinese religions that we'll study in this chapter. It represents the great concern that the people of China have always placed on maintaining harmony. One use for yang-yin was **divination**, an attempt to predict the future. Through the placement of longer or unbroken (yang) and shorter or broken (yin) pieces of wood, a fortune teller could help someone decide whether or not to purchase a particular piece of property or close a business deal. An ancient text called the *I Ching*, "The Book of Changes," is a guidebook for understanding yang-yin arrangements, if one can interpret them properly.

Even without placing any religious significance on it, the yang-yin symbol reveals much about the traditional Chinese worldview. For one thing, the symbol is a circle. That is, before it is a duality it is a unity. Within the unity of the circle two forces are at work. They are not static. The way they are configured suggests constant motion, an ebb and flow. At the very heart of one image lies an "eye" of the other, and vice versa. If reality is in con-

ACTIVITY

A. **Find out more about qualities associated with yang or yin.** Make a list of the differences. Then give examples of ways that an individual or a society might exhibit an overabundance of yang or an overabundance of yin. Finally, describe what a balance of yang and yin might be like on the personal or societal level.

B. **Describe yourself in terms of the qualities yang and yin.** (For example, are you typically more one than the other? Have you ever attempted to establish a balance in yourself?)

stant motion, as the image suggests, it is no wonder that Chinese people would seek help in divining how to maintain harmony in their lives.

A mountain is one image used in ancient China to explain yang and yin. For part of the day, one side of a mountain is sunlit and dry. Flowers are open and reaching upward to the sun. Meanwhile, the other side of the mountain is shady. Plants lean downward and are filled with dew, which moistens the earth. All qualities found in the universe represent either yang or yin. Yang is positive; yin is negative. That doesn't mean that yang is good and yin is evil. Rather, *balance and harmony are good; imbalance and disharmony are bad.* Yang is positive in the sense of being active, in motion. Yin is negative in the sense of inaction, stillness. Reflecting ancient archetypes, yang is considered the male principle while yin is the female principle. (Again, this doesn't mean that men are to be active and women passive. Everyone should develop a balance of yang and yin.) Yang is light and dry; yin is dark and wet. Yang is loud and forceful; yin is quiet and yielding. The list of associations with the two principles could go on forever. Although it is something of an over-generalization, the case can be made that Confucianism advocates more yang while Taoism clearly advocates yin in seeking harmony.

Shinto: The Japanese Way of the Gods

Shinto, or Shintoism, is the traditional religion of Japan. It shares characteristics with Confucianism, Taoism, and Buddhism, all of which have also made their mark in Japanese religious history. Since it advocates belief in supernatural beings called kami, Shinto is known as the way of the gods. Along with Confucianism, Shinto emphasizes respect for and obedience to elders. In Japan, at times this translated into uncompromising obedience to the emperor. Along with Taoism, Shinto emphasizes appreciation for nature. The Japanese landscape is dotted with archways in lakes or in front of waterfalls and mountains. These archways-without-buildings suggest that the great outdoors, nature, is in itself sacred space.

Ancestor Worship

The ancient Chinese believed that people's involvement in the affairs of the world did not end at their death. Their attitude toward the dead is typically referred to as "ancestor worship." Depending on how the term is defined, however, "worship" is not exactly the relationship that exists between the living and the dead as the ancient Chinese understood it. The living should show their respect for their elders even after they have died. Funeral rites and ongoing ritual practices existed by which the dead could be honored. Failure to perform the proper rituals could result in the dead intervening unfavorably in their family's affairs. One ancient Chinese understanding of god reflects this emphasis on honoring dead ancestors. As the emperor rules the world, so the emperor's ancestor rules the afterlife. People should honor their family's ancestors; everyone should honor the emperor's oldest ancestor, the lord of heaven. Therefore, from this perspective "god" is the ancestor of the emperor.

Belief in the existence of a spirit world is a consistent element in Chinese religious life. China had a notion of heaven, god, gods, and spirits early in its history. However, these beliefs were not so precisely conceived as they were in other traditions. For instance, Hindus can name many gods who have specific powers and symbols associated with them. On the other hand, Chinese religionists most frequently spoke of "heaven," a vague, impersonal, spiritual reality. The spirits of ancestors were not gods in the sense in which we typically understand the term but were inhabitants of the spirit world. Chinese spiritual beings resemble the spirits called *kami* in the traditional Japanese religion known as **Shinto**. Chinese history has also had myriad priests available to help people make a connection with the spirit world.

ACTIVITY

A. **Many people tend to know little of their ancestry. How well do you know yours?** How far back can you trace your family tree? Do you think it is important to know about earlier generations of your family? Why or why not?

B. **Is knowing and respecting past generations an important element of religion?** Why or why not? Does your religious tradition include honoring the past? Explain.

C. **Write a report on Shintoism in Japan, focusing especially on the belief in kami.**

Vocabulary

denominationalism: Identifying people as members of one religion.

divination: Fortune telling.

folk religion: Beliefs and practices with an unofficial or semi-official status that are popular in a religious community.

kami: Shinto gods or spirits.

Shinto: Traditional religion of Japan, which includes belief in kami, emperor worship, and respect for nature.

For Review

1. What is the Chinese perspective on denominationalism compared to the Western view?

2. What is folk religion?

3. What is divination and what ancient Chinese text was used for divination?

4. Describe the design of the yang-yin symbol.

5. Name three characteristics associated with yang and three associated with yin.

6. Why is it inaccurate to identify good or evil with yang or yin?

7. What was the relationship between the living and their dead ancestors in ancient Chinese society?

8. How did ancestor worship lead to one understanding of God in ancient Chinese society?

9. How precise was the concept of God in ancient Chinese society?

10. What is the name of the traditional Japanese religion? Who were the Kami in this tradition?

II. Confucianism
Creating Social Harmony

The human person needs to live in society. Society is not…an extra-neous addition but a requirement of [human] nature. Through the exchange with others, mutual service and dialogue with his brethren, man develops his potential; he thus responds to his vocation. (Catechism of the Catholic Church, #1879)

Zi-gong asked: "The people of the prefecture all love him—What do you think about such a man?"

The Master said: "Not good enough."

"The people of the prefecture all loathe him—what do you think about such a man?"

The Master said: "Not good enough, either. It would be best if the prefecture's good people loved him and its evil people loathed him." *(Analects 13.24, in* The Analects of Confucius, *translated by Chichung Huang [New York: Oxford University Press, 1997], 47)*

Confucius Calls for a Return to the Old Ways

Imagine living during a time when government leaders used their power to procure material pleasures and personal gain for themselves. Underlings flattered their leaders and refused to criticize them in order that they too could reap the benefits of dishonest practices. Government corruption seeped down to the lower rungs of society so that people were not treating one another with respect and no one trusted anyone else. You know that this was not the way it had been in the past. Previously, rulers ruled justly, and people knew how to treat one another. How could you cure society's ills? The only way was to *return to the values and virtues of earlier eras.* Upon this premise a philosophical movement began that would shape the Chinese worldview ever after.

The Chinese sage Confucius—K'ung fu-tzu, meaning "K'ung the Teacher" or simply "Master K'ung"—lived during such a time. His life span parallels almost exactly that of the Buddha in India, 551–479 BCE. A minor government official, he quit his job when his local ruler started to engage in immoral behavior. Confucius then spent the remainder of his life traveling from province to province seeking out a ruler who would adopt his program of ruling by ethical principles. Confucius gained a following of students who traveled with him and engaged him in discussions about living the moral life, but he never found a ruler willing to incorporate his high-minded social agenda as the basis for governing. Nonetheless, in time the ideas proposed by Confucius came to be adopted by all of China as its basis for education and preparation for government service. Confucian principles officially guided Chinese society until a little over one hundred years ago, and Confucianism influenced neighboring countries such as Korea and Japan as well.

Engraving of Confucius

Confucius did not think of his teachings as new ideas. Rather, he contended that China possessed a great storehouse of ethical teachings that had guided the country during an earlier golden age. He proposed bringing back to life the old ways that at the time lay dormant. He encouraged people to immerse themselves in classic writings, such as the books on ritual and a book of songs that contained moral teachings. From these ancient sources Confucius built a framework for living the ethical life that is the hallmark of what is known as Confucianism. The teachings of Confucius

ACTIVITY

A. Confucius believed that songs were an important part of moral education. List songs that you believe have valuable moral messages in them. For at least one of these songs, describe the message that it contains.

B. Contrast Zen koans with Confucian proverbs. Both are brief statements used for teaching. How are they different? What are the goals of each?

C. The Hebrew Bible has a Book of Proverbs, and Ben Franklin is an American known for his proverbs. Perhaps your family or teachers told you proverbs when you were a child to communicate a lesson to you. Write down three proverbs that you recall from your childhood. Then make up a proverb that could be practical guidance for yourself, friends, or family.

were collected in a book commonly known today as the ***Analects***. They are ethical discourses, records of discussions that Confucius had with students about living the moral life. They are usually written as **proverbs**—succinct sayings that contain basic moral truths. Proverbs are designed to be easily understood and remembered. Even in the West, the name Confucius has come to be associated with this teaching instrument, the proverb.

Education and Virtue: Foundations of the Good Society

The Master said: "To learn something and regularly practice it—is it not a joy?" (Analects 1.1)

Confucius proposed learning and the practice of virtue as the ways to cultivate civil society. Actually, in his view the two are the same. That is, the goal of education is learning how to be virtuous. According to the *Analects*, Confucius instructed students in four areas: culture, moral conduct, wholehearted sincerity, and truthfulness (7.24). These characteristics represent aspects of the core virtue proposed by Confucius: humanity or humane-

The Five Basic Confucian Relationships	
1.	Parents – Children
2.	Elder Brother – Younger Brother
3.	Older Friend – Younger Friend
4.	Husband – Wife
5.	Ruler – Subject

ness. (You might see the word written as *jen* or as **rén**. Typically it is pronounced more like "run.") The Chinese characters for the virtue of ren are a combination of the symbol of a person and two lines. Thus, the word literally means, "what happens when two people meet." Confucius had in mind, "What *should* happen when two people meet."

Rén is basic morality, proper interaction among people. A number of times Confucius summed up its meaning in a phrase that closely resembles what we know as the "golden rule": "Yourself, what you don't want, don't do to others" (*Analects* 15.24). Humanity, then, is benevolence, charity, and loving kindness—treating everyone the way we ourselves would wish to be treated. Following the virtue of humanity is acting the way human beings should act. Not to act humanely is succumbing to smallness: "The gentleman cherishes virtue; the small man cherishes land. The gentleman cherishes institutions; the small man cherishes favors" (*Analects* 4.11). "The gentleman is conversant with righteousness; the small man is conversant with profit" (4.16).

Practicing *rén* maintains social order and harmony; disregarding *rén* leads to chaos. Therefore, Confucius said: "People need humanity [*rén*] more than water and fire" (15.35).

A. Discuss and write up a response to the following questions:

1. Do you believe that the primary goal of education is learning how to be a good person? Why or why not?

2. Certain academic subjects lend themselves to guiding students toward becoming more moral persons. Can the following subjects serve this purpose: mathematics, the sciences, literature, foreign languages, physical education? Explain. Should fostering morality be a component of all of your courses? Explain.

3. Look at the mission of your school or workplace. Is making you a more moral person one of its goals? If so, how is that goal worded? If not, should such a goal be stated in the mission statement?

B. Morality is the central focus of Confucianism. Describe how morality fits into your own religion.

ACTIVITY

"What you do not wish for yourself, do not impose on others." (12.2)

The Five Basic Relationships: Observing the Proper Rituals

No doubt, in the schools with which you are familiar students know how to act when their instructor enters the classroom. They immediately stand and bow to the honorable teacher. Such behavior would make Confucius happy. Confucius advocated the virtue of **li**, observing the proper rituals. As you might suspect from our discussion of Confucianism so far, "ritual" here does not refer simply to religious rituals such as attending Mass or performing Hindu *puja*. Rather, *li* also means good manners and politeness. Confucianism identifies five basic relationships. Each relationship is one of inequality. The one in the superior position is to take care of and show benevolence toward the one in the inferior position. The one in the inferior position is to give obedience to the one who is superior. If the superior does not perform the proper duties and act righteously, then the person in the inferior position should practice "true" obedience, which is to disobey what is wrong. (In Chinese history, this corollary to what true obedience entails has led to the overthrow of dynasties.)

For Confucius, the model social relationship is that between parents and children. Therefore, he admonishes young people to practice **filial piety**—respect for parents and other elders. In fact, respect for elders serves as the basis for humaneness. While he does not dismiss the importance of performing the proper rituals for parents who have died, Confucius taught that people should be more concerned about showing proper respect to their parents while they are alive. Confucius especially wanted sons to honor their fathers, to the degree that he recommended that they stay at home and help their fathers rather than go traveling about a great deal.

Due partially to Confucian influence, respect for elders has been a hallmark of Far Eastern cultures for centuries. For instance, in Japan the custom of bowing when people greet each other reflects the desire to show respect to elders. A younger person is expected to bow lower and longer than his or her older counterpart. If two people meet who are relatively the same age, each one might try to outdo the other in showing respect.

ACTIVITY

A. **Rate your school or community from 1 (very poor) to 10 (very good) in terms of the atmosphere of politeness and good manners that exists there.** Explain your rating. What would you recommend to improve the atmosphere? Would you like greater emphasis to be placed on manners and politeness at schools in your area? Why or why not? What expression of politeness would you find most beneficial?

B. **Describe the major concerns of your family regarding manners as you were growing up.**

C. **If you were asked to name what is the primary social relationship, how would you answer?** Why?

D. **One dark side to Confucianism is that the more influential it became in China the more women were relegated to a lower status than men.** Why do you think this was true? Research and write a report on women in China, especially in light of its religious traditions.

Confucius and Religion

Is Confucianism a religion or merely a philosophy of moral conduct? There are four ways to address that question. (1) One answer is that in time Confucianism certainly *became* a religion. That is, Confucius came to be looked upon as something of a god. Shrines were built and religious rituals performed in his honor. As early as the second century BCE sacrifices were offered to Confucius, and he was counted among "the Immortals." However, the question remains: How did Confucius himself respond to the religion question?

(2) What is immediately striking upon reading the *Analects* is how little Confucius said about religious matters. In fact, he seems to have shared with Gautama the Buddha a fear that involvement with religion can distract us from focusing on more fundamental concerns. (For the Buddha this meant becoming awake, seeking nirvana. For Confucius it meant cultivating virtue so that everyone would contribute positively to society.) For instance, at one point the *Analects* state quite simply that: "The Master would not discourse on mystery, force, rebellion, and deity" (7.20). Confucius cautioned his students to concern themselves with the affairs of this life, not with the supernatural:

> When Ji-lu asked how to serve the spirits and gods, the Master said:"You cannot serve men yet; how can you serve the spirits?" "May I venture to ask what death is?" The Master said: "You do not understand life yet; how can you understand death?" (11.12)

(3) However, Confucius seems to have accepted the ancient Chinese belief in "heaven." Some Chinese viewed heaven as a personal god; others considered it to be an impersonal spirit world. At one point Confucius, agonizing over the poor reception his ideas were receiving, said: "I neither resent Heaven nor blame men. I learnt lower things and perceive higher things. The only one who understands me is perhaps Heaven" (14.35). Here Confucius implies that there is a reality greater than the earthly realm in which human beings live their lives. He admits that he has focused his attention on "lower things"—human affairs, while recognizing that there are "higher things." The last sentence of this saying suggests that heaven itself understands the importance of Confucius's attempts to improve the human condition during this time of immorality and corruption.

(4) Besides his few references to heaven, however, the teachings of Confucius do belong in a book on the world's great religions. His teachings represent a fundamental orientation to life. People before Confucius believed that education and virtue were pursuits proper to an elite few—leaders and those planning on being teachers or sages like Confucius. However, Confucius believed that all people should concern themselves with learning and living the moral life. For him, the true elite were those who have cultivated virtue in themselves: "Do not worry about having no office; rather, worry about whether you deserve to stand in that office. Do not worry about nobody knowing you; rather, seek to be worth knowing" (4.14). Confucius, therefore, advocated universal love and recognition of human solidarity. For him, the betterment of society began with the family and moved outward. Virtuous living was a mandate of heaven. Just as Jesus said, "Let the dead bury the dead," so Confucius felt that heaven was best served by each individual doing her or his best to make the world the best it can be.

The Master said: "Be more demanding with yourself and less so with others and you shall keep resentment away." (15.15)

A. **The Chinese teacher Mo-tzu lived shortly after Confucius. He went beyond Confucius in a number of ways. For one thing, he spoke much more about God and heaven than Confucius did. However, like Confucius, Mo-tzu was most concerned about human social behavior.** His thinking seems to have been: Even if we can't be sure whether or not God exists, we should promote belief in God since people who believe in God act more morally than those who don't. Also, Mo-tzu advocated what might be called "practical altruism." (True altruism means doing good for others regardless of the impact it has on you. Practical altruism means doing good for others because in that way you actually serve your own best interest.)

- Do you agree with Mo Tzu's assessment of the moral implication of believing in God? Why or why not?

- Do you believe that people ever act out of true altruism or are they always actually seeking their own benefit? Give examples of true versus practical altruism.

B. **Do you believe that the teachings of Confucius should be included in a course on world religions?** Why or why not?

Vocabulary

Analects: The writings of Confucius.

filial piety: Respect for parents; in Confucianism, especially a son's respect for his father.

li: Performing proper rituals, including acting politely toward others.

proverbs: Short statements containing a simple moral message.

rén: Literally, "What should happen when two people meet"; the principal Confucian virtue, usually translated as humanity, humaneness, or good-heartedness (also written as jen).

For Review

11. When did Confucius live? What were social conditions like in the China of his day?

12. How did Confucius spend his life?

13. What is the book of Confucius's sayings called?

14. What are proverbs? Why is this teaching form associated with Confucius?

15. According to Confucius, what is the purpose of education?

16. What is the principal Confucian virtue? What does it literally mean?

17. How did Confucius state the "Golden Rule"?

18. What is the practice of li?

19. For Confucius, what are the Five Basic Relationships?

20. How did the people of China come to view Confucius?

21. What did Confucius say about heaven and the afterlife?

22. What did Confucius mean when he said that his focus was on "lower things"?

III. Taoism
Harmony with Nature

Open yourself to the Tao, then trust your natural responses; and everything will fall into place. (Tao te Ching, translated by Stephen Mitchell [New York: Harper Collins, 1988], 23)

The impression of Confucius that we are left with is of a man who desperately wanted to be actively involved in politics, who traveled a great deal and talked to as many people as would listen. He wanted to transform the world as he knew it. In other words, he demonstrated some of the yang qualities mentioned earlier—activity, positive social change, the externals of ritual and proper conduct. He also gave his own slant on the two ancient Chinese concerns of venerating ancestors and harmony. More than honoring the dead, Confucius emphasized respect for "living ancestors"—that is, parents, older family members, government leaders, and teachers. When Confucius spoke of harmony, he meant social harmony brought about by people actively living virtuous lives.

Another school of thought emerged in China around the same time as Confucius. This philosophy advocated the qualities of yin to balance Confucian yang. When its teachers spoke about harmony, they meant primarily inner harmony and harmony with nature. They looked beyond the golden age of the past that Confucius appealed to and spoke instead about a reality outside of but underlying all of human history. The life story of the man associated with the founding of this school of thought closely mirrors qualities associated with yin—quietude, being unobtrusive and self-effacing, and noninterference.

Lao-tzu: Legendary Founder of Taoism

We know little about Lao-tzu. In fact, we know so little that he may not even have existed! His name means "the Old Master." Sometimes he is referred to as "the Grand Old Teacher." Legend has it that he was an older contemporary of Confucius. Stories tell of these two wise men of China meeting, although such stories seem far-fetched. Lao-tzu spent his life without notice as a minor government official. At retirement, he decided to spend his remaining days as a hermit in the mountains to the west of China. He impressed a border guard with his intention to leave society and live a hermit's life. The guard asked him if he would write down his thoughts on life. In a few days Lao-tzu returned with a collection of verse known today as the *Tao Te Ching*.

Lao-tzu is often depicted riding an ox, on his way to his mountain retreat. Like Confucius, he came to be revered as a god. The fact that we can't verify his existence and that even the stories about him reveal little reflects the worldview found in the little book attributed to him. To understand the man and his message we need to examine the central concept of his teachings—the *Tao*.

The Way and Its Power

The Tao is like a well:
used but never used up.
It is like the eternal void:
filled with infinite possibilities.... (4)

The Tao is called the Great Mother:
empty but inexhaustible,
it gives birth to infinite worlds.... (6)

It was never born;
thus it can never die.... (7)

Every being in the universe
is an expression of the Tao. (51)

Lao Tzu

Tao, pronounced "dow," means "the way." However, it is not a "way" that leads to somewhere else. Rather, it is that which underlies all that is. In that sense it resembles Hindu Brahman and Buddhist sunyatta, the emptiness from which all beings emerge. There is a "way" at work in the universe, among people, and within each person. *Tao Te Ching* (pronounced more like "dow de jing") means "the book about the way (*Tao*) and its power (*Te*)." In other words, there is a way to live that taps into the power of Tao and ways of living that thwart this energy. Spontaneity, naturalness, and unforced action characterize this way—like a child who sleeps when she's tired and bursts out in laughter when she's happy. We live in communion with the Tao when we practice the virtue of ***wu wei***.

Wu wei is the central virtue advocated by Taoism. Literally it means "not acting." The *Tao Te Ching* declares that: "Practice not-doing,/ and everything will fall into place" (3). Nonaction here means noninterference, effortless action. Colloquial expressions that capture the meaning of *wu wei* are "go with the flow" and "let it be." The *Tao Te Ching* uses images such as being like a child or an "uncarved block" to describe this attitude. The symbol used most frequently is that of water: "Shapable as a block of wood./Receptive as a valley./Clear as a glass of water" (15).

Wu wei means living in harmony with the Tao. Not to do so has drastic consequences. Here is a description of paradise that results when we live in harmony with Tao and a doomsday depiction of disharmony:

> *In harmony with the Tao,*
> *the sky is clear and spacious,*
> *the earth is solid and full,*
> *all creatures flourish together,*
> *content with the way they are,*
> *endlessly repeating themselves,*
> *endlessly renewed.*
>
> *When man interferes with the Tao,*
> *the sky becomes filthy,*
> *the earth becomes depleted,*
> *the equilibrium crumbles,*
> *creatures become extinct. (39)*

The following two examples illustrate the power of nonresistance and effortless action that is *wu wei*.

- On a hillside a large, old tree stands tall and majestic next to a young sapling that appears weak and fragile by comparison. A storm accompanied by heavy winds blows through. The old tree resists, stays stiff, and doesn't bow. The sapling bends and moves in whatever direction the winds take it. When the storm is over, the strong old tree is blown down; the sapling remains standing.

- A large rock rests in the middle of a stream. When the water bumps up against the rock, it yields and goes around effortlessly. In ten thousand years, water continues to flow; the rock has been worn down to a pebble. "Nothing in the world/is as soft and yielding as water./Yet for dissolving the hard and inflexible,/nothing can surpass it" (*Tao Te Ching*, 78).

Tao is called the watercourse way. Just as the water goes on and on flowing with no guidebooks, with no maps, with no rules, no discipline…but strangely enough in a very humble way, because it is always seeking the lower position everywhere. It never goes uphill. It always goes downhill, but it reaches to the ocean, to its very source. (Osho, Tao: The Pathless Path *[New York: Renaissance Books, 2002], ix)*

A. Describe a situation in which wu wei ("go with the flow," "let it be") would appear to be the right response. Then analyze that response.

B. One of the overriding characteristics of our culture is its excessive busyness. For instance, many Christians are so busy around Christmastime that they don't really experience the true spirit of the holiday. We are practically never "not doing." We are constantly plugged in to CD players, computers, television. We almost need to make an appointment simply to spend quiet time with our family. Practice "not doing" for a set period of time. Report on the experience.

C. Our culture also tends to place a high value on usefulness, while Taoism sings the praises of being useless. Give an example of how persons or things that are useless provide important insights into life.

D. Unlike Confucianism, Taoism advocates a "hands off" approach to governing and teaching. ("Governing a large country/is like frying a small fish./You spoil it with too much poking" [60]). The best ruler appears not to rule. The best teacher appears not to teach, and yet students learn.

1. Describe what might be differences between a school run on Confucian principles and one run on Taoist principles. Which school would you prefer for yourself? Why? If you had children, would you want the same type of schooling for them? Why or why not?

2. Have you ever had an experience in which a teacher appeared not to teach and yet you learned much? If so, describe the experience. If not, explain what you think Taoism might mean by this statement.

ACTIVITY

Christianity, especially Catholicism, also expresses the need for living in accord with the ways of nature, which it adopted from classical Greek and Roman thought. It understands "nature" and the way to interpret nature differently from Taoism. (For instance, Christianity would not advocate "go with the flow" as a reasonable moral guideline.) Nonetheless, the Catechism of the Catholic Church stresses that nature demonstrates laws that should always be followed:

The natural law is immutable and permanent throughout the variations of history; it subsists under the flux of ideas and customs and supports their progress. The rules that express it remain substantially valid. Even when it is rejected in its very principles, it cannot be destroyed or removed from the heart of man. It always rises again in the life of individuals and societies....The natural law, the Creator's very good work, provides the solid foundation on which man can build the structure of moral rules to guide his choices. (#1958-59)

A number of Chinese thinkers have tried to combine the insights of Taoism with those of Confucianism. The following passage from Wang Yang-ming (1452-1529) is one such attempt.

The great man regards Heaven and earth and the myriad things as one body. He regards the world as one family and the country as one person. As to those who make a cleavage between objects and distinguish between the self and others, they are small men. That the great man can regard Heaven, hearth and the myriad things as one body is not because he deliberately wants to do so, but because it is natural with the humane nature of his mind that he should form a unity with Heaven, earth, and the myriad things. This is true not only of the great man. Even the mind of the small man is no different...Therefore when he sees a child about to fall into a well, he cannot help a feeling of alarm and commiseration. This shows that his humanity (jen) forms one body with the child. (quoted in W. T. de Bary, ed. Sources of Chinese Tradition [New York: Columbia University Press, 1960], 412)

Applications of Taoism

Nonaction does not mean that people should literally do nothing at all. Nonaction means to not take any action that goes against nature. Do not fight against the current; instead, flow with it and you will travel a great distance without effort. For example, lifeguards advise that if you are caught in a rip current in the ocean, always swim with the current to shore, not against its pull. If a car begins to skid on a slippery patch of road, fighting the skid by steering in the opposite direction may cause the car to whipsaw back and forth, and perhaps spin out of control. Instead, good drivers carefully and sensitively turn the wheels in the direction of the skid and take their feet off the accelerator. The car will straighten out and the driver remains in control. ...stay in tune with yourself and things work out as they are meant to. (C. Alexander and Annellen Simpkins, Simple Taoism [Boston, MA: Tuttle Publishing, 1999], 69-70)

How could anyone practice Taoism, which advocates "nonaction"? To complicate matters, one of the most famous lines from the *Tao Te Ching* is: "Those who know don't talk./Those who talk don't know" (56). (Strangely enough, Taoist scholars produced a collection of scriptures so extensive that practically no one reads them all!) In fact, out of Taoism has emerged a number of practices that continue to be popular in Eastern cultures and that have grown in popularity in the West as well. Each one of them reflects the spirit of naturalness and being attuned to nature advocated by Taoism.

The Martial Arts. Taoism influenced Zen Buddhism. The martial arts reflect Taoist and Zen principles. **Tai chi chuan** is a form of martial arts that especially embodies Taoism. Although its movements mimic the actions of a warrior, they are really choreographed meditation. The key is to move from position to position without ever sacrificing physical balance and mental alertness. Tai chi applies *wu wei*, "go with the flow," to physical movement and gesture. Practitioners of tai chi repeat movements over and over again so that they are performed with complete naturalness and unity of mind and body. "**Chi**" is the inner life-force that, when tapped, enables the weak to overcome the strong and physically demure men and women to break boards or throw bigger attackers onto the ground.

The Healing Arts. In earlier times, people engaged in martial arts matches would often get hurt. Therefore, training in the healing arts accompanied training in the martial arts. **Chi kung** refers to meditation techniques and physical exercises designed to improve health. As with the martial arts, the healing arts aim to increase and utilize the energy of chi. Acupuncture and acupressure are medical techniques that grew out of Taoism. They have since emerged as healing arts in themelves, even in the West.

A great concern of many Taoists for a period of time was alchemy, the search for the one material that made up life and preserved life. (Evidence indicates that some Chinese women and men ingested what amounted to poison in the hopes of gaining eternal life.) Nonetheless, the extensive experiments that medieval Chinese alchemists performed helped them gain knowledge of healing herbs and other medicines.

The Decorative Arts. Once in Hong Kong a Western company built a large office building, but few Chinese workers wanted to work there. An expert in **feng shui** had determined that the design of the building blocked the flow of chi energy. Feng shui is based on Taoist principles. Since we are one with nature, our immediate environment affects the way we feel and function. First written about in 600 CE, feng shui refers to designing buildings and other spaces that reflect harmony, simplicity, and naturalness. When the great American architect Frank Lloyd Wright heard about the principles of Taoism, he realized that what he called "organic architecture" had been advocated in the Taoist tradition for centuries.

ACTIVITY

A. Write a report on one of the following topics:

- tai chi
- chi kung
- acupuncture
- acupressure
- feng shui

B. Go to a place of worship and evaluate its layout based on how it seeks to evoke a sense of spirituality.

C. Name a room, a building, or a space that you find uplifts your spirits. Name another such space that you find deflates your spirit. What is the difference between the two?

Is Taoism a Religion?

Taoism readily deserves classification as a religion—certainly more obviously than Confucianism does. Taoism developed into many popular expressions, many of which had religious overtones. The Tao itself came to be personalized into a god. A number of books have been written looking for points of connection between Christianity and Christ with Taoism and the Tao. Interestingly, when the American Bible Society translated the New Testament into a Chinese dialect in 1911, translators used Tao for the term "Word" in the very beginning of the Gospel of John. Thus, the translation read:

> In the beginning was the Tao,
> And the Tao was with God,
> And the Tao was God...

The great Taoist philosopher Chuang Tzu expressed a strong sense of afterlife. He told one story about noticing a skull by the side of a road on which he was traveling. Saddened at the sight of the skull, he began to question what might have led to this person's death. He nonetheless decided to use the skull as a pillow while he slept for the night. At midnight the skull appeared to him in a dream and told Chuang Tzu that his questions were unimportant from the perspective of the dead. The skull told him instead about the afterlife:

> "Among the dead," said the skull, "none is king, none is subject, there is no division of the seasons; for us the whole world is spring, the whole world is autumn. No monarch on his throne has joy greater than ours." (quoted in Arthur Waley, Three Ways of Thought in Ancient China [Garden City, NY: Anchor Books, 1959], 31)

In his most famous statement, Chuang Tzu expressed humility at making definitive statements either about this life or the next. The life we live now is like a dream.

> Once Chuang Chou dreamt that he was a butterfly. He did not know that he had ever been anything but a butterfly and was content to hover from flower to flower. Suddenly he woke and found to his astonishment that he was Chuang Chou. But it was hard to be sure whether he really was Chou and had only dreamt

that he was a butterfly, or was really a butterfly, and was only dreaming that he was Chou.

He concluded that: "Not till the Great Wakening can he know that all this was one Great Dream" (Arthur Waley, 32).

A. Explain in your own words the meaning of Chuang Tzu's butterfly dream.

B. Look over the various expressions of Taoism described in the text. Would you consider any or all of them to be elements of religion? Why or why not?

C. Write an essay on "the spirituality of Taoism."

Conclusion
Two Chinese Ways to Harmony

Even if we tried, we couldn't live in isolation from others. All of us need a sense of social harmony, a sense of how we should treat one another in the myriad interactions we have each day. Confucius recognized this need and built a framework to guide people in developing and maintaining social harmony. All of us also need to experience inner harmony and harmony with the forces of the universe. In the bigger picture, our social harmony or disharmony is merely one small portion of the great, all-encompassing unity of which we are a part. We gain some sense of this great "way" by noting the ways of nature. Taoism helped instill in China a spirit of respect for nature and for inner harmony that has always been so evident in its culture. These two strains of Chinese thought—Confucianism and Taoism—flourished side by side for centuries; a yang and yin of Chinese religious life.

Vocabulary

acupressure: Applying pressure to various points in the body, serving the same purposes as acupuncture.

acupuncture: Traditionally, insertion of needles into various points in the body in order to foster proper flow of chi and restore balance of yang and yin. It is now used for a variety of purposes, such as pain relief.

chi: The life force that flows naturally within people.

chi kung: Traditional Chinese healing practices utilizing meditation and exercise.

feng shui: Designing spaces that reflect harmony and naturalness and allow proper flow of chi energy.

tai chi chuan: A martial arts program designed to maximize balance and one's inner energy.

Tao: The way of nature and the universe.

wu wei: Literally "nonaction," the principal Taoist virtue.

For Review

23. What is the focus of harmony in Taoism in contrast to Confucianism?

24. In what sense does the life of Lao-tzu reflect his worldview?

25. What is the Tao? What is the meaning of Tao Te Ching?

26. What is the principal Taoist virtue? Name three ways that the term can be translated.

27. What are three symbols used for this virtue in the Tao Te Ching? Explain why one of these symbols exhibits Taoist qualities.

28. What is chi? How do tai chi chuan and chi kung seek to use chi?

29. What are acupuncture and acupressure?

30. What is the purpose of feng shui?

31. What term did the American Bible Society use for "Word" in its translation of the Gospel according to John?

32. How did Chuang Tzu describe this life and the afterlife?

CHAPTER 8

OTHER RELIGIONS
Old and New

If we confined our study simply to the largest or the most famous religious traditions, we would overlook religions that have sustained groups of people for many centuries or that are currently growing in membership. All of the religions we have studied so far originated in Asia. What can we say about religions originating elsewhere, such as on the world's second largest continent—Africa? Evidence exists that people of Africa engaged in religious activity many thousands of years ago. There are still people in Africa who practice forms of religion that pre-date Christianity and Islam on the continent. People in other parts of the world, especially in the Southern Hemisphere, also continue to practice ancient forms of religious expression. In addition, in the past couple of centuries a number of new religions have emerged. Despite often facing persecution or discrimination, they not only survive but also thrive. Often they build on one of the world's dominant religions, such as Christianity, and give a unique spin to its message. In this final chapter we will look at some of these religions old and new, seeking to identify how they view the world and their place within it.

Overview

■ Tribal religions share a belief in an intimate interconnection between the spirit world and the world of everyday reality.

■ In recent centuries, new religions have emerged that have added greatly to the world's religious landscape.

Before we begin...

Traditional tribal cultures did not have religions. Rather, everything that members of a tribe did had religious significance. List five to ten major events that typically occur in your life, in your family's life, or in the life of your school or community.

■ **Choose one of these events and describe how it could be celebrated so that it has religious significance.**

■ **Explain why you would celebrate the event in this way.**

I. Tribal Religions
Ancient Spiritualities That Live on Today

Before four thousand years ago, religious expression was tribal. That is, people identified with a particular tribe. Religious beliefs and practices were an integral part of tribal culture; they were not to be shared with others. Since the religion of one tribe was unique and different from that of every other tribe, we must be cautious in making generalizations about religions whose origins are in the distant past. (In Africa alone, there are some three thousand ethnic groups, each with its own traditional language and religion!) Also, we would be mistaken to view ancient tribal religious practices as relics from the distant past that are no longer active in today's world. They remain vital expressions of human spirituality today in three ways: (1) Groups of people continue to follow traditional tribal practices. (2) Some people, disillusioned with what they perceive to be a lack of spirituality in the modern world, look to ancient religious practices to guide them in their spiritual quest. (3) Some ancient beliefs and practices came to be subsumed into major universal religious traditions and are now a significant part of religions we have already studied in this course.

Concerning this last point, in time major religious traditions became dominant in most parts of the world. Except for perhaps Judaism, these religions were universal in appeal and were not tied to a particular tribe or ethnic group. (As you may recall, Judaism is "the religion of Jews" rather than one that seeks to be the religion for everybody.) However, popular elements of tribal religions often continued to be practiced within the context of one of these newer religions. For instance, Advent wreaths, Christmas trees, and Halloween have pre-Christian European origins. Arabs went on pilgrimage to Mecca long before Islam declared the practice one of its Five Pillars. Hinduism and the Chinese religions blended older beliefs and practices with newer interpretations so thoroughly that it is almost impossible to separate the old from the new.

It is also important to keep in mind that the exchange between tribal and universal religions has been a two-way street. That is, many people have adapted elements of Christianity or Islam into the beliefs and practices of their tribal traditions. For instance, an American Indian holy man named Black Elk, whose ideas were written down in the popular book *Black Elk Speaks*, was also a Catholic catechist for his tribe.

Even though tribal religions are by definition unique to particular tribes, we can identify certain characteristics frequently shared by these ancient forms of religion throughout the world.

ACTIVITY

Here is a brief description of tribal religious life in Africa:

For the traditional African, the Sacred is an organized and hierarchized universe filled with invisible beings, which include God, spirits, the spirits of ancestors, myths, legends, ceremonies, elaborate rituals, and cult objects.

(Georges Niangoran-Bouah, in Mary Pat Fisher and Lee W. Bailey, *An Anthology of Living Religions* [Upper Saddle River, NJ: Prentice Hall, 2000], 44)

Find out whatever you can about one traditional tribal group (for example, a Native American, African, Pacific Islander, or Siberian tribe). Try to determine the various dimensions of the religious life of that tribe.

Humanity, Nature, and the Supernatural: The Integrated World of Tribal Societies

As we begin our exploration into the religions of traditional tribal groups, it is important to realize that members of these groups do not make clear distinctions commonly made in modern societies. Instead, they view matter and spirit, natural and supernatural beings, as members of one family—an integrated and interconnected whole. In this perspective, while animals are creatures who roam the jungles and forests, fly in the sky, or inhabit the rivers and seas, they are also creatures of spirit. Individual persons and tribes might identify with a particular animal and its spiritual powers.

Since the sacred permeates all of life, the wellbeing of tribal people depends upon their being attuned to the many forces at work in the world. Religious activity is not separate from hunting and fishing, growing crops, marriage and family life, birth and death, warfare and politics. Everything has a sacred quality to it, and much of a tribe's life centers around working with and seeking help from the spiritual elements lying behind the world of nature and human society.

Totems and Taboos

"Totems" are animals or objects that have special significance for a tribe or with which members of a tribe identify. Something can be "taboo"—to be avoided—either because it is perceived to be too holy to approach or because it is unclean.

ACTIVITY

Spend at least fifteen minutes seeking to cultivate a spirit of reverence while:

■ observing people in a busy place such as a shopping mall,

■ being alone in nature, or

■ spending time in a religious building.

Describe the experience in art, song, or poetry.

God and Spirits: A Richly Populated Spirit World

In the beginning was God,
> *Today is God*
> *Tomorrow will be God.*

Who can make an image of God?
He has no body.
He is as a word
> *which comes out of your mouth.*

That word! It is no more,
> *It is past, and still it lives!*

So is God.

> (traditional Pygmy hymn, in John S. Mbiti, African Religions
> and Philosophy [London, UK: Heinemann, 1988], 34-35)

Do people who adhere to their traditional tribal religion believe in a Supreme Being, God who is creator and overseer of the universe? You may be surprised to know that most tribal religions do recognize a Supreme Being. Most groups who adhere to tribal forms of belief recognize that there is a God who is the cause of all things, one who has no equal and who is above all other beings. African tribes and Native American tribes use many names for God. God is creator, Great Spirit, the maker of souls, the one who is met everywhere, the all-seeing, the one who brings round the seasons. Just as in other traditions, tribal notions of God typically represent God as both transcendent (beyond the earthly, human realm) and as immanent (evident and involved in the earthly, human realm).

Whether or not particular tribal cultures recognize one almighty God, it is clear that ancient religious traditions accept the reality of a spirit world filled with a rich array of gods, ancestors, and other sacred beings. The spirit world is very important in such cultures; the beings who inhabit it influence events that happen in everyday reality. For instance, Native Americans known as the Tetons or Lakota Sioux refer to the spirit of a person, object, or even an event as **wakan**, or sacred. The spirits of trees, rivers, animals, and human beings have power. For the Tetons, everything sacred is **wakan tanka**, which is often translated as "Great Spirit" and personified as God. Disregarding the inhabitants of the spirit world would be disastrous for an individual or a tribe. Therefore, tribal societies have various techniques available to call upon the power of spirits.

The Hopi Indians of the American Southwest call the spirits who live among them *Kachinas*. Kachinas represent forces of nature or perhaps an ancestor who has died. Men dress up as Kachinas during religious ceremonies, and Kachina dolls depict the many varieties of Kachina spirits.

One term used to explain the concept of God found in most tribal religions is **diffused monotheism**. The term suggests that there is one God whose power is diffused through many lesser gods. For instance, an African rainmaking ceremony invokes the god of rain to bless the tribe with rain during a drought. Those who participate in the ceremony appear to direct their prayers toward the rain god directly and to the one, almighty God indirectly. In the spirit world, one step below the various gods but just as important are the spirits of ancestors. Tribal consciousness considers both living and deceased to be active members of a family. Tribal life, therefore, includes ways to maintain contact with ancestors ranging from simple gestures to elaborate rituals.

Every object in the world has a spirit and that spirit is wakan. Thus the spirits of the tree or things of that kind, while not like the spirit of man, are also wakan. Wakan comes from the wakan beings. These wakan beings are greater than mankind in the same way that mankind is greater than animals. They are never born and never die. They can do many things that mankind cannot do. Mankind can pray to the wakan beings for help…. The word Wakan Tanka means all of the wakan beings because they are all as if one. (Sword, a Dakota Indian, quoted in Ninian Smart and Richard D. Hecht, editors, Sacred Texts of the World *[New York: Crossroad, 1982], 349)*

We see God in Water, Sun, Air—everywhere.

(George Goodstriker, Kainai (Blackfoot) Elder, in Native Wisdom for White Minds *[New York: One World, 1995], np)*

Make a list of names and characteristics of God and the gods found in various tribal religions.

ACTIVITY

Myths: Stories That Explain and Sustain

A tribe is a group of people who share a common identity. One source of its communal identity is its myths, the stories describing a tribe's origins and its place in the world. Myths are sacred to a tribe, its sacred stories. Myths are so tied up with tribal identity that, if members of a tribe left them unattended, the tribe itself would die. Tribal cultures began as oral, non-literate societies. Therefore, tribal myths have been handed down through song, dance, festivals, and storytellers. Myths are so tied up with tribal identity that, if members of a tribe left them unattended, the tribe would die. (By comparison, can you imagine Catholicism without the Eucharist? Catholics who attend Mass enter into the "sacred mysteries" of their faith. They enact through word and action the central story of their faith that "Christ has died, Christ has risen, Christ has come again.")

Mythic stories spell out the connection that members of a tribe have with God. One of the most popular types of myth is the **creation myth**, a story describing the origins of the world. North American Indian myths often speak of the earth as originally covered with water. The earth is formed when a particular animal dives into the water and brings up earth out of which the land is formed. For instance, the Seneca Indians of New York State talk about a woman who lands on the back of a turtle floating on the great expanse of water. Many animals attempt to dive to the bottom of the water and bring up mud out of which to build the land. When one animal succeeds in accomplishing this task, the Creator expands this tiny bit of soil to make the earth on the back of the turtle. From this land base, the woman gives birth to a daughter, the mother of corn, and to twin sons who as forces of good and evil constantly struggle against each other.

This story reveals much about how the Seneca view reality. For instance, the earth is a divine gift. Animals are allies. From the beginning, corn has sustained them. And the battle between good and bad has been around for a long time. We might suggest that this account of creation is "only a story"—as if to label it a story makes it less impor-

Aborigines of Australia speak of creation taking place while God is dreaming. Therefore, they seek to return to or enter into "dreamtime" by going off alone into the wilderness or by engaging in other activities. Dreamtime is the mythic realm, the spirit world behind their everyday reality.

tant that "the facts." However, mythic stories hold much power and tap into the depths of the human psyche that facts cannot reach. For instance, most modern Westerners may have heard about the "big bang" theory and evolution. Nonetheless, when they think about "creation" they often still call to mind the stories found at the beginning of the book of Genesis in the Bible. Part of the reason for this is that the biblical creation accounts speak about God and the relationship among God, people, and the rest of creation in ways that scientific accounts do not.

Write a mythic story about your family's origins that would describe its "supernatural" character. As part of your story explain why your family has certain characteristics (such as red hair or friendly personalities).

ACTIVITY

Shamanism: Using the Spirit World for Healing

The Altaic shaman in Siberia wore brown leather and elaborate decorations of metal disks, bird feathers, and colored streamers. He entranced himself by sitting astride a horsehide-covered bench or a straw goose and beating a drum rhythmically for hours, the beat being the pounding of the hooves or wings of these spirit-steeds as they bore him to the parallel realm of the spirits. Finally, the shaman would dismount and, flushed with ecstasy, climb nine steps notched in a tree trunk. At each stage in the ascent he would relate the difficulties of his journey, address the gods of that level, and report what they were telling him about the coming events. (Robert S. Ellwood and Barbara A. McGraw, Many Peoples, Many Faiths *[Upper Saddle River, NJ: Prentice Hall, 1999], 37)*

In the perspective of ancient cultures, sickness was never just a physical problem. Every physical ailment or misfortune had spiritual and what we would call psychological causes as well. Therefore, the healing arts practiced by tribal groups blended together the physical and the spiritual. There are indications that some healers in tribal cultures actually knew a great deal about the medicinal benefits of certain herbs and other natural substances. They often used a variety of remedies in their practice. Some practices performed by Native American and African tribal healers appeared to

A Native American medicine man

fall into the category superstition so that when Europeans encountered them they called such healers "medicine men" or "witch doctors." These labels typically had a negative connotation since the practices tribal healers performed often did not conform to modern, scientifically verified medical practices.

One type of healing agent found in most tribal groups is the **shaman**. The term itself originated in Siberia and means "one who sees in the dark." Shamans possess the ability to see into the spirit world (which is unseen or "dark" to most people) and as such can bring a message of healing to people who seek them out for help. Shamans use various techniques to make their journey into the spirit world. In most cases drumming serves as the catalyst for a shaman to journey from the world of ordinary consciousness to the spirit world, although mind-altering drugs also have had a place in some cultures.

The widespread presence of shamanism in tribal societies indicates once again that people in these cultures view the boundaries between what we might call "ordinary reality" and the deeper, spiritual reality to be very porous. Many doors exist through which messages, objects, and people can travel from one realm to the other. Shamans typically undergo rigorous initiation rites preparing themselves for their important role in the community. However, ultimately a person becomes a shaman because a god or spirit chooses her or him. A shaman needs the direction and help of this spirit, sometimes in the form of a particular animal, in traveling back and forth between the worlds of ordinary consciousness and of the altered consciousness he or she enters into during trances.

Some scholars of religion find shamanism as so pervasive in the ancient world that they label all ancient religion "shamanism." The phenomenon is difficult to assess for two reasons. For one, shamans often deny or poke fun at their special powers. Also, in many tribal societies shamans are predominantly women who have frequently been overlooked in anthropological studies.

A. Research and write a report on shamanism as it exists in a particular tribal culture.

B. Write a report on shamanism as it is practiced in the world today.

C. Describe how a shaman is similar to or different from religious
   figures found in other traditions, such as a Catholic priest, a
   Protestant minister, a Buddhist monk, a Hindu yogi, a Jewish
   rabbi, or a Muslim mullah.

Religious Rituals: Celebrations and Communal Identity

Becoming an Adult Member of the Tribe: An Initiation Rite

*The young man approached his initiation with both trepidation
and excitement. He knew nothing of what was to transpire.
Secrecy added to the experience.*

*His father led him outside where he began singing in praise of
the spirits. His father invoked the ancestors of the tribe to offer
guidance and protection as the young man made his transformation into adulthood.*

*The elders arrived, dressed in ceremonial robes similar to
those worn for generations. Their faces and bodies were painted
so that they looked strange and fearsome. The leader of the group
stood in the middle of a circle and began walking slowly around
the young man about to be initiated.*

*The leader sang a chant that told the story of the origins of
the tribe and the great exploits the ancestors had made. He alert-
ed the young man that if he made the journey successfully he
would take on the identity of the tribe; he and the tribe were
about to become one. Wherever he would go he would carry the
tribe with him.*

Soon the boy would be a man.

Religious rituals are the lifeblood of tribal societies. Through ritual, community members cement their identity as a people, celebrate their place in the
universe, reinvigorate their connection with the spirit world, and keep alive

their essential stories. In tribal societies, important events such as births and deaths are marked by religious ceremony. One of the most important events for a community is the transition of a child into an adult. Tribes around the world have **initiation** rites especially for boys marking that time when they are to take on adult responsibilities. Often the boys also receive the tribe's secret knowledge or undergo some trial so that they receive a vision, which they bring back and share with the rest of the community.

We may think of singing and dancing as pure fun. However, in tribal societies the singing and dancing that take place during important ceremonies are not just for fun. Usually accompanied by a drum, a tribal dance can last for days. During that time, all members of a tribe participate, at a faster or slower pace than the others. Nonetheless, through the dance everyone is transformed, everyone feels connected to everyone else, and everyone seeks contact with the power of the spirit.

Today the Plains Indians of America continue practices aimed at achieving deepened awareness for themselves and for their tribe. For instance, in isolated sections of Arizona we might fine a young Native American man engaging in a **vision quest**. By spending days in isolation, fasting and meditating, he seeks a vision that offers guidance, insight, or an experience of the divine. Among Plains Indians, participating in a sweat lodge can serve the same purpose.

ACTIVITY

Write a report on a Native American religious ritual or practice, such as:

- vision quest
- sweat lodge
- sun dance
- pow-wow

Vocabulary

creation myth: An account of creation of the world in story form that reveals fundamental beliefs and perspectives of a particular group.

diffused monotheism: Belief in one God who is manifest through many lesser gods.

initiation rite: Ritual or ceremony marking transition from one life stage to another. In tribal societies, it typically refers to the process whereby a child becomes an adult member of the tribe.

shaman: Term originating with a Siberian tribe referring to a person who allegedly can heal by entering into a trance and receiving communication and assistance from a spirit.

wakan: Lakota Sioux word for that which is holy. Wakan Tanka is often translated as "Great Spirit" or God.

For Review

1. List three ways that ancient tribal religious beliefs and practices remain present in the world today.
2. Give an example of an ancient tribal practice that is now found in Christianity.
3. In what sense do members of traditional tribal societies view the world differently from the typical modern worldview?
4. What are totems and taboos?
5. What position do most tribal groups have regarding belief in a Supreme Being?
6. Define diffused monotheism.
7. What role do myths play for a community of people such as a tribe?
8. What are creation myths?
9. How did ancient cultures typically view the causes of physical illness?
10. What ability are shamans believed to possess? What does this belief suggest about the way tribal people view the relationship between physical and spiritual realities?
11. What is an initiation rite?
12. What do Plains Indians of America seek to achieve through a vision quest or sweat lodge?

II. New Religions Broaden the World's Religious Landscape

In 1851 the French historian and philosopher Ernest Renan announced to the world that Islam was "the last religious creation of humanity." He was more than a bit premature. At about the time he was writing, the Bahai faith, Christian Science, Mormonism, the Seventh-Day Adventists, and a major Japanese religious movement known as Tenrikyo were all just coming to life. Falun Gong and Pentecostalism—both of which now have millions and millions of members—had yet to emerge. (Toby Lester, "Oh, Gods!" Atlantic Monthly 289 [February, 2002], 37)

In the nineteenth century, Ernest Renan was not alone in predicting that no new religions would emerge on the world scene. Actually, a number of people believed that even currently existing religions would either die out or slip to the margins of society. Some scholars traced the history of religion in three stages. During the first stage, humans engaged in primitive, superstitious practices centered on polytheism and nature worship. Then around 900 to 500 BCE a major shift occurred in a number of sectors of the globe. (This was the time of the Buddha, Confucius, the early Greek philosophers, and the compilation of the Hebrew Scriptures.) The great axial period, as it came to be known, saw the emergence of more highly developed beliefs such as the concept of one God and reliance on sacred scriptures. "Religion" was replacing superstition. The third period of human religious history began with the Enlightenment in Europe beginning around the eighteenth century CE. The Enlightenment placed science above religion as source of truth. Some Enlightenment thinkers believed that, in time, religions would die out among rational, sophisticated people just as primitive superstitions had. Places of religious worship would no longer serve active communities of believers but instead would become museums, containing mementos of the past. People who still practiced religion would be a quaint curiosity similar to storefront palm readers or fortune tellers.

A. Find out about the perspective on religion held by one or more of the following:

Karl Marx   Albert Schweitzer

Friedrich Nietsche   John Henry Newman

Sigmund Freud   Peter Berger

Carl Jung   Madelyn Murray O'Hare

Albert Einstein

B. Some scholars suggest that, rather than an end to religion, we are entering a new "axial period," that is, a radically new stage in human religious development. Write an essay describing changes that a religion might undergo during the twenty-first century.

New Religions in the United States

Even while people were predicting the demise of religion, new religions were emerging. The United States of the nineteenth century proved to be fertile ground for new religious movements. Typically the founders of these movements gave their own spin to Christianity based on new insights they had gained or even new revelations they had received from supernatural sources. Each in its own way proposed that Christianity as currently practiced had been corrupted and needed purifying. Four such movements are Mormonisn, Adventists, Christian Science, and Jehovah's Witnesses.

The Church of Jesus Christ of Latter-Day Saints

In the early nineteenth century, Western New York was a hotbed of evangelical Christian activity. A young boy named Joseph Smith was enthralled with but confused by the many preachers who made their way through the area. In 1820, at age fourteen, he asked God which branch of Christianity was the true one. God the Father and Jesus appeared to him, telling him that none was correct and that he should await further guidance. That guidance came three years later when a heavenly being named Moroni directed him to a place where golden plates were buried and told Smith to dig them up and translate them into English from the ancient, unknown language in which they were written. Over the next few years Smith dictated the translation of the text to his wife and two neighbors. When completed, the angel took the golden plates away. In 1830 the *Book of Mormon* was published.

Temple Square in Salt Lake City

The book tells about two groups of people who migrated to America during ancient times. One group was godly; the other was evil and cursed by God. After his Resurrection, Jesus visited America where he preached to members of the godly group. Nonetheless, around four hundred years later they were wiped out by their evil neighbors. The last survivors, the prophet Mormon and his son Moroni, recorded all these events on the golden plates later made known to Joseph Smith.

In 1830 Smith began his church, calling it simply the Church of Jesus Christ. Later the term "of Latter-Day Saints" was added to distinguish the group who accepted the revelations made to Smith from earlier "saints" or so-called Christians who followed a corrupted version of Christianity. As membership in the church grew, so did the intensity of opposition it attracted, causing the group to move westward a number of times. In 1844 a mob killed Smith and his brother while they were in jail in Illinois. Brigham Young gained control of the main body of the church and, from 1846 to 1847, led its members to the Great Salt Lake valley in present-day Utah. (A splinter group remained in Illinois.) Persecutions of Mormons, as they were known, continued for the remainder of the century. One reason for opposition to Mormons was their practice of **polygamy**, which was outlawed by the United States government. In 1890 the head of the church proclaimed that its members should abide by the law of the land regarding marriage, eliminating polygamy as a tenet of the faith. In fact, an emphasis on the sacredness of family life has always been a central teaching of Mormons, and church members are known for adhering to traditional morality.

Mormons believe in the Bible but depend upon new revelations, such as the *Book of Mormon*, to clarify its meaning. Christianity had become corrupted and the true priesthood had ended until Joseph Smith founded the true Church of Jesus Christ of Latter-Day Saints. Even after Smith's death and down to the present time, the head of the church can receive new revelations to clarify teachings. Mormons believe in the Trinity but consider the Father and the Son to have separate physical bodies while the Holy Ghost is a spiritual entity. Since baptism and membership in the church are necessary to enter the glory of heaven, Mormon temples make available a baptismal ceremony whereby a living member of the church can receive baptism on behalf of a dead ancestor. Another practice for which Mormons are noted is their missionary work. Young adults typically give up to two years of their life to spread the message of the church, often going door-to-door seeking converts.

Read about current beliefs, practices, and membership numbers of the Church of Jesus Christ of Latter-Day Saints.

ACTIVITY

Seventh-Day Adventist Church

One point of focus among a number of American Christian preachers during the eighteenth century was the Second Coming of Christ. Many people came to believe that Christ would return to earth to establish his kingdom, saving those who believed and condemning nonbelievers. Some Christians studied the Bible to find indications about when exactly the Second Coming would take place. A collective name for those who anticipated the Second Coming in the near future was **Adventists**. One such group also understood that the Bible specified Saturday as the Sabbath and thus held worship services on Saturday rather than Sunday. At a conference in Battle Creek, Michigan, in 1860, a number of congregations who held these two beliefs took the name Seventh-Day Adventists.

Adventists understand the writings of Ellen G. White (1821-1861) to be inspired, although they do not consider them to be on the level of the Bible. White received numerous visions during her lifetime and wrote prolifically about how Christians could prepare themselves for Christ's coming. She and members of the church emphasized healthy living, abstinence from alcohol and tobacco use, vegetarianism, and the promotion of hospitals and health centers. Adventists consider themselves Christians and do not condemn other Christians for different practices, such as Sunday worship. They do differ from mainstream Christian thought in that they believe that the saved will remain in the grave until Christ's coming when they will be resurrected to eternal life while non-believers will simply cease to exist.

Although the church began in the United States, today less than ten percent of its members are found in North America. The church has experienced phenomenal growth worldwide, with baptisms taking place regularly in over two hundred countries.

Christian Science

Mary Baker Eddy

If you live in a city or a fairly large town, you may come upon a building identified as a "Christian Science Reading Room." Christian Science is another movement emerging out of the United States in the nineteenth century that emphasizes healing and the written word. Its founder, Mary Baker Eddy, was a sickly child. In her forties, with the help of a faith healer, she was cured of a spinal disease. Later, in 1866, she injured herself when she slipped and fell on a patch of ice. Reading the Bible about Jesus healing the sick, Mrs. Eddy sensed the healing power of faith, arose from her bed, and felt in better health than ever before.

Christian Scientists identify this incident as the beginning of their movement. Like other religious movements of the time, Christian Science considers itself to be a restoration of the original spirit of Christianity. (For instance, in the Bible in the book known as the Acts of the Apostles several accounts of the disciples healing in Jesus' name are recorded.) Christian Scientists read from the Bible at Sunday services. However, they also include readings from Mary Baker Eddy's *Science and Health with Key to the Scriptures*, first published in 1875.

Christian Science applies its message of healing in situations beyond those involving physical illness. It believes that by taking on the mind of Christ other ills can be cured as well, such as family and social problems. Christian Science considers evil and sickness to be a matter of perspective. They can be overcome because only God, the good, is truly real. Prayer, which leads to absolute faith in God, makes all things possible. Sin and hell also are nonexistent. The true human being is the one who possesses the mind of Christ.

Christian Scientists are not alone in advocating the power of prayer and mental attitude in healing and overcoming problems on all levels. Imagine, for instance, pausing to pray before an activity such as a class, a game, or a meal. Explain what difference praying can make.

Jehovah's Witnesses

The group that took the name Jehovah's Witnesses in 1931 is perhaps best known today for the door-to-door missionary work carried out by its members. It grew out of the **millennialist** spirit popular in the United States during the late 1800s. That is, its founders were among the many people who believed that Christ would soon appear and begin a thousand-year (millennial) reign as described in the Book of Revelation, chapter 20. A number of dates actually were determined when Christ would visibly appear. After a number of disappointments, the leader of the Witnesses proclaimed that Christ's coming would be invisible. Nonetheless, the religion is based upon the core belief that the end times are near.

Like other new American religions of the period, Jehovah's Witnesses base their teachings on the Bible. However, members of the movement have created their own translation of the Bible, the *New World Translation*, which supports their beliefs. The publishing operation of the church, the Watch Tower Bible and Tract Society, regularly produces materials for use by its members.

Witnesses believe Jesus to be inferior to God, whom they call Jehovah. Also, the Holy Spirit is not God but a term for God-in-action. When Christ returns, a select group of 144,000 will go to heaven while the remainder of the Witnesses will stay on earth and be ruled. Since they are against armed support of any earthly government, Jehovah's Witnesses refuse to fight in wars. They also refuse to give or receive blood transfusions.

- *Jehovah is the name of the only true God, the Creator of all things.*

- *Jesus…is the Son of God….Jesus never claimed equality with God and thus is not part of a Trinity.*

- *Jehovah's Witnesses do not use religious symbols, such as the cross, in their worship.*

- *God's Kingdom...is the heavenly Kingdom for which Jesus taught all his followers to pray. Soon it will become the one government over all the earth and will solve mankind's pressing problems. The Bible does not give a date for these events, but it provides evidence to show that we are living in "the last days" of this troubled world....Those judged righteous will be given everlasting life on a paradise earth. Those judged unrighteous will not be tormented but will die and cease to exist. (Authorized Site of the Office of Public Information of Jehovah's Witnesses [http://www.jw-media.org])*

ACTIVITY

Christian groups who believe that Christ will soon bring about a dramatic transformation of the world are called millenarian. Find out what various Christian churches believe about the Second Coming of Christ. If you are a Christian, how does your church view the Book of Revelation in the Bible?

New American Religions of the Twentieth Century

Many new religions gained followers during the twentieth century. Africa and Japan were two places where many new groups formed. A number of religious movements either began or found a home in the United States during the last century, especially during the counter-cultural days of the 1960s. A number of them actually were variations on one of the Eastern religions described in this book. Three groups that have continued to grow and gain influence in the United States are the Unification Church, the Church of Scientology, and the New Age movement.

The Unification Church

One of the most famous new religious organizations to appear in the United States during the second half of the twentieth century was the Family Federation for World Peace and Unification, or the Unification Church. Actually begun in Korea by Reverend Sun Myung Moon, the movement gathered momentum in the United States in 1972 when Moon moved to New York State.

The church considers itself to be Christian, although it does not consider Jesus to be God. Jesus was the messiah, but his work remained incomplete. In 1992 Reverend Moon announced that he himself was also the messiah, called upon to restore God's original plan of peace and unification. The trinity is really God, Man, and Woman together in love and harmony. The biblical story of the Fall describes the disruption that occurred in this harmony intended by God. Marriage is an essential building block in God's plan. A major feature of the religion is wedding ceremonies of thousands of couples at a time. Members of the church itself typically have their spouse chosen by Reverend Moon or now by other leaders.

Scientology

L. Ron Hubbard was one of a number of people during the latter half of the twentieth century who offered a self-improvement program. He originally called his theory of how the mind works the science of Dianetics. Essentially he proposed that the unconscious mind stores mental images, called engrams, of pain and suffering. Engrams hinder a person from reaching his or her full potential. Many of the most troublesome engrams are the result of experiences that took place even before birth. Someone trained in Dianetics can help a person identify incidents that caused engrams, which erases their negative power. Once all engrams are erased, a person becomes "Clear."

> When a person becomes Clear, he loses all the fears, anxieties and irrational thoughts that were held down by pain in the reactive mind and, in short, regains himself. Without a reactive mind, an individual is much, much more himself. ("What Is Scientology?" Quoted in David V. Barrett, The New Believers [London: Cassell & Co, 2001], 449)

In 1955 Hubbard and his followers incorporated their organization as the Church of Scientology. The church included an understanding of the world and of the human person based on science fiction stories written by Hubbard and the Dianetics techniques he had developed. He established a series of programs aimed at helping people become ever more fully developed human beings. Scientology claims to be a religion because it views humans as spiritual beings. However, Scientology proposes that it is able to use technologies and psychotherapeutic techniques never before available to help people perfect themselves. According to Scientology, self-fulfillment is now available to everyone, which can also lead to transformation of the world.

ACTIVITY

Discuss and debate the following statement: Self-help programs that claim to lead to perfection are compatible with Christianity, Buddhism, Islam, and Judaism.

The New Age Movement

The term "new age" describes the hopeful spirit of personal and global transformation that motivates many seekers. (Bruce G. Epperly, Crystal & Cross *[Mystic, CT: Twenty-Third Publications, 1996], 3)*

In the 1980s, book and music stores began to include sections labeled "New Age." Materials offered in these sections are not linked directly to any one religion. Actually, they often combine references to any and all religions indiscriminately. The New Age seems to be aimed at people interested in spirituality but turned off by organized religions. Music is meditative, and books address topics such as "getting in touch with the inner self." Not a religion in the strict sense, nonetheless the New Age movement does offer alternatives to traditional religious practices for the spiritual seeker. Many New Age ideas and materials are compatible with or even complementary to a religion such as Christianity. (After all, meditative music can help people's prayer life, regardless of their religious affiliation.) Behind the wide variety of beliefs and practices, common themes run through the works of most proponents of New Age spirituality. One author, Bruce G. Epperly, lists four such themes characteristic of the New Age.

The first theme Epperly identifies is belief in the unity of all life. Here New Age reflects the monism of Hinduism, Buddhism, and Taoism. However, New Age writers often support their views on the oneness of all reality by referring to modern physics, the ecology movement, and psychology. A second theme is belief in a higher self. In other words, we human beings are much greater than we appear to be. We are like an eagle living like a chicken, or a lion believing it is a goat. Our true self, our inner self, is god-like. The third theme is the power of mind. Through a change in attitude or perspective we can uncover our true self, and we would then function at a much more developed level. This "mind over matter" stance resonates with Christian Science discussed above. Finally, New Age offers a variety of spiritual technologies. That is, the movement aims to be practical, providing techniques aimed at tapping into a person's spiritual energy.

New Age religion often incorporates modern physics, the ecology movement, and psychology

A fifth theme running through New Age literature not listed by Epperly is the link between recent developments in science and religion. For instance, some scientists who study quantum physics appear to be speaking about spirituality more than science. If nothing else, they blur the distinction between materiality and spirituality. In that sense, they seem to be echoing the worldview commonly held among tribal religions.

New Age tends to be individualistic and optimistic. One does not have to be a member of a church or a community to practice it. Underlying the New Age movement is the belief that if enough people changed their attitudes and performed certain practices, then the world would be a better place. New Age tends to dismiss the dark side of life; it is ultimately illusion. Any darkness we experience can be overcome by right thinking and right living.

How would you critique New Age thinking? What positives does it offer?

ACTIVITY

Conclusion

The Ongoing Religious Quest

From ancient cave drawings to modern explorations into the workings of the universe, humanity has been on a religious quest. Some groups of people hold onto their old ways of maintaining contact with the spiritual dimension of life even as others search for new forms of religious expression. Religion seems to be as old as humanity itself. Contrary to predictions of its demise, the vast majority of the world's population continues to look to religion and religions for hope and meaning in their lives.

Vocabulary

Adventists: A term for Christians who believe Christ's Second Coming will soon occur.

millennialism: Belief in the Second Coming of Christ, when he will begin his Thousand-Year Reign.

polygamy: The practice of one man marrying more than one wife.

ACTIVITY

A. Debate or discuss the following statements:

1. Tribal religions are not compatible with the modern world.

2. Tribal religions have much to offer people in the modern world.

B. Choose one of the new religious movements discussed in this chapter. Write about why you think many people find it appealing.

C. Access a website dedicated to one of the topics or one of the religions discussed in this chapter. Describe the points of emphasis addressed in that site.

D. Interview a member of one of the religions discussed in this chapter.

E. Look at United States history textbooks for references to religions discussed in this chapter. Describe the perspective given on one of the religions mentioned in the history text.

For Review

13. Describe the three stages of religious development that some eighteenth-century scholars proposed.

14. Who founded the Mormon religion?

15. What was the source of the Book of Mormon?

16. What practice led to early persecution of Mormons?

17. How do Mormons perceive Christianity?

18. What two beliefs are implied in the name Seventh-Day Adventists?

19. What experience serves as the starting point for Christian Science?

20. What was the millennialist spirit popular in the United States during the late 1800s?

21. What is the name of the publishing arm of Jehovah's Witnesses?

22. How do Witnesses view Jesus?

23. What do Witnesses believe about Christ's Second Coming?

24. Who founded the Unification Church? How does he view his role in human history?

25. What is the trinity according to the Unification Church?

26. What unique wedding ceremonies have been performed in the Unification Church?

27. What does Scientology mean by "engrams" and "Clear"?

28. What four themes are characteristic of the New Age movement?

God of all creation
  who loves all people
  we pray for peace and understanding
  within our hearts
  in our communities
  between nations
  among the world's religions.

Fill us with wonder and wisdom
  so that we may see you
  everywhere.
Guide us along our journey
  from you
  to you
  within you
  with all your people.

In our encounters
  may we discover
  and create
  shalom, salaam, shanti, peace. Amen.